FRECKLETON

The History of
Freckleton

PETER SHAKESHAFT

Carnegie Publishing Ltd

Published by Carnegie Publishing Ltd
Carnegie House, Chatsworth Road
Lancaster LA1 4SL
publishing website: www.carnegiepub.co.uk
book production website: www.wooof.net

British Library Cataloguing-in-Publication data
A CIP record for this book is available from the British Library

ISBN 1-85936-084-X

Typeset in Adobe Garamond by Carnegie Publishing
Printed and bound in the UK by
The Cromwell Press, Trowbridge, Wilts

Contents

Acknowledgements

In writing this history of Freckleton I have been helped by many people in different ways. I especially thank my wife Maureen who has assisted me throughout the research and writing of the book. For their encouragement and advice I would like to thank Dr A. Crosby, Dr M. Duggan, and Mr R. Watson. I am most grateful to the many people of Freckleton who gave freely of their time and lent me their personal property deeds and other important documents. I particularly thank Mr R. Banks, Mr P. Hall and Mr H. Hall whose constant help and interest has led to the discovery of many facts that might otherwise still remain unknown. Also Mr D. Kirby for the loan of the important old township books now in his custody, and Mr H. Robinson for his work during the 'Millennium 2000' celebrations. I would also like to acknowledge the assistance of the County Archivist and staff of the Lancashire Record Office from where much of the material used has been drawn, also Dr A. Piper of the University of Durham for his transcripts of the Lytham Priory charters.

Many of the photographs and illustrations have come from private collections. I am very grateful for being allowed to reproduce them and would like to thank Mr and Mrs R. Banks, Mr and Mrs T. Butcher, Mrs E. Dollin, Mr and Mrs C. Fare, Mr and Mrs H. Fisher, Mrs J. Foster, Rev. J. Gibson, Mr H. Hall, Mr and Mrs P. Hall, Mr R. Hardy, Mrs R. Jolly, Mrs A. Kay, Mr M. Lancaster, Mr E. Lightbown, Mr and Mrs M. Rossall, Rev. N. S. Saul, Mrs M. Townsend and Mrs M. Wright. I apologise if I have unknowningly infringed copyright in the use of these photographs. Illustrations for which copyright still exists, or for which special permission has been given for their use, have been credited accordingly beneath the actual item.

I would like to thank the staff at Carnegie Publishing for an excellent production. With regard to the actual text, whilst every effort has been made to ensure that all the facts are correct any errors are entirely my own. Finally, I hope you will have as much pleasure in reading this book as I have had in writing it.

Glossary

Amercement	A fine paid in a manorial court.
Appurtenances	The rights and duties appended to an agreement over holding land attached to a house.
Caul	A type of groyne but built parallel to the river to direct the flow of water and control the channel. The early cauls appear to have been made up of sod banks wrapped together to form the wall of the river. One of the definitions in the *Oxford English Dictionary* of the word *caul* is 'a net for wrapping something up'.
Court Baron	Assembly of the freehold tenants of a manor under the direction of the lord or his steward where in addition to manorial administration changes in tenancy were recorded.
Court Leet	Court held in the manor before the lord or his steward where the local bye-laws were enforced. Usually held at the same time as the court baron.
Demesne	Belonging to the lord. A lord's demesne consisted of those manorial lands which were reserved for his personal benefit and on which tenants gave free service.
Distraint	Seizure of goods or animals for debt or other reason.
Dungeon	From the Middle English word *dongeon* meaning a secure or guarded place.
Emendation of Bread and Ale	The right to control the standard of bread and ale, and fine those who did not maintain the standard.
Entrepot	A port where mechandise can be temporarily received for dispatch elsewhere.
Fealty	An oath of loyalty taken by a tenant concerning customary services and payments.
Feoffment	A free grant or conveyance of a tenement.
Frankalmoign	Land granted by a lay person for the benefit of an ecclesiastical foundation.
Habergeon	A sleeveless coat or jacket of mail or scale armour.
Haketon	A stuffed jacket or jerkin worn under the mail. A jacket of leather or the like plated without mail.

Hannings	From the word *hainings* (meadows) divided amongst the community into narrower strips.
Infangenthef	The right to hang thieves if taken within the lord's demesne.
Infeudation	The granting of land to a vassal.
Inquest	An inquiry.
Inquisition Post Mortem (I.P.M.)	An inquest held on the death of one of the Crown's tenants to determine the date of death and the lands held at the time and to confirm the identity and age of the heir.
Knights Fee	A feudal obligation by which the tenant was required to pay for his land through the performing of military service.
Messuage	Dwelling house and its appurtenances.
Rack Rent	Practice by landowners of offering annual agreements rather than long leases to their tenants.
Recusant	A person who declined to attend his or her parish church. After 1570 the term usually applied to Roman Catholics but could apply to any non-conformist.
Scutage	Payment of a fine in lieu of Knights Fee.
Seisin	Lawful possession. The right to hold.
Selion	Parallel strips of arable land in an open field.
Settlement	Not just the buildings but also the land which supported it.
Stint	To regulate the number of cattle to graze on a common.
Tenement	Rented land or dwelling.
Thegn	An Anglo-Saxon Noble.
Tithe	A tax of one tenth, specifically a tenth part of the annual produce of land or labour, formerly levied to support the clergy and the Church.
Weyf	The right to take any wandering cattle.

Old-style money is presented in the following manner: £6 6s. 6d.

To convert to decimal currency, please note that there were 12 pence (*d.*) in each shilling (*s.*), and 20 shillings in each pound sterling (£).

For example:	1s. 0d.	=	£0.05
	10s. 0d.	=	£0.50
	£3 15s. 6d.	=	£3.78.

Preface

During the past eighty years there have been several publications dealing with various aspects of the history of Freckleton but only one – *A Short History of Freckleton* by Philip Rogers – published in 1947 attempted to record the continuous history of the township from earliest times. It was the book which first alerted me to the fascinating story of Freckleton's past, but, as Rogers himself wrote in his prefatory note, there were many records which, due to lack of time, he had not inspected. This present book continues the work begun by Rogers, although unlike him I have attempted to access and study the numerous documents available, at the Lancashire County Record Office and elsewhere, that relate to the history of Freckleton.

Monastic charters provide an insight into thirteenth-century life and from the mid-sixteenth century there is an ever-increasing written historical record. With the departure of the Sharples family in the late seventeenth century 'township' affairs were determined by men and women from within the community. One of the results of this communal responsibility was that Freckleton township developed quite differently from any other in the parish of Kirkham, with evidence of an independent spirit being particularly present in the Quaker movement of the late seventeenth and eighteenth centuries. For over one hundred years, from the mid-eighteenth century onwards, industry co-existed side by side with traditional farming with the port of Freckleton as a centre for the distribution of coal throughout the Fylde region and beyond. In the nineteenth century Freckleton witnessed perhaps more than its share of social and economic distress, particularly among its handloom weavers and their later contemporaries in the cotton factory.

Everywhere in Freckleton there is history, whether it be in the shape of the fields, the plan of the streets or in the houses and buildings, old and new. There is still much to see and discover and it is hoped that care is taken to preserve as much of this surviving past as is possible. Wherever possible I have endeavoured to tell the story of Freckleton by using either the written or spoken word of the men and women directly or indirectly involved with events or incident being described, and have hopefully thereby achieved, in the words of Professor F. W. Maitland, the nineteenth-century historian, 'By slow degrees, the thoughts of our forefathers, their common thoughts about common things, will have become thinkable once more'.

Part I

Early and Medieval Freckleton

CHAPTER I

Origins of the Township

The First Settlers

Although almost nothing is known of the early occupation of the part of the Fylde that included Freckleton, this apparent scarcity of evidence does not necessarily mean that settlement† was limited and more archaeological investigation may help to extend the story. Evidence of human presence in the Fylde around 10,000 BC was revealed in 1970 when the almost complete skeleton of an elk (*Alces alces*), a species whose European range is now restricted to Scandinavia, was unearthed two and a half feet below the surface of a site at Carleton, near Poulton. Beside the remains of the animal was a barbed spearhead that had been fashioned by the hand of one of the early Mesolithic hunters and foodgatherers who had been directly or indirectly responsible for the death of the animal.

From about 4500 BC Neolithic people began to occupy Lancashire and evidence of their presence in the Freckleton area, probably dating from the late Neolithic period (around 2400 BC), was provided by the discovery of a large stone axe, measuring 10¼ inches, that had been 'used as an adze or axe for wood working, or as a hoe for agricultural pursuits'.[1] Although the picture is not clear, evidence of some form of a settlement near to Freckleton during the Bronze Age period (between 2400 and 700 BC) was discovered in 1885. During the excavation for the then new Preston Dock, only a few miles upriver from Freckleton, 24 human skulls, a bronze spearhead, two dugout canoes, over sixty antlers of red deer, forty three skulls of wild cattle, five horses heads, skulls of

---

† For a definition of items marked with a dagger (†), see Glossary on pp.ix–x

the pilot whale and a skull of a bottle-nosed dolphin were identified. There are, however, no known sites from anywhere in the western Fylde for the period known as the Iron Age (between 800 BC and AD 43) and the beginnings of the Romano-British period, and therefore no evidence to suggest any form of settlement at Freckleton at this time.

The Roman Occupation (AD 78–410)

By the time of the Roman occupation the district may have been settled by a branch of the Celtic tribe of the Brigantes called the Setantii but again no evidence of their presence in Freckleton has ever been found. Nor is there any evidence, despite the claim of the Rev. Whitaker,[2] that in AD 79 Freckleton Naze was the site of 'Portus Setantiorum', a still unidentified Roman port that was drawn on a map of Britain by the geographer Ptolemy in the second century AD. However, it is probable that ships were able to reach a point at or near to the Naze and that a road led from there to Kirkham. Alternatively, as the raised sea-levels of 2,000 years ago meant that the Ribble at Freckleton 'must have covered, at least on the tide, the embayment of Freckleton Marsh'[3] the then tidal waters may have reached much closer to Kirkham than at present. Consequently it has been suggested that the Roman fort at Kirkham was established in the early AD 70s as 'a potential entrepot'† thereby providing 'an invaluable staging point allowing sea-borne goods relatively rapid and easy access to the road system via Ribchester'.[4]

The only evidence of an actual Roman presence at Freckleton comes from seventeen silver *denarii* coins found in the early 1990s. The find is probably the whole or part of a hoard or cache of savings, and represents approximately three weeks' pay for a Roman legionary soldier. The coins fall into the period AD 60 to 165 and similar small hoards have been found at Ribchester in 1978 and at Clitheroe in 1990. It is generally thought that some kind of military, political or economic upheaval occurred in the 160s and archaeological evidence suggests that the fort at Kirkham was also abandoned at this time. It may therefore be one of these events that caused the individual concerned to bury his savings and his failure to retrieve them at a later date. During the remaining two hundred and fifty years of the Roman occupation little is known of their activity in the Fylde, nor when they finally left the Kirkham area.

Angles and Scandinavians

After the final departure of the Romans from Britain in AD 410 the remaining Romano-British people in the Fylde probably formed part of a small British kingdom, with local populations surviving beyond the advance of the Northumbrian Angles in the early seventh century. It was possibly soon after the Anglian settlement that the township of Freckleton first acquired its present name, and although the commonest settlement term 'tun' is well represented in the Kirkham area it is only at Freckleton that the name of an individual forms the first part of the place name.

It should not be assumed, however, that because Freckleton is an Anglo-Saxon place-name it was founded during that period, and it may have had a Celtic or even earlier name. The interpretation currently favoured by place name scholars of the origin of the name Freckleton is that it means 'the settlement of Frecla'. Names which mean 'x's tun' are likely to be 'take over' names of established settlements granted to a particular thegn† following the Anglian conquest. Because of its strategic value to the Anglian settlement of the Fylde, as access point on a crossing over the Ribble, the settlement now known as Freckleton was possibly granted to the individual called Frecla whose social status was such that it resulted in the permanent establishment of the name.

Until recently it had been thought that it was settlers of Norwegian descent, who arrived from their settlements in Ireland in the early tenth century, that had had the greatest Scandinavian impact on the North West but, based on place name evidence, it now seems that people of Danish or Anglo-Danish origin were also involved.[5] The area known as Amounderness, which encompassed the whole of the Fylde and beyond, incorporates the name of Agmund, a Scandinavian who must have had considerable authority. Evidence of the integration of the Scandinavian people with the existing Anglian population is again provided with the association of Anglian and Scandinavian place names such as Newton with Scales, Bryning with Kellarmergh and Clifton with Salwick, in which the first part is Anglian and the second part Scandinavian.

However, no Scandinavian name appears to have been added to that of Freckleton, even though there is plenty of evidence provided by the later twelfth-century monastic charters that such integration must have been taking place. Scandinavian personal names, such as Ketel, Elvive and Tustehorn form part of the descriptive field names or furlongs of the period and it was this Anglo-Scandinavian population that was working the land in Freckleton at the time of the Norman Conquest.

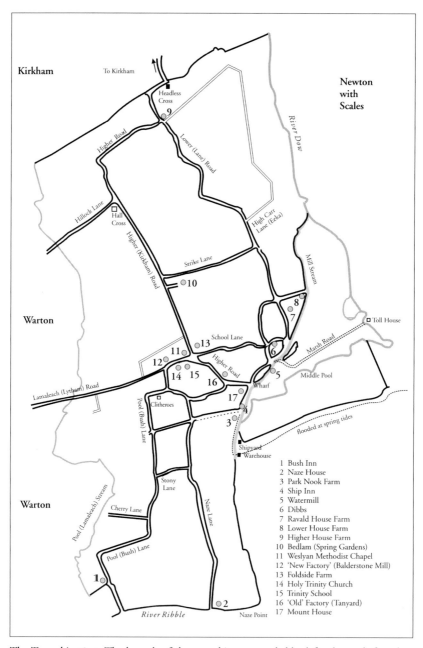

Kirkham

To Kirkham

Newton
with
Scales

Headless
Cross

9

River Dow

Higher Road

Lower (Lane) Road

Hillock Lane

Hall
Cross

High Carr Lane (Eeka)

Higher (Kirkham) Road

Strike Lane

Mill Stream

10

Warton

8
7

Toll House

School Lane

13

11

6

Marsh Road

12

Higher Road

14   15

16

5

Middle Pool

17

Wharf

Lamaleach (Lytham) Road

Pool (Bush) Lane

Clitheroes

4

3

flooded at spring tides

Shipyard
Warehouse

Stony
Lane

1 Bush Inn
2 Naze House
3 Park Nook Farm
4 Ship Inn
5 Watermill
6 Dibbs
7 Ravald House Farm
8 Lower House Farm
9 Higher House Farm
10 Bedlam (Spring Gardens)
11 Weslyan Methodist Chapel
12 'New Factory' (Balderstone Mill)
13 Foldside Farm
14 Holy Trinity Church
15 Trinity School
16 'Old' Factory (Tanyard)
17 Mount House

Pool (Lamaleach) Stream

Warton

Cherry Lane

Naze Lane

Pool (Bush) Lane

1

2

River Ribble

Naze Point

The Township 1840. The bounds of the township were probably defined even before the
Norman conquest of 1066. This map, based on the 1840 Ordnance Survey shows how
natural features such as the River Ribble, Lamaleach Brook and Dow Brook determined
the southern, western and eastern boundaries.

CHAPTER 2

Medieval Freckleton

The Domesday Survey

The Norman Conquest of 1066 was a watershed in English history and under the Normans the feudal system was refined into a new social order. The basis of Norman power was land, and ownership of land was held at the disposal of the King who divided out the country amongst his favoured barons. In the years following the Conquest the Hundred of Amounderness, which included Freckleton, was granted to Roger of Poitou and was intermittently retained by him until his final expulsion from England in 1102.

The first surviving documentary reference to Freckleton is the entry in the Domesday Survey of 1086 when the township (spelt *Frecheltun* in the original) was said to contain 4 carucates of land. The carucate was the basic unit of taxation and originally was the amount of land that a team of eight oxen could plough each year. The actual acreage ploughed varied throughout the country and historically a Lancashire acre tended to be larger than in most other counties, even varying from township to township. Assuming, however, a figure of 120 acres per carucate then perhaps about 480 acres of land were being worked in the township, although this acreage may well have included adjacent moor and marshland as the production of corn on nearby Clifton Marsh is recorded as early as 1256.[1]

The Early Manor

Early in the twelfth century the Bussel family were granted the barony (or fee) of Penwortham and in a charter dated between 1153 and 1160 Richard Bussel confirmed to the Abbey of Evesham the grant in frank-almoign† made by his father, Warine, of 'two thirds of the tithe† of his demesne† in Freckleton and Warton together with the right of fishing in the Ribble with one net'.[2] The Bussel family made various grants of manors within their barony and in the mid-twelfth century there is the first mention of a manorial lord at Freckleton when Jordan, son of Richard, acted as a witness to a charter dated sometime

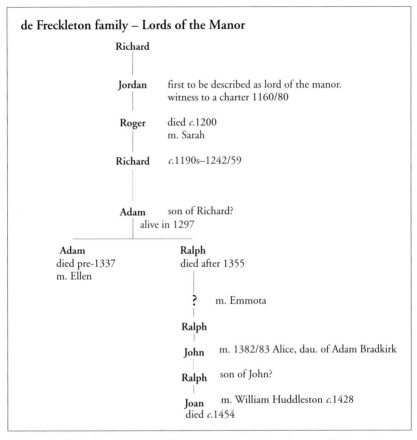

de Freckleton family – Lords of the Manor

Richard

Jordan   first to be described as lord of the manor.
                  witness to a charter 1160/80

Roger   died *c*.1200
                  m. Sarah

Richard   *c*.1190s–1242/59

Adam   son of Richard?
                  alive in 1297

Adam   Ralph
died pre-1337   died after 1355
m. Ellen

                  ?   m. Emmota

                  Ralph

                  John   m. 1382/83 Alice, dau. of Adam Bradkirk

                  Ralph   son of John?

                  Joan   m. William Huddleston *c*.1428
                  died *c*.1454

The de Freckleton family tree is based on information in the charters of Lytham Priory and other published documents. It shows the line of descent of the family who were the medieval lords of the manor. Other families also called Freckleton continued to reside in the township until the early nineteenth century.

between 1160 and *c*. 1180.[3] It was this family that became known as de Freckleton.

A manor has been described as an estate, 'a unit of English territorial organization originally of the nature of a feudal lordship'.[4] It was the key unit of social and economic organisation, and from within it were appointed various officials such as steward, bailiff, hayward, pinder and reeve. The reeve, nominated by his fellow tenants, acted as village foreman and arranged the day-to-day business of the manor. For the medieval peasants who cultivated the manorial land, work would have been the ruling fact of life. Their staple diet would have been oats eaten in the form of oatmeal porridge or oatcakes whilst barley would have provided the main ingredient for their ale.

If a medieval manorial court was held at Freckleton then the records, as in much of Lancashire, have not survived. However, as the appointment of the township constable and transfer of certain lands were still being recorded at the court baront and court leett of Penwortham as late as the early nineteenth century it may be that such matters had always been determined at Penwortham rather than at Freckleton. The only glimpse we have of an manorial appointment in medieval times is from a charter in 1230 when one of the witnesses is named as William, son of Nicholas the reeve of Freckleton.

The de Freckleton family however were the recognised lords of the manor and in addition to the 4 carucates of land mentioned in the Domesday survey they had been granted lands in Whittingham, Elswick and Newton, totalling in all 9 carucates. These lands were held by service of knights feet, a feudal obligation introduced by Henry II in 1181 and a form of landholding by which the tenant held his land through the performance of military service. It did not mean that the person became known as 'Sir' and in fact the de Freckleton family never acquired this title.

Their newly acquired status did not deter others from contesting entitlement to land and property and in 1200–01 Roger de Freckleton was deprived by Theobald Walter of a (now unidentifiable) pasture called Brethoughmoor.[5] The background to this particular incident probably had wider implications and could have been connected to a dispute between Theobald Walter, brother of Archbishop Walter of York, who had been granted lands in Amounderness, and the King. At a subsequent assize Roger was found to have been removed from his pasture 'without justice' and King John instructed the sheriff to return the land to him. The matter seems to have been finally resolved the following year when William de Winwick and his wife gave (returned to?) Roger his nine acres in Brethough(moor), which they presumably had been given by Theobald Walter, whilst at the same time Roger confirmed to them the lands they held in Whittingham and Elswick.

Roger was succeeded by his son Richard who, though still a minor at the time of his father's death and in ward under the guardianship of the archdeacon of Stafford and William de Harwood, had been recognised as lord of the manor by 1212. Richard retained this status until his death, which occurred sometime between 1242 and 1259. In the years before his death he subdivided his manorial holding by a process of infeudationt and an inquest† ordered by Henry III in 1242, to ascertain the names of those responsible for military service, reveals that whilst Richard remained the principal landowner Gilbert de Meols, Roger de Nottesagh, William de Pul, Alan de Singleton and Warin de Whittingham also had estates in Freckleton.[6] It would seem though that by this date the performing of military service as a requirement of the knights fee had been commuted to a fine, and that in fact the manor was then being held in return for performance of duty at Lancaster Castle known as 'castleward'.

Monastic Charters

After about 1100 it became standard for larger landowners, including monasteries, to preserve the evidence of their title to land in written form, and hence the making and keeping of charters became usual. Grants of land to such monasteries were most numerous in the twelfth and thirteenth centuries and in Freckleton both the de Freckleton family and others had begun making such grants by the late twelfth century. As will be seen these charters are very detailed and provide information about people and locations in thirteenth-century Freckleton that would otherwise be unknown. Richard de Freckleton made several grants of land to Cockersand Abbey, a practice begun when his father made a testamentary grant to Cockersand about 1190:

> Testamentary grant in frankalmoign from Roger de Freckleton, son of Jordan (to the monks of Cockersand) for the health of his soul, of two acres of land in the southern part of Freckleton, with a common of pasture and the appurtenances.†[7]

At various times during the next sixty years Richard de Freckleton and others made six further grants to Cockersand Abbey. One grant dated 1210–50, with its mention of the personal name Lyulph from the Old Norse 'Liolf', provides further evidence of the pre-conquest Scandinavian settlement mentioned earlier.

> Grant in frankalmoign from the said Richard of that land in Freckleton called Lyulph's croft, with the toft, together with the bank up to the Pool; and four selions† of his demesne land at the Moor, next to the land belonging to the Hospital of St John [of Jerusalem] with common of pasture and the appurtenances†.[8]

Cockersand Abbey like many other monastic institutions combined contemplation and prayer with successful commercial activities, and in order to protect and extend their economic interests attempted, whenever possible, to gain local political and judicial control. When therefore in 1292 the abbot of Cockersand claimed the privilege of weyf,† infangen-theft† and emendation of the assize of bread and ale† in Freckleton and other parts of Lancashire he was, in effect, claiming a right or power equal to that of a baron. As a consequence of making this claim a warrant was issued by the King (Edward I) summoning the abbot to appear before Hugh de Cressingham, Justice at Lancaster, to answer by 'what warrant' he claimed such rights.

In reply the abbot said he did not claim weyf and other rights but 'to be quit of common fines and amercements† of the county and wapentake [hundred] as is contained in the writ of King John'. The jury, however, decided that although the abbot was not liable for fines imposed by the county or wapentake he ought not to be, nor used to be, exempt from common fines except only in two carucates of land in Newsham and the

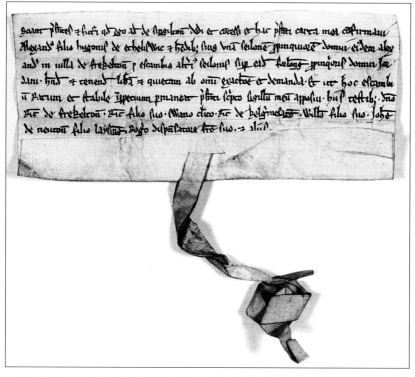

Lower House deed. A deed of 1240 that refers to both the 'house of Alexander' and the 'house of Jordan'. The deed was found with other documents relating to Lower House Farm. *(Courtesy of Lancashire Record Office – DDNw Box 4)*

manor of Pilling. The jury also decided that the abbot was liable to a tax calculated on the land he then held, and this presumably included that which he had already been granted in Freckleton.[9]

Grants of land and property in Freckleton were also made to the Benedictine priory at Lytham, a dependent daughter house of the great cathedral priory of Durham, and during the half century from 1215 they received some thirty such grants of land and property, including the lordship of four tenants.[10] Richard de Freckleton, whose parents Roger and Sarah had been buried at Lytham, made 12 grants. On one occasion Richard described himself as 'brother of the house St Cuthbert of Lytham' and it is therefore possible that he may have become an oblate, whereby he became associated, and chose to live in close connection, with the Benedictine community, integrating the spirit of the priory rule into his daily life. Alternatively, as was often the case, it may have been that, as an influential person, he had been granted 'honorary' brethren status. One particular charter (appendix A) appears to be a composite of the grants made by Richard de Freckleton and others to Lytham Priory and provides evidence of the extent to which these grants were made and also confirmation of the prevailing farming practices to be described in chapter 21. Several of the locations mentioned in the charter can still be identified today. The present-day Strike Lane is presumably derived from the word 'strik' and, although the lane now effectively ends at Strike Lane School, a trackway continues until it joins with Lower Lane. On the 1838 tithe map the majority of fields on both sides of this track still had the word strike as part of their descriptive fieldname and in medieval times it almost certainly formed one of the large townfields.

Another location mentioned in the same charter was Longerodes (rodes being the northern English dialect word for land which had been cleared from woodland), which lay in the area between the present Avalon Drive and Lower Lane and adjoined a field referred to in another charter called Kettleswra (or Kettleswick: from the personal name Kettle), which bordered Preston Old Road between the Sports and Social Club and Rigby Close. The nearby Croftebutts is now perpetuated in the modern lane of that name. The location of 'the butt on which the pound fold stands' cannot be pinpointed with any certainty but was said, in another charter, to run north-south. Foldside Farm, demolished in 1966, stood in the centre of the village adjacent to the road leading north, and might have acquired its name from its proximity to the fold.

A southward route is also referred to when Richard de Freckleton granted land 'between the land of Adam de Singleton and the way out of the vill in the south'; a route presumably along the original course of either Naze Lane or Pool (Bush) Lane leading to the fording point across the Ribble in the area of the Naze. The significance of this important river crossing is discussed in chapter 24. The reference to 'by the land of St John' in other Lytham charters show that by the late thirteenth century the Knights Hospitallers too had been granted land in the township, whilst sometime prior to 1297 Dieulacres Abbey in Shropshire had been given lands 'in the field called Hwldismont upon Ribblebank' with 'appurtenant easements in the vill of Freckleton' by Adam de Singleton.[11]

Principal Families

In 1259 Richard le Boteler (the name by which the descendants of Theobald Walter were then known) 'obtained' a portion of the manor from Richard de Freckleton.[12] The means by which this portion was obtained is not clear but may have been connected to the dispute of 1200 and could also have had some bearing on subsequent events in 1323 when there was clearly ill feeling between the Butler and de Freckleton families.

The Butler residence in the township was almost certainly a house on the site of the present Higher House (Higher House was known as Butlers House until at least 1577) though as the principal family house was Rawcliffe Hall the Freckleton property was probably occupied by a junior member of the family. In 1364–65 the younger brother of Sir John Butler, who was high sheriff of Lancashire on three occasions, was described as Richard Butler of Freckleton. In 1572 the Butler estate in Freckleton was divided amongst the representatives of the four daughters of John Butler and during the 1570s the inherited properties, land and manorial rights were sold.

By the late thirteenth century the Banastre family, too, had acquired land and property in the township. Their possessions had descended from the estate of Alan de Singleton and parts were subsequently granted to the earls of Derby. In a deed dated *c.* 1240 [13] Adam de Singleton (son of Alan) exchanged with Alexander son of Hugh of Etheliswic (Elswick) one selion near to the house of the said Alexander in the town of Freckleton for another selion in the same furlong near to the house of Jordan. As this deed was listed in a catalogue of documents relating to Lower House Farm it is tantalising to wonder if one of these properties stood on the site of the present day farm.

The site of Orchard House in Kirkham Road may also have been part of the original Singleton estate as it too was owned by the Earl of Derby until the mid-nineteenth century when it came into the possession of the Park family, and later, the Throp family. The same area is also the reputed site of an 'apparition' known locally as the 'Bannister Doll'. The origins of this tradition are unknown but may well preserve the memory of some incident that occurred there at some time in the distant past.

The Fourteenth and Fifteenth Centuries

To return to the de Freckleton family we find that in 1297 Adam de Freckleton held a knights fee for the manor of Freckleton and paid 10s. 0d. yearly in lieu of castleward at Lancaster Castle. Around this date he gave to his son, also called Adam, and Ellen his son's wife, a messuage† (dwelling house) and 3 oxgangs of land in Freckleton bought from Sir William de Clifton. During the period 1315–23 Lancashire was the scene of a series of family feuds that were part of a wider political conflict between Edward II and Thomas, Earl of Lancaster and Robert de Holland, who had risen to fortune in the service of the Earl. The de Freckleton family were directly involved in these feuds and in 1315 Adam (the son) was convicted, with two others, of the murder of Sir Henry de Bury. Because he did not attend the assizes, to which he had been summoned, he was outlawed, but later pardoned on the grounds that his indictment had been procured by his enemies.

His conviction, however, was presumably the reason why, in 1322–23, Adam released to his brother, Ralph, all right to his land in Freckleton, except for an oxgang held by Edmund and Joan de Rigby, and shortly afterwards Ralph was described as:

> The heir of Adam de Freckleton holds of Alice, daughter and heir of Henry de Lacy, formerly Earl of Lincoln, in demesne and service the manors of Freckleton, Whittingham, Newton, Elswick as of the fee of Penwortham by the service of 10s. 0d. yearly for the ward of Lancaster Castle at the term of Midsummer, and by the service of one Knights Fee, and he does suit at county and wapentake for the manor of Freckleton.[14]

In addition to the de Freckleton family the identity of other landowners in Freckleton at this time is provided by a rental, taken at Michaelmas 1324, of the lands which had passed to the crown following the attainder of Thomas, Earl of Lancaster and Robert de Holland.[15]

Rent of Nicholas le Botiler for a culture called Roaker
  [Raker?] in Freckleton   4s. 2d.

Rent of Robert de Shireburne for 2 oxgangs, 3r[oods]
  in Freckleton   3d.

Rent of Adam de Banastre of 1lb of cumin for 2
  oxgangs of land in Freckleton   1¼d.

Rent of Edmund de Riggeby and Joan his wife one pair
  of gloves for tenements in Freckleton   1¼d.

Ralph de Freckleton himself appears to have been somewhat fortunate in retaining his manorial status as he too had been involved in the troubles and had been accused of being in the company of Sir William de Bradeshagh, who with 'many more armed men on horse and on foot' went to the county court at Lancaster held on 8 August 1323, and so intimidated Cecilia, the widow of Richard le Botiller (Butler) that she was 'afraid to come to that county court to prosecute [Sir William] through fear and terror'. At the time Ralph de Threkelton (sic) 'came armed with haketon† and habergeon† and plate armour'.[16] As a consequence of his act he was initially imprisoned and is also recorded as having to pay a fine of 10 marks.

By 1300 the population of England and Wales was estimated to have been about 3 million, or double that of the Norman Conquest. The last two decades of the thirteenth century and the first decade of the fourteenth century were relatively prosperous and even in 1332, despite the troubles of the previous twenty years, twelve individuals from Freckleton were required to contribute to the Exchequer lay subsidy. This was a subsidy based on a fraction (usually one-fifteenth in the shires) of moveable property and income and was a change from a taxation based on knights fee. It reflected the way the economy was changing and the extension of wealth lower down the social scale. Even three hundred years later a reference to this method of taxation is contained in a deed dated 22 December 1666 which refers to 'the usual way of assessing the Fifteenth upon and within the said township of Freckleton'.[17]

In 1332 the following individuals were named as having paid the tax in Freckleton.[18] The presence of a dikeman is a possible indication of his importance in relation to the extensive marshland adjacent to the township, where control of the waters by means of a dyke or dykes would have been necessary to effect maximum use for livestock grazing.

| Robert de Freckleton | 2s. 0d. | William de Mithop | 2s. 6d. |
| Ralph de Freckleton | 2s. 0d. | Richard de Kendale | 3s. 0d. |

Robert de Hodersale	2s. 0d.	Nicholas Bussell	2s. 0d.
William son of William	3s. 0d.	Thomas de la More	2s. 0d.
Robert son of Michael	2s. 0d.	John de la More	2s. 0d.
William Dikemon	2s. 4d.	Richard son of Margery	16d.
		Total	£1 6s. 2d.

Within twenty years, however, this economic and social progress had been checked by the devastation caused by the arrival of the Black Death. It has been estimated that between September 1349 and January 1350 over 3,000 people died in the parish of Kirkham – a figure that represents perhaps 30% to 40% of the population.[19] Although there are no specific references to Freckleton at this time it is unlikely that the village suffered any less than its neighbours. Evidence of a late outbreak of the plague in about the year 1400 was provided by 'Rawlyn of Cowburne' when in 1427 he gave evidence in a dispute concerning the watermill. Although the connection between the two events is unclear the details provide a graphic account of the death of his uncle, Richard Bannister of Warton.

> Be it known to all men that I Rawlyn of Cowburne in my whole mind because of sothfastness [truth] and truth witness this underwritten also I shall answer before God that it is true that I foresaid Rawlyn of Cowburne in age of 17 years went with my mother to Warton to her brother decon [Richard] Banaster for he lay sick in the pestilence and there my mother and I dwelled there all night with him and about midnight the spots were broken out of him and his wife saw the token and said decon thou thinkest little on Janet thy daughter and anone [in the first place] they send after a priest Sir John of Cornay and believe they send after a clerk one Thomlyn Johnson of Warton and made a deed to Sir John and took seisin† [lawful possession; the right to hold] whether it was known to the sick man or not I wote [know] not never the less it was all done betweene midnight and cockscrow for the foresaid decon banaster that was sick was dead before day verily knowing to me that I suppose the sick man wist [knew] not thereof and well I wote [know] there was nothing done as touching this matter before that night.[20]

In the years immediately following the outbreak of the Black Death the de Freckleton family continued to be the leading family within the township. In 1355 Ralph de Freckleton – presumably the same Ralph who had acquired the manor from his brother Adam in 1322–23 – was still alive. Ellen, the wife of Adam, had by 1337 become a widow but continued to make claims for land against various members of the de Freckleton family until 1354. Also still present were the Butler and

Banastre families together with Richard de Shireburne [of Stonyhurst] whose ancestor, perhaps as a consequence of the troubles mentioned previously, had been given land in Freckleton by Adam de Freckleton. By 1441 another Richard Shireburne was recorded as having 40 acres of land, 20 acres of meadow and 100 acres of pasture in Freckleton. Only in 1717 did the Shireburne family connection with the township finally appear to cease.

The Black Death, however, had struck a fatal blow to the manorial system and, as elsewhere, in a world of acute labour shortages the Freckleton villagers who had survived would have been able to break their servile ties and other obligations. These new economic forces may have been the cause of the financial constraints in which a younger Ralph de Freckleton, grandson of the previously mentioned Ralph, found himself in 1369 when he made a feoffment† of his lands in Freckleton and Elswick. Though the manor was re-granted to him in 1371 he himself then granted, in the same year, 'the whole of his fishery in the township of Freckleton with sufficient ingress and egress' to John the Botiller of Marton at a rent of one rose at the Nativity of St John the Baptist yearly for 16 years, and thereafter £20 yearly.[21] In 1374 Emmota, the mother of Ralph, released to him the 40 acres she had received at the time of her marriage.

In 1382–83 an agreement was made for the marriage of John, son of Ralph, to Alice daughter of Adam de Bradkirk and in the following year Ralph made a further feoffment of the manor of Freckleton, perhaps on this occasion to finance the marriage. It is not known whether the marriage of John and Alice took place nor when the deaths of Ralph and John occurred. The location of the medieval residence of the de Freckleton family is also unknown. The only archaeological evidence of a building dating from the period comes from the excavations carried out by Lancaster University in 1990–91. In the area now covered by the new bypass roundabout a moated site was identified, but at the time of the excavations it was considered that the moat was too small to have served as as a defence around a manor house and was more likely to have surrounded a barn or a fishpond.

By 1428 William Huddleston and his wife Joan, daughter and heiress of a later Ralph, were in possession of the manor and were recorded as still in possession in 1446. Joan appears to have died about 1454 but it was not until 1496 that the estate was sold to the Earl of Derby.

Part II

Freckleton in the Sixteenth and Seventeenth Centuries

CHAPTER 3

The Tudor Township (1485–1603)

In 1489 the Earl of Derby was granted the Freckleton estate of his step-father Sir Thomas Pilkington who, as a supporter of Richard III at the battle of Bosworth in 1485, had suffered forfeiture of his Lancashire estates by Henry VII. As a result of this acquisition and together with the subsequent purchase of the former de Freckleton estate from the Huddleston family in 1496 the Earl became the principal and most influential landowner in Freckleton. The Lathom rental of Thomas, Earl of Derby, shows that in 1522 109s. 9½d. was received from the estate, including 2s. 4d. for fisheries in the Ribble and 4s. 4d. profits of the court held during the year,[1] and this latter profit would seem to indicate that the earls of Derby had continued to hold some form of a manorial court in Freckleton up to, at least, that date.

The Dissolution of the Monasteries during the 1530s, however, brought about a fundamental change in social and economic affairs when land previously held by religious orders passed to the Crown. Shortly after the Dissolution the possessions of Lytham Priory were granted to Sir Thomas Holcroft and when Thomas Clifton, of Clifton, died in 1584 a schedule of his property included the following entry: 'Divers messuages and tenements with appurtenances in Freckleton are held of Thomas Holcroft Esquire ... by fealty† and rent of 4 pence'.[2]

In May of the same year an inquisition held in the queens court at Garstang refers to the lands previously held by the Knights Hospitallers:

Whereas John Sharples, Henry Robinson and Richard Robinson of Freckleton or their assigns do now occupy certain lands and tenements there, late in the tenure of one William Tomlynson deceased, we find and do present that the said John Sharples, Henry Robinson and Richard Robinson have and hold the said lands in fee simple to them and their heirs, and that the rent of threepence is and ought yearly to be paid unto her Majesty out of the said lands as in the right of St Johns, and that relief is to be paid for the same after the death of every heir thereof.[3]

By 1700 the payments seemed to have lapsed and the last known mention of the rents is in 1717 when, following an Act of Parliament that required all Catholics to register their names and real estates, Sir Nicholas Shireburne of Stonyhurst recorded that he had 'All the rents called St John of Jerusalem rents from lands in Freckleton'.[4]

There is also a reference to the lands previously held by Dieulacres Abbey when 'By an Inquisition Post Mortem† taken at Preston on 11 January 1587–88 it appears that John Cowburne died seized of a messuage and twenty acres of land in Freckleton, which was held of the Queen, as of the late Abbey of Dieulacres, by fealty, and rent of 8½*d.* per annum'.[5]

By 1588 the then Earl of Derby had suffered an economic setback in his affairs and in order to ease his financial difficulties found it necessary to attempt to improve the yield from his estates. In Freckleton it was

Naze House. One of the three properties leased by the Earl of Derby to Richard Harrison on 18 November 1598. Although most probably in the ownership of the Kirkham and Coulborn families its subsequent history is not definitely known until the late eighteenth century. In 1795 James Coulborn was the owner and in *c.*1807 he sold the house to the de la Pryme family who were Blackburn merchants.

reported that the steward William Skillicorn, and his bailiff Peter Mosley, used simple surveying techniques to enclose land, much to the annoyance of the local townspeople who saw them about to 'set down wickers ... in order to measure the same ground with cords and lines'.[6]

Perhaps also part of the same innovations was the sale in September and October 1590 of parcels of freehold land to George Brown, William Browne, John [1] Sharples, Henry Robinson, Gregory Freckleton, Nicholas Badger, Henry Cowburn, and Richard Robinson. Eight years later Richard Harrison also acquired his land and properties in the township.

Although the Earl of Derby remained an important landowner during the reign of Elizabeth I the emerging influence of other families, some of whom were to play an important role in township affairs over the next two hundred years, was already evident and of these it was Sharples family that was to become the most influential in Freckleton during the seventeenth century.

CHAPTER 4

The Sharples Family

The earliest mention of the Sharples family in Freckleton is in 1547 when George *[1]* and his son James *[1]* purchased from John Brown of the city of London 'a messuage and tenement in Freckleton in the holding of Richard Tomlinson which John Brown among others lately purchased of Sir Thomas Butler, Knight'.[1] The cost was £12.

Writing about this property in 1623 John *[2]* refers to George *[1]* as his 'grandfathers brother' whilst a schedule compiled about the same time describes Tomlinsons House as 'alias Hall Cross House'. This property would appear to have stood on or near to the site of the present house located on the west side of Kirkham Road just before the junction with Hillock Lane and formerly known as Grimbaldestons House. The 1777 datestone incorporates the initials of Henry and Margaret Grimbaldeston, whilst the deeds to the property contain details of a sale in 1804 when the building was referred to as Hall Cross House 'now in the possession of Henry Grimbaldeston'.[2]

On 30 November 1573 the Earl of Derby granted John *[1]*, who had married Elizabeth Colebrand (sic), the lease of Lower House. In a renewal of the lease on the property in 1582 John *[1]* is described as 'servant of the Earl' and may therefore have been steward for the earl's property in the area. In the 1570s he began to acquire other properties in the township and in 1573 two messuages were purchased from James Anderton, one of the representatives of the four daughters of John Butler. When in 1577 John *[1]* purchased two further messuages, one of which was Higher House, James Anderton also sold him 'all that his purparty part and portion of the manor, lordship or seignourie of Freckleton' that had been obtained by Richard Butler in 1259.

By 1585 the social position of John *[1]* was sufficient for him to be entered in the list of local gentry. This list included all those who were lords of the manor, receiving the title of esquire, and the lesser landowners who had the title of 'gentleman'. As one of the 57 free tenants residing in Amounderness John *[1]* is described as gentleman – the only entry for a resident of Freckleton. Further evidence of his status is provided

---

[1] Numbers in italics within square brackets refer to the genealogical tables.

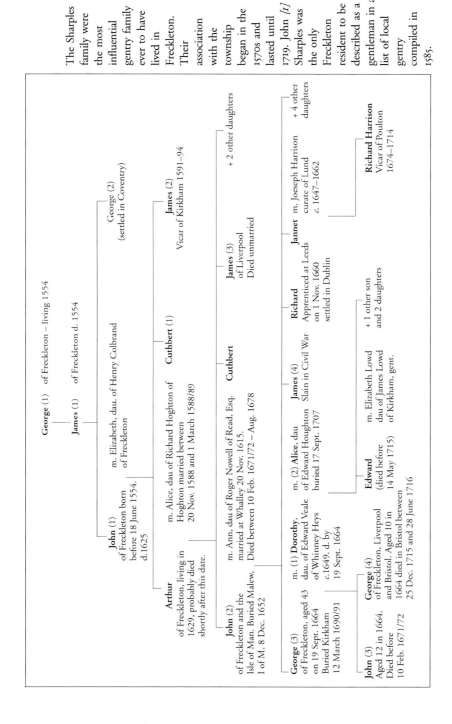

The Sharples family were the most influential gentry family ever to have lived in Freckleton. Their association with the township began in the 1570s and lasted until 1719, John [H] Sharples was the only Freckleton resident to be described as a gentleman in a list of local gentry compiled in 1585.

George (1) of Freckleton – living 1554

James (1) of Freckleton d. 1554

John (1)
of Freckleton born
before 18 June 1554.
d.1625

m. Elizabeth, dau. of Henry Colbrand
of Freckleton

George (2)
(settled in Coventry)

Arthur
of Freckleton, living in
1629, probably died
shortly after this date.

m. Alice, dau of Richard Hoghton of
Hoghton married between
20 Nov. 1588 and 1 March 1588/89

Cuthbert (1)

James (2)
Vicar of Kirkham 1591–94

John (2)
of Freckleton and the
Isle of Man. Buried Malew,
I of M, 8 Dec. 1652

m. Ann, dau of Roger Nowell of Read, Esq.
married at Whalley 20 Nov. 1615.
Died between 10 Feb. 1671/72 – Aug. 1678

Cuthbert

James (3)
of Liverpool
Died unmarried

+ 2 other daughters

George (3)
of Freckleton, aged 43
on 19 Sept. 1664
Buried Kirkham
12 March 1690/91

m. (1) Dorothy,
dau. of Edward Veale
of Whinney Heys
c.1649. d. by
19 Sept. 1664

m. (2) Alice, dau
of Edward Houghton
buried 17 Sept. 1707

James (4)
Slain in Civil War

Richard
Apprenticed at Leeds
on 1 Nov. 1660
settled in Dublin

Jannet m. Joeseph Harrison
curate of Lund
c. 1647–1662

+ 4 other
daughters

John (3)
Aged 12 in 1664.
Died before
10 Feb. 1671/72

George (4)
of Freckleton, Liverpool
and Bristol. Aged 10 in
1664 died in Bristol between
25 Dec. 1715 and 28 June 1716

Edward
(died before
14 May 1715)

m. Elizabeth Lowd
dau of James Lowd
of Kirkham, gent.

+ 1 other son
and 2 daughters

Richard Harrison
Vicar of Poulton
1674–1714

on the occasion of the marriage in 1589 of his son Arthur to Alice, daughter of Richard Hoghton of Hoghton when John *[1]* was recorded in the parish book as 'Churchwarden this year'.

John *[1]* continued to prosper and on 9 October 1590, at a cost of £90 2s. 6d., he purchased Lower House from the Earl of Derby and thereafter the property remained in the ownership of the family until they left the district in the early eighteenth century. A further lease of the same property for 1,000 years was taken out in March 1597 by Cuthbert *[1]*, the second son of John *[1]*, and in September 1598 Cuthbert assigned the lease to trustees.

Some idea of the extent of the family estate in the early seventeenth century can be obtained from documents compiled on the occasion of the marriage in 1615 of John *[2]*, the son of Arthur and grandson of John *[1]*, to Anne, daughter of Roger Nowell of Read. At that time the Sharples estate was described as:

> all their manor of Freckleton, and all their messuages and lands in Freckleton now in the several occupations of the said John Sharples and Arthur Sharples reputed and taken to be the demesne of them or either of them. All their messuages and lands in Freckleton in the tenures of the following:

Grimbaldestons House (Hall Cross). It is probable that this is the house referred to in 1623 as 'Tomlinsons House'. The 1777 datestone incorporates the initials of Henry and Margaret Grimbaldeston. This was the year of their Silver Wedding and was possibly the event which occasioned the (re)building of the present house.

William Cowbron rent	6/–		George Freckleton rent		1/–
Robert Wade	"	16/–	Widow Cowbron	"	4/–
Henry Harrison	"	2/–	John Galter	"	4/–
Widow Singleton	"	3/–	Widow Mewerley	"	5/–
Bartholomew Cowbron		4/–	Widow Mercer	"	2/–
Thomas Wawen	"	2/6	the late wife of		
			Myles Sharples	"	7/–

a messuage and all those houses, smithy and parcels of land in the several tenures of Richard Tomlinson and Thomas Freckleton called Tomlinsons House rent 4/6.

All their parcels of land in Freckleton in the tenures of:

Margaret Freckleton rent   2/–
Thomas Freckleton   "   4*d*.

and all other their messuages and lands in Freckleton.

In addition to the above compilation Roger Nowell added a memorandum which provides an even more comprehensive valuation of the Sharples estate:

Imprimis [First]	The demesne lands in Freckleton being above c [100] acres are worth £100 per annum
	Item the ancient rents and other lands in the same Town which are set up the rack amounteth to £10 per annum
Item	the lands in Kirkham are £4 per annum
Item	the ancient rent of the tenants of the Manor of Warton is £12 10*s*. per annum besides the boones and Fishing in the same Lordship
Item	the lands which are now upon the rack after the rate of 13*s*. 4*d*. the acre within the same Towne the lease whereof doth determine at Candlemas [2 Feb.] AD 1619 and do then come into possession are 44 acres of land of the long measure
Item	the rente charge issuing of Mr Butlers lands is £4 19*s*. 10*d*. per annum all which premises are conveyed and estated upon my son Sharples and the issue male which he shall have by my daughter. So that it appeareth the lands of inheritance aforesaid amount in present to the value of £166 6*s*. 6*d*.

Roger Nowell also estimated the value of corn produced at the water and wind mills and the worth of six acres of moss and concluded that 'the revenues of the whole means to be £200 per annum'.

In 1625 John *[1]* died aged about 80 and the estate passed to his grandson John *[2]*. There are no documents that provide an explanation as to why his son Arthur did not inherit the estate but it was almost certainly due to Arthur's earlier financial difficulties. In 1619 his goods had been forfeited by law and were only returned to the family following their re-purchase by his own son.

In addition to the apparently strained relationship with his father, John *[2]* also had to contend with the creditors of his late father-in-law who were pressing for payment of debts. In a letter to his legal adviser he writes about 'these my greatest troubles and miseries that ever befell me, or I hope that ever will'. These troubles were probably the reason behind the fine of 6*s.* 8*d.* that was imposed at Penwortham Court on 17 April 1626 on the servant of his brother-in-law, Roger Nowell, 'for having on the first of September last at Freckleton made an affray upon Anne Sharples wife of John Sharples of Freckleton, gent, and Richard Harrison of Freckleton, yeoman, and with his sword drawn blood'.[3]

However, whilst there might have been financial problems to resolve concerning his late father-in-law the monetary wealth of John *[2]* himself was not in doubt and in the Lay Subsidy of 1626[4] he was assessed for a larger amount of goods than any other person in the Hundred of Amounderness. Like his grandfather before him John *[2]* entered the service of the Earl of Derby and held office under him in the Isle of Man. In 1630 he was comptroller of the island and in 1636 was named also as deputy governor. He continued in office throughout the English Civil War of 1642–49, although he must have moved between Freckleton and the island because in 1644, following the skirmish on Freckleton Marsh (described in the next chapter) and the subsequent siege of Lathom House, then occupied by the countess of Derby, he was sent by the Earl of Derby to 'let them know what was his Lord's pleasure about yielding it'. The defenders however would not surrender to the Parliamentary forces and 'Mr Sharples thereupon was permitted quietly to return to the Island'.[5]

When the Royalist Earl of Derby left the safety of the Isle of Man in 1651 to fight for Charles II a rebellion took place and the island was surrendered to representatives of the Commonwealth. John *[2]* was later implicated in this rebellion and during the trial in 1662 of the former receiver-general of the island, it was stated that 'Comptroller Sharples was privy to the rising'. It is probable that John was a reluctant participant in the rebellion and did so only to protect his Freckleton estate which otherwise would have been sequestered by Parliament. Whatever his reason he never faced trial as he died on the Isle of Man in 1652 and was buried at Malew, near Castletown.

The Freckleton estate then passed to George *[3]* who, unlike his father, does not appear to have taken any active part in the national politics of the period. Born in 1621 he completed his education at Brasenose College, Oxford, where he matriculated in 1640. He married firstly Dorothy, daughter of Edward Veale of Whinney Heys in Layton who was the leading justice of the peace in the district and a man of great influence. His second wife was Alice, daughter of Edward Houghton of Ramsgreave. Throughout his life George *[3]* was one of the leading men in Kirkham parish and his public duties included that of one of his majesty's coroners for the county and trustee for the free school at Kirkham, a role that involved journeys to London. His social status is evident from entries in the rolls of the Preston Guild Merchants where his name appears as a foreign guild burgess in 1662 and 1682.

Within the township of Freckleton he appears to have been greatly respected and whenever there was a dispute amongst his tenants it was he who took responsibility to resolve the matter. He also acted in other matters and, for example, in 1661 he was named as a trustee in the will of George Marcer, who bequeathed him 'five shillings and my hunting staff with a thrown [throne?] head'.[6] In 1652 his grandfather had authorised the sale of the Warton estate but thereafter George *[3]* took great interest in and continued to add to the Freckleton estate. In 1666 he secured certain lands which were part of the (Ravald) estate that had been leased originally to Richard Harrison in 1598. These eighteen acres were added to the forty two acres of Lower House and sold as a single unit to Newton Charity in 1719.

In 1664 George *[3]* entered into a financial agreement with John Veale of Whinney Heys and others concerning his 'manor, messuages, lands etc in Freckleton in the occupation of George Sharples and Anne Sharples, widow, his mother'. At that date Higher House was described as the 'capital messuage' and appears to have been occupied by Anne Sharples who, in accordance with the terms of the agreement, had the use of the house 'for life'. In the same agreement Lower House was described as a mansion house and, in the event of his death, was for the use of George's widow Alice during the lifetime of his mother. On the death of his mother Alice was to occupy Higher House.

In 1664 Lower House was described as comprising 'the Kitchen, the Brewhouse, the new buildings, the new barn, the hay barn, the little shippon, the orchard next the marsh, the garden next adjoining to the West end thereof, the half of the hempyard'. The earliest surviving description of Higher House is that of 1691 when, following the death of George *[3]*, an inventory was made of his goods. In the inventory the apprizers named the rooms as 'the Larder, the red Chamber, the Hole, the Cannamie [?] Chamber, the entrie, the garding chamber, the passidge chamber, the Blue Chamber, the Knod [?] Chamber, the Little Chamber, the pastery and milkhouse, the servants chamber, Mrs Sharples Chamber, the Kitchen'.[7]

From 1664 until the month before his death in March 1691 George *[3]* made a series of agreements and leases on his various properties, all of which were necessary for the purpose of securing his financial affairs. The last was made in February 1691 when, in order to raise £1000, he mortgaged his estate to Robert St Claire of Gravesend, Kent. In his will, made in the week of his death, George *[3]* refers to 'my manor or reputed manor of Freckleton'.[8] In fact all manorial 'rights' had long since ceased to be recognised by the township and this is the last known occasion when anyone claimed to possess such title in Freckleton. George *[3]* also directed that his estate was to be sold, at any time one year after his death, to discharge the mortgage and other debts and

In 1664 Lower House was described as the mansion house of the Sharples family and clearly had recently undergone some rebuilding as there is mention of 'new buildings' and a 'new barn'. Further rebuilding took place in the late eighteenth century. This photograph of the farmhouse was taken in *c.* 1944. (*Courtesy of Lancashire Record Office – DDNw Box 4*)

legacies. Despite his somewhat straitened financial circumstances his family ensured his funeral befitted his social position in the community and the funeral expenses included:

To John Sharples the Drinking House	£4	18s.	0d.
To a cask of ale at Walkers of Kirkham	£0	13s.	0d.
To ditto at Burrowes	£0	10s.	6d.
To sheep, calves, fish, bacon and pullets and capons	£2	8s.	0d.
To 3 quarters of Mutton from Wildings	£0	9s.	0d.
To Butcher Houghton	£0	5s.	0d.

In addition Mr Clegg (the Vicar of Kirkham) was paid 10s. 0d. for preaching a sermon, whilst the coffin cost 10s. 6d.

The estate then passed to his second son George *[4]* who at the time of his father's death was a surveyor in the Customs House at Liverpool and from where in 1695 he was transferred to Bristol. In his absence the estate was managed by his cousin, Richard Harrison, vicar of Poulton. By 1694 all his father's debts and legacies had been paid off, though this had necessitated the sale of all property in Newton with Scales, together with Higher House in Freckleton and several closes of land. Writing in 1702, George *[4]* recalled the events of the 1690s as a time when he was 'under a necessity of selling and forced to make large pennyworths'. It is also clear that at same time he gave serious consideration, much to the consternation of his tenants, to selling the remainder of the Freckleton estate. In a letter from Richard Harrison he was advised that 'your tenants hear that you intend to sell the inheritance of their several tenements and would take it a favour to be each one purchaser of his own'.

However, no further sales were made until after his death, which occurred in Bristol sometime between December 1715 and January 1716. Three years later, on 2 February 1719, Lower House was sold for £1,375, to the Trustees of John Hornby's Charity School at Newton. The remainder of the estate, including the property at Hall Cross, was sold to William Shaw for £415, thus ending almost two hundred years of family influence in the township.

CHAPTER 5

The Stuart Township (1603–1714)

Principal Families

Foremost after the Sharples family was the Harrison family[1] whose association with Freckleton also had its origins in their connection with the earls of Derby. Cuthbert Harrison, born about 1553, was the son of Grace Harrison. As a widow, Grace married Peter Mason of Lathom, who owned property and land in Freckleton and whose brother was secretary to the Earl of Derby in 1572. Cuthbert married in 1573 but does not appear to have come to live in Freckleton until some years later where he died in 1588. In his will Cuthbert bequeathed to his son Richard 'one great chest' but there is no mention of any property and it is not until 18 November 1598, when the Earl of Derby granted Richard Harrison leases on what was later known as Ravald House,[2] Naze House,[3] and at Hall Cross (on the east side of Kirkham Road),[4] that we have any definite information about the properties the family owned or leased.

The acquisition of three such important dwellings clearly indicates that Richard was a man of some means and influence, and in 1638 he was elected to represent Freckleton as one of the Thirty Men of Kirkham. He died in 1657 and his estate passed to his son Cuthbert who had married Alice Coulbourne of Freckleton in 1622. When Cuthbert died in 1661 his son Richard succeeded to the estate, but when Richard himself died in 1675 he directed in his will, in spite of having a large family, that the whole of his property was to be sold and the proceeds given to his wife and children. His Ravald estate was sold to Henry Jackson but, in the absence of documentary evidence, the purchaser(s) of his properties at Naze House and Hall Cross remains unknown.

Although the family ceased to own property in the township the descendants of Richard continued to be active locally. Joseph the youngest son of Richard became minister of Lund Chapel in 1645 and in 1650 the parliamentary commissioners reported that he was 'a godly, diligent and painfull [painstaking] minister'. However, as a consequence of the 1662 Act of Uniformity he was ejected from his living, presumably for his puritan convictions, though he continued to live in Newton with

Scales. He married Jennet, the sister of George *[3]* Sharples, and it was their son Richard, the vicar of Poulton, who was entrusted by George *[4]* Sharples to manage his Freckleton estate.

Although the last mention of a male de Freckleton, as lord of the manor, had been Ralph in *c.*1427 it seems clear that when the senior male line died out junior branches of the family remained in the township and prospered. Even the favoured christian name of Ralph was perpetuated and in 1587 a Ralph Freckleton died leaving two messuages which were inherited by his son Henry. Henry died in 1626, his heir being a nephew also called Ralph, who, according to a deed, subsequently leased a messuage, which almost certainly stood on the site of the present Mount House in Preston Old Road, to his own brother Henry.

When a James Freckleton died in 1586 he too was in possession of a dwelling in the township and it was probably this property that his son Gregory acquired from the Earl of Derby in 1590. Members of the Freckleton family continued to have a presence of relative importance throughout the Stuart period, and the family association with the township that gave them their name did not cease finally until 1840 when the Raker estate was sold.

In addition the Badger, Browne, Cowburne and Robinson families were also already present in the township by the sixteenth century and were soon after joined by a branch of the Hall family. The earliest mention of the Brown family occurs in 1313–14 when Robert Browne unsuccessfully claimed a messuage against Adam, son of Alan de Pool.[5] A similar time span applies to the Cowburne (alternatively spelt Coulborne) family who acquired their surname from an estate in Warton where a Roger Culban lived in 1332,[6] though an even earlier possible corruption of the name occurs in one of the Lytham Priory charters of 1210–50 where there is a reference to 'land in a field in Freckleton between that once Calbayn's'.[7]

The Township

Although there is no official estimation of the population of the township at the commencement of the Stuart period there are two events which may provide a rough estimate. In 1642 all adults were required to sign the Protestation Oath,[8] and based on the number of men taking the oath attempts have been made to estimate the total population of townships. If the method used is reliable then the population of Freckleton in 1642 would have been approximately 217. Altogether 149 men and women took the Oath and of the thirty surnames entered on the return the four most numerous were Browne (20), Freckleton (18), Cowburn (12) and Hall (10).

The other possible source is the Hearth Tax returns which record the tax of one shilling levied on every hearth in each residence on Lady Day and Michaelmas Day from 1662 until 1689. In the return of 1664 the number of properties assessed in Freckleton was 49 of which 37 appear to have been chargeable.[9] Exempt from payment were those in receipt of poor relief and those inhabiting houses worth less than 20 shillings per annum and not paying parish rate. By multiplying the figure of 49 by an average household size of 4.5 a population of 220 compares favourably with the 1642 estimate of 217.

The number of surnames entered on the Hearth Tax return of 1664 was 21 and, as in 1642, it was the same families that were the most numerous – Browne (9), Cowburn (6), Freckleton (5) and Hall (4). In addition there were 6 entries for the Sharples family, with George *[3]* Sharples occupying the property (presumably Higher House) with the largest number of hearths. Nearest in number to his six hearths were the homes of Lawrence Cowburn and Butler Cowburn each with three, and apart from William Cowburn, Joanne Cowburn and Henry Robinson with two hearths each, all the others had only the one.

The majority of the population would have been engaged in agriculture, and work, family life and township affairs would have been their main topics of interest and conversation. Survival was the primary objective and in the seventeenth century people had to contend with various diseases and disasters. The crisis of 1623 was one of the most severe for almost 300 years and in that year fifteen Freckleton residents were buried at Kirkham, compared with six in 1620 and none in 1625.[10] Although fifteen may not now seem excessive it represented perhaps 7% of the population and the present day equivalent would be 490 deaths in one year. This crisis was the result of either famine or disease, or possibly both, and was found throughout north-west England. In May 1631 came the great plague and although separate township figures were not recorded the total number of burials in Kirkham parish that year was 304, of which 193 occurred in the months of August and September.[11]

Under the Poor Law Act of 1601 the township was responsible for certain functions and at an annual meeting the overseers of the poor, the surveyor of the highways and the constable were chosen by their fellow ratepayers as the township officers. As the name of the Act implies

Cottage, School Lane. When demolished in 1966 this cottage was almost certainly over 300 hundred years old. It was cruck framed, walls were made of wattle and daub and thatch was still present beneath the tin roof. The last occupants were the Hawthornthwaite family who lived there until the 1950s.

the work of the overseers and the constable was primarily the relief of the poor and this ever present problem is dealt with in more detail in chapter 7. Money for both poor relief and other expenses would have been raised through local taxation, probably by the levying of the poor rate on properties above a particular rental value.

In Freckleton the office of constable appears to have been considered a symbol of the independence of the township from any local manorial control, and whenever the marsh gate owners took their grievances to law they invariably prefaced their submission with the words 'the said Township of Freckleton is and for the time whereof the memory of man is not to the contrary hath been a Township ... and hath constantly had Constables and other rights ...'

However, despite this apparent independence the constables were still required to attend the baronial court of Penwortham, an obligation that originated from the days when the manorial lords of Freckleton held their manor at the behest of the barony of Penwortham. In 1626 Thomas

Freckleton, together with James Sharples, was chosen by the inhabitants to be constable, but his appointment was disallowed by the steward at the Penwortham court leet following an initial refusal by Thomas to undertake the office. However, after representation to the magistrates at the quarter sessions Thomas Freckleton 'was sworn as Constable Of Freckleton on the abovesaid day [22 April 1626] in the abovesaid year before us'.[12]

National events were probably of little general interest to the majority of the population although one exception would have been the days leading up to 18 August 1644, when Freckleton was the centre of a minor skirmish between opposing sides in the English Civil War. After his defeat at the battle of Marston Moor in June 1644 Prince Rupert, the Royalist leader, retreated into Lancashire. Although he himself did not stay in the county his forces remained for a month afterwards, and by mid August numbered about 2,700 in the Lytham and Kirkham areas, nearly all cavalry.

Monday 18 August was appointed as the day for these forces to rendezvous on Freckleton Marsh when, presumably referring to the day before, it was reported that the Royalist leaders and many others:

> lay that night about the house of Richard Harrison [presumably Ravald House], having their provisions brought to them from Mr Westbie's House at Moulbreck [Mowbreck Hall]. They brought with them out of the North and other places divers droves of Cattle which they carried along, yet some they lost in the County. They lay upon that Marsh and in the town till after one of the clock, the other day, for the Flood was so there was no passage over the Ribble till that time.[13]

In response Sir John Meldrum – in charge of the local Parliamentarian forces – marched to attack them, but being unsure of the countryside wasted much time and was forced to return to Preston. He then marched along the north bank of the Ribble and at Lea Hall the Royalists were seen crossing the river at Freckleton – possibly at the point near to the present Naze House – when

> For more expedition, command was given that horsemen should take behind them musketeers: who rid up speedily to Proud Bridge in Freckleton, where some [Royalists] remained. And coming up within musket-shot of them, killed one or two, and the rest fled. But it being marsh ground, and many pools and holes, not very passable for strangers, there was not pursuit of them, so that all got over [the Ribble] in safety.[14]

During the remaining years of the Civil War and throughout the

Commonwealth period, Freckleton appears to have passed through a period of relative tranquillity and the office of constable seems to have rotated, without dissent, among those eligible to serve. In 1675, however, the year of the disruptive Quaker meeting described in chapter 13, there is an indication of friction within the township, and Lawrence Webster and William Robinson felt it necessary to petition the magistrates at Preston about the length of time they were being expected to remain in office. In his petition Lawrence Webster said that:

> your petitioner and one William Robinson of Freckleton hath already Served one year and a quarter in the office of a constable for the town of Freckleton and ought to have been dismissed the last general sessions here holden but it is that Mathew Kirkham and Ralph Freckleton both of Freckleton ... Should by usual custom have served for this present year being their time to serve by house row but would not come to the last Sessions to be Sworn nor as yet will not so that your petitioner and the said William Robinson are like to serve two years.[15]

In response the magistrates agreed to provide an allowance to the petitioners for serving 'this time more than they should have Served'. Although we do not know the background to the dispute it seems probable that Ralph Freckleton and Mathew Kirkham were reluctant to serve in 1675 because of events then unfolding in the township, though whether this was due to their sympathies towards the Quakers or straightforward avoidance of responsibility will never be known.

In the remaining forty years of the Stuart period township affairs, apart from the continuing matter of non payment of tithes by the Quakers, appear to have run smoothly and there are no known cases of disputes over accepting township offices, nor indeed of any other problems.

Wealth and Status in Later Stuart Freckleton

From the wills and probate inventories available at the Lancashire Record Office it is possible to trace the wealth and status of some of the many people who lived, worked and died in Freckleton during the years 1657 to 1714. An inventory was a central part of proving the will and was a list of personal goods credits and debts compiled under oath by friends and neighbours. Personal estate comprised of both household goods and livestock and crops. It did not include real estate (property). The inventories also provide a picture of the farming practices carried on within the township and this aspect is looked at in more detail in chapter 21.

Altogether 69 wills and inventories have been analysed and from the

Inventory of George *[3]* Sharples, 1691. The inventory forming part of the will of George [3] is the most detailed of all the surviving seventeenth-century inventories. As the leading farmer of his day George and his family lived in relative comfort. (*Courtesy of Lancashire Record Office – WRW (A) 1691*)

54 which give rank or status, only George *[3]* Sharples, whose inventory was valued at £208 19s. 4d., was described as 'gentleman'. The next in order of status were the 25 yeoman. Yeoman has been described 'as the status name of the most successful of those who worked the land' and 'the men who held it under the old order became farmers under the new'.[16] Thirteen other men were referred to as husbandmen, an occupation described as 'an extremely common term of men in the old world, because it was the description of what so many of them were engaged in, tending the animals and tilling the soil'.[17] Of the eleven women ten were described as widows and one a spinster. In addition there were two linen websters (weavers), a blacksmith and a tailor.

The valuations from the 54 inventories can be seen in the following table:

Up to £20	– 15 persons	£151–£200	– 1 person
£21–£50	– 17 "	£201–£250	– 2 persons
£51–£100	– 13 "	£251–£300	– 1 person
£101–£150	– 5 "		

and although providing an interesting insight into a section of the community they only tell us about the men and women in the township who had sufficient money and possessions of some value to justify making a will. The day to day existence of the rest of the population, including the various tradesmen necessary to keep the township self sufficient, can only be gleaned from other sources.

Between 1657 and 1688 the average amount for fourteen yeoman inventories was £79 and ranged from a high of £179 14s. 6d. for James Sharples in 1663, to £21 9s. 2d. for William Tomlinson in 1662. Between 1689 and 1714 the average of eleven inventories increased to £90, with the goods of Andrew Freckleton the younger being valued at £273 1s. 0d. in 1710, but only £18 6s. 6d. for Matthew Kirkham in 1703. In the first of the same two periods the average amount for ten husbandman inventories was £28 and ranged from £45 8s. 3d. for Henry Browne in 1667 to £4 8s. 4d. for Jeffrey Freckleton in 1674. In the latter period the average of three husbandmen inventories increased slightly to £39, with the goods of John Johnson valued at £55 15s. 10d. in 1696 and those of Butler Browne at £27 17s. 8d. in 1693.

What does emerge from these figures is confirmation that in this period yeomen were wealthier than husbandmen, and that the term 'yeoman' not only indicated social status but also wealth. There was, however, some overlapping and some yeomen were obviously determined to retain their social status whatever their financial situation.

A comparison of the value of the inventories for the ten widows reveals that four were in excess of £50 and ranged from that of Jane Smalley, with £83 1s. 5d. in 1685, to the £55 6s. 2d. of Bridget Freckleton in 1710. None of the inventories of the other six women were valued in excess of £18. Being widows many women must have been concerned about the future prospects of their children, particularly those of a young age, and others for whom they had had some responsibility. This concern is sometimes reflected in the bequests made in their wills.

After specifying bequests to members of her family, including Katherine Sharples 'my niece who now dwelleth with me', Agnes Browne also gave £3 to her servant John Singleton 'with one bed and all furniture belonging to it and the broad Chest with one chair and one cushion'. One of the bequests made in 1667 by Margaret Marcer, the widow of George Marcer, suggests that she had acted as the village midwife, as in addition to her family members she also gave 'to all the rest of [the] Children I took into the World every one six pence'. In 1670 Jennett Gawlter left her tenement to her eldest son John but bound him 'to pay the sum of seven pounds & ten shillings ... for the apprenticeship of his Brother William my youngest son at the 25 June next ensuing', whilst Anne Smith in 1679 divided her personal estate, that included livestock and household furniture, item by item amongst her three children Richard, Elizabeth and Margery.

Not one of the inventories of the four tradesmen exceeded £13 12s. 0d. James Hargreave the blacksmith left just £5 6s. 8d., of which his working tools – 'bellows, hammers, vice and other little tools' – were valued at £4 0s. 0d. Richard Browne the tailor was slightly more prosperous and left personal estate of £12 0s. 9d., of which £8 13s. 4d. was for three kine and one calf, but there is nothing in his inventory relating to his occupation.

Debts and Loans

As private country banks did not begin to develop until the mid-eighteenth century it was necessary for each community to organise its own credit system, and from the mid-seventeenth century inventories begin to record debts either 'owing by' or 'owing to'. The sums recorded were in bills or bonds often noted as either by 'speciality' or 'without speciality' and whilst the latter method gave higher interest rates it also carried a higher degree of risk. This practice would seem to have been in operation all over the country and 'The provision of credit enabled people in the countryside to purchase more land, to erect new buildings and to survive bad harvests and misfortune on their farms. It attracted the men who lived in retirement, and the widows and spinsters who had money to spare, and who were able to live on the interest of their capital'.[18]

Alice Freckleton, a widow, was the provider of both types of loan and when she died in 1674 her inventory recorded … 'Due to the decedent by speciality £3 0s. 0d., Due with out speciality £1 0s. 0d., All her apparell £0 13s. 4d.' Total £4 13s. 4d. In 1677 William Browne left personal estate to the value of £87 15s. 2d. of which 52% was represented by the £45 5s. 0d. due to him, including £40 5s. 0d. without speciality. At the other end of the scale the £7 0s. 0d. owing by speciality to John Kirkham in 1693 was only 18% of his personal estate.

The largest amount owing to any one person was that due to Andrew Freckleton the younger, whose personal estate, as already mentioned, was valued at £273 1s. 0d. Included in this amount was £62 2s. 0d. for 'the several sums of money owing unto the decedent upon bonds, bills and account book (some of which said sums are debts desparate [i.e. over-due])', and £146 0s. 0d. for 'the several sums of money formerly owing unto Andrew Freckleton senior, late of Freckleton aforesaid, yeoman: But was owing unto the decedent (some of which said sums being also debts desparate)'. Also included in the £273 1s. 0d. was the £30 0s. 0d. that Andrew Freckleton the younger had in ready money.

Both sets of outstanding monies are itemised with the name of the borrower and the amount loaned. The earliest outstanding loan is dated 1696 and others then commence on an almost yearly basis until 1709, and it seems clear that many of the farmers in the township looked to both Andrew the younger and his uncle as the men who would provide them with necessary finance when they required it. Although described as yeomen it is probable, as we will see later, that the wealth of both men had been acquired as a result of their involvement in the linen industry. Andrew the elder died in April/May 1709 followed in March/April 1710 by his nephew, and as the widow of Andrew the elder also died in April 1710 the monies finally came to Bridget and Thomas, the children of Andrew the younger.

Part III

Freckleton in the Eighteenth Century

CHAPTER 6

The Georgian Township (1714–1837)

The Eighteenth-century Township

The end of the Stuart period in 1714 coincided with the departure of the Sharples family and with them the last vestiges of any paternal influence within the township, and it was not until the end of the eighteenth century when the Mayor family, through their commercial success, rose to prominence that any one particular family once more came to dominate township affairs to such a degree. For most of the eighteenth century the various township offices were filled by the leading men of their day who came from families such as Brown, Coulborn, Goodshaw, Hardiker, Mayor, Smalley, Wade and Willacy.

The absence of any known eighteenth-century township minute books makes it difficult to assess the influence of particular individuals, but Robert Smalley, a tanner who died in 1780 and whose family had been associated with Freckleton for almost two hundred years, was probably as influential as any. Part of his former extensive estate is still identifiable today by the house in Preston Old Road called Smalley Cottage.

A more representative picture of the township as a whole is partially provided by the occupations of thirty eight Freckleton men who were married at Kirkham church between the years 1755 and 1771. In that period twenty were described as husbandman, nine as weaver, two as flax dresser and two as yeoman together with a blacksmith, carpenter, labourer, mariner and a tanner, and these occupations reflect the way in which the township changed during the eighteenth century from one that was predominately agricultural to one combining both agriculture and manufacturing.

76 Preston Old Road. Unfortunately nothing is known of the early history of this Grade 2 listed three-storey building. Built with hand-made brick it has a tiled roof with gable chimneys. The 1780 datestone would appear to incorporate the initials of John and Alice Mayor who were married in 1768 and who possibly resided in the house until John rebuilt 'Lorimers' in 1793.

Township Administration

Probably throughout the eighteenth century and certainly during the first third of the nineteenth century township affairs were carried out by a committee chosen at the town's annual meeting. This committee appears to have then nominated the men who were to be overseers of the poor, constable and the surveyor of the highways. Throughout this period the constable was still required to attend the medieval baronial court of Penwortham and there are annual references in the township disbursement records of dues being paid for 'service' at Penwortham Court until at least 1827.

Amongst the few surviving township documents from the mid-eighteenth century are the township accounts for the years 1738 and 1739, 1741 [1] and 1744.[2] The accounts for 1738 show that the disbursements totalled £38 2s. 5d., but as the constable received only £33 15s. 5d. from the various assessments he was £4 7s. 0d. out of pocket. The following year the disbursements increased by 68% to £55 14s. 5d., but as £56 2s. 9d. had been collected from the ratepayers the constable had 8s. 4d. 'in his hand'. In 1741 the amounts were £61 2s. 3d. collected and £64 8s. 3d. disbursed and in 1744 £59 6s. 2½d. and £54 8s. 7½d. In the latter year Robert Smalley and Thomas Freckleton were chosen as constables and granted a (joint?) wage of £3 10s. 0d., and at the same meeting £4 6s. 7d. was received from the purse of William Brown, the retiring constable.

Although there are no documents to show the pattern of population growth during the eighteenth century the social consequences brought about by an increasing and changing population may have been one of the reasons why in 1754 forty-six ratepayers decided to form an 'Association for the Prosecution of Felons' when it was stated that:

> Whereas divers Thefts Larcenys Trespasses and other Misdemeanours are frequently committed in the Township of Freckleton ... and the persons committing such Misdemeanours frequently escape punishment by reason of the Charges and Expences attending such prosecution to the great Encouragement of the said offenders and the evil Example of others
>
> Now we whose Hands and Seals are hereunto set & subscribed being inhabitants owners or occupiers of Lands within the said Township do hereby ... covenant grant and agree to & with Mathew Ryley [&] James Crookhall both of Clifton in the said County Gentlemen ... that when any of the offences aforesaid shall be committed or done within the said Township the Constable there for the time being shall prosecute such offenders at the Expence and Charge of the said Township of Freckleton and that in order to reimburse himself the Charges of such prosecution it shall and may be lawful to and for the said Mathew Ryley and James Crookhall ... at the Request of the said Constable to lay a Rate or assessment upon the Inhabitants of the said Township ... which Rate [made] of the said parties subscribing ... hereby binds & oblige him or herself to pay the said Constable or to the said Mathew Ryley & James Crookhall ... upon Demand.[3]

There is no subsequent information relating to the number of years that the association functioned, although a possible connection with the days when the township constable was responsible for law and order is provided with the building situated in Preston Old Road and formerly known as 'the Cage'. Although partially rebuilt in the 1986 it was reputed to have been 'where drunks and other minor offenders were locked up for the night'.[4] The township also had to contribute towards maintaining law and order within the county and in 1773 the constable was instructed by the high constable of Amounderness to raise money for the repairs to the Preston House of Correction.[5]

The Township Highways

An Act of 1555 required the annual appointment of a surveyor of the highways for each township. The surveyor was empowered to raise local rates and was also responsible for the supervision of statute labour whereby each able-bodied householder or tenant was required to give four days statute labour a year, a requirement that was increased to six days a year from 1691.

As we will see in chapter 19 the earliest surviving township highway accounts are those beginning in the late seventeenth century and concern the road across the marsh, which appears to have been the responsibility of the township until the late eighteenth century. Amongst the few surviving eighteenth-century township highway documents is one dated October 1730 in which the magistrates at the quarter sessions granted a

'The Cage', Preston Old Road. In 1754 forty-six ratepayers decided to form an 'Association for the Prosecution of Felons' but it is unknown whether the building on Preston Old Road was used as a lock up at that time. An Act of Parliament passed in 1842 ordered that 'lock-up houses, strong rooms or cages' be appropriated for the purpose of the Act. The building was rebuilt in 1986.

certificate of 'Good repair of Highway' which stated that 'Whereas the Highways in Freckleton Stand presented for being out of repair These are therefore to certify his Majesties Justices of the Peace that the same have been lately repaired and are now in good order and Condition'.[6]

During the late eighteenth century there are also frequent references in the records of Penwortham Court to certain roads within Freckleton, as in 1779 when Edward Mayor, as surveyor of the highways, was presented for 'not repairing and amending the bottom part of a certain Lane called Strike Lane which part of the said Lane wants Earth throwing into the middle in order to raise the said Lane containing forty yards in Length or thereabouts'.[7]

It was not only the roads but also the repair of bridges that was the responsibility of the township and in a letter dated November 1801 Thomas Willacy, in his post of constable, wrote to Thomas Crookall of Lytham, the high constable of Amounderness, informing him that the number 'of Bridges within our Town are':

The Lamaleach Bridge repaired by Freckleton & Warton
The Headless cross Bridge repaired by Freckleton & Kirkham
Beside two other Bridges in the High roads leading to Kirkham and repaired by our Town only'.[8]

It is, however, the township highway account book for the years 1802 to 1818[9] that provides the clearest picture of how roads were maintained and financed. The money inevitably came from yet another assessment placed on the ratepayers and varied from 2s. 0d. in the pound in 1802 to 7½d. in 1808. The amounts raised by these assessments ranged from £147 10s. 4½d. in 1814 to just £22 11s. 7d. in 1812, but as this latter year was also the year when £530 had to be raised by the marsh gate owners – amongst whom were many ratepayers – for the repair of the Clow, it was probably thought enough was enough!

It seems clear from the accounts that ample use was made of the option that enabled any ratepayer who was required to perform statute labour to provide a substitute, and James Hargreaves, who had previously been landlord of the *Ship Inn*, was regularly employed on maintaining the roads in the early years of the nineteenth century. In 1802 he was paid 6d. a day for general maintainance work and for additional work such as 'pulling up 941 yards of Pavern[men]t at 7½d. per score' he was paid £1 9s. 4½d. In the year 1807–08 he was paid a total of £5 3s. 9d. for 207½ days' work and it is therefore not surprising that he and his wife Mary were also in receipt of regular poor law payments for items such as money for relief, payment of house rent and clothing and clogs. On one occasion there is an allowance of 2s. 0d. for 'a pint of rum for James'.

On the evidence of the materials purchased by the township it would seem that roads were made up of a layer of gravel that was placed on top of stone blocks. In May 1802 John Counsel was paid £4 4s. 0d. 'for 4 Flatt Loads of Gravel' for which there were additional costs of £3 12s. 0d. for '9 Men Loading' and £2 2s. 0d. for '7 Men Discharging', all of which took six days to complete. In September the same year George Richardson was paid 13s. 0d. for 3½ tons of stone. Whenever this sort of work took place there was usually an allowance for ale and in October 1802 William Nickson, Innkeeper, was paid £1 3s. 0d. for the ale he had supplied during the 'Loading and Discharging of Gravel'.

With the notable exception of Higher Road (Kirkham Road) the accounts also provide information as to when and where work was carried out. A possible reason for the omission of Higher Road may be that following a special appeal for its repair in 1774 sufficient money had been raised, through subscription, to build it to a standard that eliminated the need for regular repair.

6 March 1805	To Richard Holiday for Carting and other work in the Croftbutts Lane as per Bill		£3	6s.	0d.
2 Dec.	1809	Roger Allanson 1½ day Pool House Lane [Bush Lane] at 3s. 8d.	£0	5s.	6d.
25 Dec.	1809	Robert Hall's Bill for Brook Lane [the area of Preston Old Road adjacent to the marsh gate?]	£1	2s.	6d.
	[1809]	To Lammaleach Bridge	£41	10s.	0d.
6 Jan.	1815	To Thomas Dugdale for plat covering Stones for Strike Lane	£1	12s.	10½d.
2 Dec.	1815	To ½ expence repairing Headless Cross Bridge	£0	9s.	6d.
7 Dec.	1816	To John Garlick 7 Tons little Stones		14s.	0d.
		" " " Spreading [Stones] Hillock Lane 2s. 0d.	£0	16s.	0d.
28 Dec.	1817	To Robert Hall 12 Stoops Lamaleach Lane [Lytham Road]	£1	16s.	0d.

This method of maintenance continued until 1835 when an Act passed that year abolished statute labour, permitted the levying of a highway rate, and allowed for the employment of a paid district surveyor.

Local and National Taxes

In addition to the taxes raised to pay for the relief of the poor, money was also raised through local taxation to pay other dues such as the annual payment to the high constable and the church tax (rate). There were also annual payments made for 'Birds & Eggs' (?) and from 1803 to 1807 the catching and destroying of Mouldwarps (Moles) for which Thomas Thompson was paid the considerable sum of £13 12s. 4d. on 6 April 1805. Among an almost bewildering range of miscellaneous payments the following entries may provide some images of life in the early nineteenth-century township:

10 April	1804	To Thos Threlfall & Jas Mayor Marking the Carts within the Township	3s.	2d.
19 Nov.	1804	To a Journey to Preston with Returns of Boats Barges etc.	4s.	0d.
26 Nov.	1808	To Richd Coulbron for a Coffin for Drowned Man	18s.	0d.
		To Funeral Expences	£1 2s.	8d.
7 Jan.	1811	Thos Adamson for Liquor at taking the Inquest of Rymer Porter's Child	5s.	6d.
29 June	1811	Journey to Preston about Population [the Census]	5s.	0d.
25 Oct.	1817	To paid Mr J. Grimshaw for his opinion and Case about the Coal Hills	6s.	0d.
21 Dec.	1818	Willm Lambert printing lists of Paupers	11s.	6d.
27 July	1821	Journey to Preston with returns of Lunaticks	5s.	0d.
30 July	1822	Extra Meeting of Committee R. Clifton's [the Ship] about Smithy	3s.	6d.
23 Dec.	1826	Doct Warbrick attending the Inquest etc. of Dead Child	15s.	0d.
19 Apr.	1827	Wages Serving Officer	£20 0s.	0d.

As well as the poor law and highway assessments there were also national taxes to be paid and in 1797 Thomas Willacy and Thomas Threlfall were appointed assessors for duties on clocks and watches, horses, inhabited houses and male servants.[10] In 1808–09 the same two men carried out a further assessment[11] and identified 48 persons who were liable in respect of various taxes relating to:

Houses & Windows (i.e. no. of windows)   43 persons

Inhabited Houses (i.e. £ rent)	2	" [both Innkeepers]
Male Servants at 5/–	3	"
Two Wheel Carriages drawn by one horse	2	"
Two Wheel Taxed Carts	2	"
Horses for riding or drawing Carriages		
(Private use)	4	"
Horses & Mules at 12s. 6d. each	18	"
Dogs at 6s. 0d. each	9	"
Dogs at 10s. 0d. each	8	"

Land Tax Return 1810. A tax collected between *c.*1692 and 1832. The returns from 1780 to 1832 name the people paying the tax but unfortunately do not identify the property or the land in question. Nevertheless it is often possible to deduce the location by linking the returns to other records. (*Courtesy of Lancashire Record Office – QDL 1810/A/24*)

The entry for 'Houses and Windows' almost certainly refers to the window tax that was first introduced in 1696. A new Act in 1747 provided that households with between ten and fourteen windows paid 6*d.* per window on top of the old basic 2*s.* 0*d.*, and the tax was not abolished until 1851. In Freckleton an annual payment, usually 10*s.* 0*d.*, was made to 'Window Peepers' whose job, presumably, was to count the number of windows in each property. From 1799 there were also demands for income tax, whilst the land tax which had been collected since 1692, at the usual rate of 4*s.* 0*d.* in the pound, was not abolished in its original form until 1832.

The Militia and Army of Reserve

Prominent amongst township expenses during the early nineteenth century were the costs of the militia, a military force usually raised from the civilian population to supplement regular troops in an emergency. At such times the township constable was ordered to draw up lists of all able-bodied men of a certain age. A ballot was then held to decide which of these men should be called up or else pay for a replacement. Following resumption of hostilities with Napoleonic France the township constable and others were kept busy during the summer of 1803, complying with the regulations concerning the militia and the army of reserve, as the following extracts show:

10 June	To a Journey to Preston to ballot for Militia	3*s.*	6*d.*
	To Thos Noblet giving Militia Men Notice	1*s.*	6*d.*
18 June	To Sundry expence at ... Preston Swearing in the Militia	3*s.*	10*d.*
	To Thos Threlfalls Journey [to] " " "	5*s.*	0*d.*
	To Thos Willacy Ditto	3*s.*	6*d.*
29 July	To a Journey to Preston with Returns for the Army of Reserve	3*s.*	6*d.*
2 Aug.	To Thos Noblet giving Notice for the men to meet at School	1*s.*	6*d.*
6 Aug.	To a Journey to Preston to ballot for the Army of Reserve	3*s.*	6*d.*
13 Aug.	To Mr Moon for 100 Papers for Volunteers	5*s.*	0*d.*

In addition there were two further journeys to Preston on September 17 and 24, both incurring costs of 3*s.* 6*d.*, together with unspecified payments of £7 15*s.* 6*d.* for the militia and £45 9*s.* 7*d.* for the army of reserve. Even twelve years after the end of hostilities with France the disbursement books record annual journeys to Preston with the militia returns and in 1827 William Riley was paid 3*s.* 0*d.* for 'giving Notice for Militia to Meet'.

Wealth and Status in the Eighteenth Century

Towards the end of the eighteenth century the practice of combining wills and inventories ceased, so for the years 1714 to 1782 a total of only 36 wills have been analysed, resulting in the following valuation break-down:

Up to £20	– 11 persons	£201–£250	– Nil
£21–£50	– 4 "	£251–£300	– Nil
£51–£100	– 6 "	£301–£350	– 3 persons
£101–£150	– 6 "	£351–£400	– 1 person
£151–£200	– 2 "		

The remaining three inventories totalled £414, £530 and £667 and of the 34 men represented in the survey there were 21 yeomen and nine husbandmen, together with a tailor, a blacksmith, a tanner and a labourer. The two women were both widows of wealthy yeomen.

The three highest inventories all belonged to yeomen, two of whom were Quakers. The inventory of William Brown was valued at £530 2*s.* 0*d.* and that of Joseph Lancaster, after allowing for funeral expenses, at £667 8*s.* 0*d.* As we will see in chapter 13 William Brown bequeathed a substantial amount of money in 1724 towards the building of the Quaker meeting house and school. Joseph Lancaster must have lived comfortably, if frugally, because in 1782 the bulk of his personal estate of £656 was in securities, whereas his household goods totalled just £11 17*s.* 0*d.* together with £13 13*s.* 0*d.* in cash. His only other possession was a horse valued at £1 9*s.* 0*d.*

In 1724 the inventory of Richard Baine was valued at £414 7*s.* 0*d.*, of which £252 was owing in bonds and bills, and a further £100 'by several conveyances or instruments in writing'. He left numerous bequests to an extended family and evidence of his 'sound and disposing mind and memory' with regard to the money he had previously loaned is contained in his will, when he gave £10 to 'Thomas son of Peter Robinson deceased in case a pretended bond forged by the said Peter Robinson against me be destroyed'.

The clear distinction in wealth that was evident in the late Stuart period between a yeoman and a husbandman becomes somewhat blurred on the evidence provided by these later wills. Of the remaining eighteen yeomen inventories the amounts ranged from £15 1s. 0d. to £374 3s. 0d. with an average of £171, but if the three highest are eliminated the average reduces to £110. However even that does not necessarily convey a full picture since eight of those were under £50. The inventories of the nine husbandmen also fall into distinct categories with five under £50, including four under £20, and the remaining four ranging from £100 to £147. The overall average is £64 but for four of the nine the average is only £15.

The inventory of James Smith, a yeoman who died in 1726, was valued at £374 3s. 0d., an amount that included 'The decedants Apparrell & some other goods sold at £203 18s. 0d.' Amongst the recipients of the numerous individual bequests made by James Smith were the Browne, Coulborne, Freckleton, Goodshaw and Salthouse families. In contrast the value of the inventory of John Buck, also described as a yeoman, was just £21 18s. 6d. when he died in 1727, of which £1 8s. 6d. was for 'goods in the firehouse [living room]', and £2 5s. 0d. for 'goods in the upper room'. It is probable, however, that John Buck was wealthier than his inventory supposes as in his will he states that his nephew John Foster was to have a messuage lately purchased from James Smith on condition that John Foster made certain payments to other family members. In his own will John Foster, who died in 1783, describes one of his properties as 'a Dwelling House and Barn part of which said Barn hath lately been converted into a House and garden at the back thereof ... formerly called James Smith'. Although the house described cannot be pinpointed with absolute certainty there is evidence to suggest (see chapter 24) that it stood near to the present Stanley House in Preston Old Road.

At the opposite end of the scale was Robert Noblet who died in 1725 and left just £10 11s. 0d. Apart from the 2s. 0d. he bequeathed to his sister Margaret the remainder went to his nephew who lived at Treales. Amongst his belongings there were a feather bed and a chaff bed valued at £1 10s. 0d., a chair and four cushions at 1s. 6d. and two pair of sheets at 8s. 0d. There was also one desk and box, value just 1s. 0d., and it is intriguing to wonder whether this was the same desk on which he had worked almost thirty years previously whilst serving as township constable. When William Smalley died in 1749 he left a cottage in Freckleton called 'Nobletts' to his sister, but whether this was the same cottage in which Robert Noblet had lived is not known.

The value of the personal estate of William Smalley amounted to £179 18s. 0d. of which £105 10s. 0d. was 'by Bonds, Bills and Securitys' and he clearly lived in some comfort, as the following inventory extracts reveal. In the room over the parlour there was a bed, bedstocks and hangings value £1 5s. 0d. whilst similar items in the room over the buttery were valued at £1 15s. 0d. In the room over the house there was another bed, bedstocks and hangings which together with other furniture amounted to £3 10s. 0d. In the same room there were also seven chairs, one table, a looking glass and some pictures. Items in the kitchen included one great pan and one iron pan also other brass pans and a cheese press. In the parlour there were six chairs, a map and some pictures with a total value of £1 8s. 6d. and in the dwelling house there was one spice box, one maiden, one clock case, a warming pan, four chairs, a table, one squab, one settle, one little table with a total value of £4 19s. 0d. In the same room there were also some pictures and two brass candlesticks valued at 13s. 0d.

Thomas Freckleton, the grandson of Andrew Freckleton the younger, was a blacksmith and almost certainly carried on his trade at Dibbs Farm.[12] His inventory compiled in 1752 came to £54 11s. 8d. and in addition to the usual household furniture there was a clock and case valued at £2 10s. 0d. and a looking glass and picture at 2s. 0d. His 'Smithy working tools' were valued at £6 4s. 0d. and 'Debts appearing upon the Smithy book' amounted to £27 6s. 0d.

Of the remaining inventories the highest in value was the £343 3s. 0d. of Thomas Hall, a tanner who died in 1758 and whose will is discussed in more detail in chapter 21. William Whalley, the first Freckleton labourer recorded as making a will, had an inventory valued at just £15 15s. 0d. when he died in 1754, and even that included one cow and a stirk valued at £7 10s. 0d. His household goods amounted to only £4 0s. 0d., his wearing apparrell to £1 10s. 0d. whilst his purse contained £2 15s. 0d. Nevertheless he had laid the foundation for a family that continued to prosper in Freckleton for at least the following two generations and was representative of emerging families whose wealth derived either directly or indirectly from the new commercial ventures taking place in the township.

The Early Nineteenth-century Township

The ten-year censuses of 1801 to 1831 provide evidence of a village which was expanding due to the opportunities provided in the manufacturing trades and in the same period the number of houses in the township increased from 114 to 174. However, since it is not until the census of

1841 that individuals are named and occupations given, the Militia List of 1823 offers an important alternative source of information with regard to the occupations of males aged between 18 and 45.[13]

Of the 109 men whose names appear on the list 36 were described as weavers followed, in terms of numbers, by 21 labourers. No yeoman or farmer appears on the list, probably because they were older men and therefore exempt, but there were nine husbandmen. One merchant (Robert Mayor) and two manufacturers (John Mayor Jnr and Robert Mayor Jnr.) were listed, as were three bookkeepers. Tradesmen included two blacksmiths, three bricklayers, two joiners, two millers, three rope-makers, one starcher, two tailors, two twinespinners and one wheelwright. Among those supplying the retail needs of this expanding community in 1823 were George Richardson, shopkeeper and Thomas Catterall, butcher, and in 1828 Edward Brown and John Garlick are also described as shopkeepers and Thomas Gaulter and George Richardson as dealers in sundries.[14]

Part IV

The Poor, 1601–1834

CHAPTER 7

The Poor Law

Origins and Administration of the Poor Law

Following the Dissolution of the monasteries the responsibility for maintenance of the poor passed to each parish or township. An Act of 1563 required that 'two able persons or more shall be appointed gatherers and collectors of the charitable alms of all the residue of people inhabiting in the parish', and in 1572 the office of overseer of the poor was created to supervise endowments and other charitable funds. The 1590s saw a catastrophic series of bad harvests and high food prices, and from 1597–98 all parishes were allowed to levy a poor rate with a view to providing work for their paupers.

It was, however, the Poor Law Act of 1601, amended by the Act of Settlement in 1662, that was the basis of Poor Law administration until 1834. In accordance with the 1601 Act the poor rate collected by the overseers was to be spent in four ways: 'for setting to work the children of all such whose parents shall not be thought able to maintain them'; 'for setting to work all such persons, married or unmarried, having no means to maintain them, and who use no ordinary or daily trade of life to get their living by'; 'for providing a convenient stock of flax, hemp, wood, thread, iron, and other ware and stuff to set the poor on work'; 'for the necessary relief of the lame, impotent, old, blind, and other such among them being poor and not able to work'. In practice the poor were effectively divided into the two categories of deserving and undeserving and whilst the deserving were to be given money, clothes and other necessities, the able-bodied and feckless were expected to work.

During the Commonwealth period (1649–60) it would seem that in Kirkham parish the care of the poor became the responsibility of the churchwardens.[1] However, in July 1660 the Thirty Men agreed that each township should be responsible for keeping their own poor.[2] In addition to the money collected through the rating system the marsh gate owners had authority, under an ordinance of 1670, 'to distribute amongst the poor of the Township of Freckleton' the sums due and forfeited by any livestock trespassing on the marsh. This payment to the poor was probably the origin of the later creation of the fictional half gate, the value of which was distributed annually to the poor. In 1824 the Charity Commissioners reported that Thomas Willacy (the constable) retained 35s. 0d. yearly from the monies he collected from the marsh gate owners, but added that when the marsh rate had been insufficient the deficiency was paid out of the poor rate.

The Act of 1662 amended the law by stating that everyone had a place of settlement. Legitimate children inherited their father's place of settlement and married women took their husband's place of settlement. Illegitimate children legally belonged to their place of birth and consequently, in order to avoid having to maintain them, the overseers took a great interest in trying to ensure that illegitimate children were not born within their township. The constable, in addition to his responsibility for the maintenance of law and order, was also responsible for a wide range of other duties that included the apprenticing of pauper children, the supervision and removal of itinerant strangers and beggars, and the collection of child maintenance from the fathers of illegitimate children.

One of the dilemmas for township officers, and particularly the overseers, was how to define 'deserving poor', requiring as it did the need to balance the ratepayers' wish for low rates against a decision as to whether or not to grant relief to those requesting it. If a request for relief was refused the applicant could appeal to the magistrates at the quarter sessions, and in 1655 Jane Cowburn was allowed 20s. 0d. a year on such an appeal.[3] In at least one instance relief was provided as a result of a bequest in a will and in 1681 Jennet Singleton gave to Ellen Singleton 'who is kept by the towne fourty shillings & my bed & beddinge & a bit of new cloth'.[4]

The petition of John Hall in 1694 describes in detail his background and the reason for his appeal:

> That the petitioner is a very labouring industrious man and endeavoureth as much as in him lies to maintain his wife & 3 children with his hardy labour, but all falls short & will not maintain [th]em & the petitioner has applied himself to the Overseer of the poor of Freckleton for some help & weekly allowance but they have denied unless the petitioner can

obtain an order for release from this Court, & your petitioner has likewise applied himself to Mr Justice Parker who recommended his case to the said overseers but they did not at all regard it.

Your petitioner humbly begs an order from this court for some weekly allowance and will ever pray etc. [5]

Unfortunately, as in many such similar petitions, the decision of the Court is not noted on the document and so we do not know whether John Hall was successful or not with his appeal.

Overseers were ever vigilant and when in 1708 Mary Salthouse, a widow, was reported to have 'lately fled from the said township into the south country & hath left behind her two small children but no sort of provision for their maintainance' the overseer went to the justices and requested that the sum of twenty shillings a year 'payable unto the said Mary Salthouse from Lawrence Coulborne her brother, which twenty shillings a year was given unto the said Mary by the last Will of Christopher Coulborne her late father' should be paid to the overseer in order for him to maintain the children.[6] In their judgement the magistrates agreed with the request and ordered that Lawrence Coulborne pay the twenty shillings to the overseer.

In 1716 the justices ordered that Thomas Allanson, described as 'very poor and not able to maintain himself and family without your relief', was to be granted twelve pence a week.[7] Three years later, when he appealed again for 'the relief of himself and [his] sons poor helpless children', he was granted ten pence a week and also reimbursed the sixteen pence charges of the order.[8]

In view of the obvious desperate family circumstances it is not surprising that in June 1728 a Thomas Allanson, probably the grandson of the above named Thomas and described as 'a poor child of the said Township of Freckleton', was apprenticed by James Sharples and James Coulborn, overseers of Freckleton, to Thomas Grimbaldeston, the then tenant of Lower House Farm until he, Thomas, attained his full age of twenty-one years. However, within six months Thomas Grimbaldeston consented to assign Thomas Allanson to William Davis, a tailor at Kirkham. It was agreed that Thomas, who would have had no say in the matter:

shall well and truly serve the said William Davis as his Master and his commandments lawful and honest shall do and from his service shall not absent himself day or night during the Term aforesaid provided that the said William Davis shall well in treat and use the said Thomas Allanson providing for and allowing unto him meet competent and Sufficient Meat Drink Apparrel Lodging washing and all other things necessary and fit for an Apprentice during all the said Term. And at the end of the said Term make provide allow and deliver unto the said Apprentice double apparrel of all sorts good and new (viz) a good new Suit for the Holydays and another for the working Days. [9]

In 1736, for some unknown reason, William Davis discharged Thomas Allanson and he returned to Freckleton to serve his step-father James Sanderson, a husbandman, 'the remainder of his time and what he earned was to be given to Sanderson'. [10]

In addition to the money raised through the rating system the poor of Freckleton also benefited from the bequests made by several local benefactors. In 1674, under the terms of the will of Henry Coulborn, the township received 'every fifteen year' £5 10s. 0d. 'for binding poor children apprentice', [11] and in 1693 John Kirkham willed that five pounds be paid to Ralph Kirkham 'which five pounds I give freely to the poor in the Township of Freckleton forever that is six shillings yearly year by year'. [12] About 1706 Lawrence Webster, notwithstanding his complaint a quarter of a century earlier about having to serve an additional term as constable, appears to have had some empathy with the poor with whom he had had to deal during his period in office. Although there is no mention of it in his will he apparently left 10s. 0d. a year for distribution amongst the poor of Freckleton. [13] The money was paid from the profits of a close of land called the Swainson Butts (now Swinza Butts) situated along Lower Lane.

In 1709 Andrew Freckleton the elder gave 'for the use of the poor of Freckleton the Sum of twenty pounds and it is my Will and mind that James Smalley and Edward Sharples of Freckleton and their heirs shall have the management of the said Sum of twenty pounds for the poors use yearly'. [14] In 1730 Roger Rigby gave 'Ten pounds to the poor of the Township of Freckleton' [15] and in 1765 William Coulborn gave twenty shillings to his Executors 'to be by them distributed to and amongst such poor inhabitants of the Township of freckleton as they think most objects of Charity and who have no relief from the Overseers of the said Township'. [16]

In 1722 the Workhouse Test Act allowed parishes to erect their own workhouses and in 1726 the inhabitants of Kirkham unanimously agreed to such an undertaking. Freckleton, despite being one of the townships within the parish, seems to have refrained from participating in this arrangement until 1738 when:

at a public meeting in the township of Freckleton after public notice given to the Inhabitants from house to house and so assembled has thought

Poor Law Payments. A typical page from the account book of 'Sundry Disbursements within the Township of Freckleton from 10 April 1817 to 26 March 1818'. It must always be remembered that not all recipients were necessarily feckless and many were suffering genuine hardship.

proper to join in the workhouse at Kirkham for the term of three years for the imploying their poor.[17]

In the same year Freckleton paid a total of £11 to six of its inhabitants described as poor, although none appears to have been sent to the workhouse.[18]

Throughout the eighteenth century the many quarter sessions orders and apprenticeship agreements provide ample evidence that the overseers and constables of Freckleton were fully occupied maintaining and enforcing the requirements of the Poor Law. From 1738 to 1784 at least fifteen settlement or removal orders were issued, and involved the removal of persons from Freckleton to other townships. Usually these were within the Fylde but occasionally it was even further afield, as in 1784, when Ellen Whittle, the wife of William Whittle, and her three children were removed to Liverpool. A journey in the opposite direction likewise had to be undertaken by anyone whose place of settlement was Freckleton, but who were found to be without means of supporting themselves in another township.

Whilst much of the information about the recipients of Poor Law payments can be obtained only from the records kept by the overseers and constables, there are other occasions when those in distress appealed direct to the group or organisation of which they were a member. Correspondence between the Quakers in Freckleton and their brethren in Preston provides a first hand account of the circumstances some Freckleton people were experiencing at the end of the eighteenth century. In an undated letter, written sometime between 1794 and 1802, R. Harrison wrote from Freckleton to Agnes Abbet at Preston concerning the situation of Isabel Brown of Freckleton (she died aged 80 in 1802):

> I found Isabel Brown in which was truly moving her immed[iate] necessity speak fondly for Compassion and your assistance and as far as I am capable of forming my judgement of her wants a few [clot]hing apparrell such as a gown petticoat and shifts she is in great need of ... and what per week or month you may judge proper ...[19]

In 1800 William Coulborn, who died in 1810 aged 91, appealed personally for assistance, even being prepared to go to Preston in order to plead his case:

> Dear friends the time is so hard that my income will not afford me meats and clothes I have none worth anything and I am near 80 years old I am not able to work so if you please to send me a few Clothes is all I want at present to keep me warm and Clean. If you want to see me I will come over so I am your friend.[20]

Township Disbursements Books 1803–1834

At Easter 1803 a return,[21] relating to the year 1802–03, was completed in the name of the overseers and gives some idea of how the poor law was then being administered in the township:

Total money expended for the maintenance and relief. Out of [Work]house.	£137 18s. 4d.
In the House.	Nil
Money expended in purchasing materials for employing the Poor.	
Out of House.	Nil
In the House.	Nil
Number of persons relieved from the Poor's rate permanently, not including children of such Persons.	

Out of House. 24

In the House. Nil

Number of children of persons relieved permanently.

Under 5 years of age. 14

From 5 to 14 years of age. 22

Number of persons relieved occasionally. 4

Number of persons relieved who are 60 years of age, or disabled from labour by permanent illness, or other infirmity. 11

Number of Friendly Societies who hold their usual meetings within the Parish or place. 1

Number of members in the said Societies including members not belonging to the place, as well as those belonging to it. 74

It is, however, the township disbursements books for the years 1803 to 1812[22] and 1817 to 1827[23] together with the vestry relief book for 1831 to 1834,[24] that provide a wealth of detail and insight into the human stories that lay hidden within the statistical returns. Throughout these three periods the general administration of the Poor Law and setting of the poor rate was carried out by a committee composed of between seven and nine of the leading men in the township, of whom members of the Mayor family were usually prominent, together with Thomas Willacy the constable.

From 1803 to 1812 a total of 41 men and 25 women received some sort of relief payment. Some received assistance on only one occasion in a year, in contrast to five individuals who were given almost continuous payments for eight years and six others who likewise needed assistance every year. Whilst it is difficult to determine the number of other family members directly affected by an individual claim, if we assume that each of the 66 claimants had an average of two dependants then perhaps 200 individuals, approximately one third of the population, were reliant on either short or long term assistance. This included payment for such diverse reasons as house rent, relief, doctors bill, confinement, clothing, clogs, coals, blankets, coffin and funeral expenses, and loans.

In the same period between 37% and 60% of the money raised through the poor rate was spent annually on the direct relief of the poor, whilst for the years 1817 to 1826 the amount increased to between 55% and 71%. The poor assessments varied between 5*d.* and 10*d.* in the pound, were levied up to five times a year, and could produce, in Freckleton, approximately £540 annually.

Thomas Rose who, in 1800, lived in a cottage in Hillock Lane, received relief every year from 1803 to 1812. In 1803–04 he received a total of

£7 1s. 2d., of which £4 8s. 6d. was relief at 1s. 6d. a week between May and November, increasing to 2s. 0d. thereafter. In addition he received an extra 1s. 0d. for the week in February 1804 when he was ill, and 10s. 8d. for 10 b(ags?) of coal on 21 December 1804. In 1804–05 his house rent was again paid and he received relief at 3s. 0d. a week, as well as 12s. 6d. for a pair of blankets. Similar payments continued throughout the years 1805 to 1810, but in the latter year his name also appears in the highway account book where he is recorded as having been paid 6d. a day for 75 days' labouring work. In 1811–12 he is again receiving relief at 3s. 0d. a week and having his house rent paid, though it appears that by this date he had moved from Hillock Lane. In addition to these payments Mary Richardson was paid 10s. 0d. for 7½ yards of cloth and 1s. 4d. for making his shirts, whilst Nanny Mayor was paid 9s. 6d. for fustian and flannel and Edward Kirby 2s. 6d. for making his breeches.

Septimus Helm 1794–1878. The only known photograph of a Freckleton handloom weaver. In the years 1831–32 he requested Poor Law relief on just five occasions – other families were on almost continuous weekly relief. On the 1841 census Septimus is described as 'Handloom Weaver – Sacking'. For the last seventeen years of his life he was the sexton at Holy Trinity Church.

Thomas Eaves' solitary but sad appearance in the records illustrates the tasks involved, for the overseers, in the pursuit of their work. In December 1805 Thomas received payments from Freckleton of £1 0s. 0d. and 10s. 6d. 'when at Liverpool'. On 21 January 1806 Henry Hardman was paid 10s. 10d. for bringing him from Liverpool and on the same day John Noblet was paid 5s. 0d. for Thomas' victuals, and 2s. 0d. for (providing) his crutches. Whether or not Thomas was a sailor who had had an accident on board his vessel is not known, but whatever the reason on 26 January George Brown was paid 8d. for 'fetching Doctor'. By 1 February Thomas Eaves was dead and his funeral expenses were recorded as:

To Ale & Bread at Kirkham	£1 5s. 0d.
To Church dues & Bier	£0 3s. 8d.
To Ale & Bread at Freckleton	£0 3s. 0d.
To Richard Coulborn Coffin	£0 18s. 0d.
To Thos Threlfall fetching and bringing Herse [sic]	£0 2s. 6d.
Other payments, including the 11s. 6d. paid to Dr Knipe, resulted in the township having to meet costs that amounted to	£7 3s. 2d.

From 1803 until 1806 payments made to Ellen Ball were for the upkeep of herself and her three children, and comprised her annual house rent of £2 10s. 0d. and 4s. 0d. weekly relief. On 18 October 1807 she was given an additional 2s. 0d. as her daughter Ann was ill, and when Ann died soon after the funeral expenses came to £2 7s. 3d. Later the same month Ellen was given 17s. 6d. in cash 'towards potatoe Ground', for which purpose 10s. 0d. was also given to her the following year. In 1809 and 1810 Ellen only received money for her house rent and following a payment to John Sharples, on 15 November 1810 'for Ellen Balls' shop window', she received no further disbursement.

The workhouse used by Freckleton was not, as might be expected, at Kirkham but at Brindle and in most years the township committee paid an annual rent of £1 15s. 6d. to the workhouse there. Throughout 1817 Ellen Taylor received relief in Freckleton and this continued until May 1818 when William Moon was paid 7s. 6d. for taking her to Brindle workhouse, where the bills for her upkeep for the remainder of the year amounted to £20 2s. 4½d. She appears to have remained at Brindle until March 1820 as after that date no further payments are recorded.

Brindle workhouse seems, however, to have been little used by Freckleton, which perhaps was fortunate for the poor, as it was one of the more notorious, being described as being 'for the support of the poor of any township that may choose to contribute towards the support of the house'. About 80 townships sent their poor to Brindle and for years it 'was used as a general receptable for the pauper lunatics, and the idle and refractory poor'. It was said that 'a severity of discipline was thus introduced', which was not done away with until the building of the county asylum at Lancaster 'and the subsequent interference of several Magistrates'.[25]

The disbursement books for the years 1817–18 to 1826–27 mirror the same pattern, and in those ten years 92 men and 46 women received some form of assistance. In 1821 the population had risen to 875, an increase of almost 25% compared with 1811, of which a sizeable proportion were employed in handloom weaving. As we saw in the previous chapter the 1823 Militia List for Freckleton recorded 109 men aged between 18 and 45, of whom 36 (or one third) were weavers.[26] Of these a total of 22 were considered poor and exempt from militia service and it is the family size and ages of the children of these exempt men that perhaps provides some of the answers as to why so many applied for assistance in the years 1817 to 1827.

The exempt men were all aged between 33 and 42 and the average number of their children aged under sixteen years was 5. It would appear therefore that in the 1820s and 1830s a high proportion of the population was of a young age and this assumption tends to be confirmed by the 1841 census when 31.4% of those living in Freckleton, and born in Lancashire, were aged between ten and twenty years. Assuming that the majority of these young people were also resident ten years earlier (the overall population increased by only 86 between 1831 and 1841) then in 1831 about one third of the population of Freckleton was under the age of ten. For a modern comparison to these statistics just 13.4% of the population of Lancashire was aged under ten years in 1991.

James Tomlinson was a weaver born in 1787 and who by 1823 had a family of four boys aged ten, eight, six and three, and one girl aged twelve. He received assistance in seven of the ten years between 1817 and 1826, beginning in 1817 when he was given additional pay of 3s. 6d. a week during the summer months. In addition his house rent of £3 16s. 0d. was paid to T. Mayor Jnr. In May 1817 he was given 10s. 6d. for 'three bushels potatoes for sets' and in October 16s. 0d. in cash 'towards potatoe ground'. In January 1818 he was given 4s. 0d. 'when wife ill' and similar payments were made on two other occasions in the same year. When he was ill himself for four weeks in October 1821 he was given 5s. 0d. a week, but by the following May his fortunes had improved and he then only required half his house rent to be paid.

Thereafter he sought no further assistance until March 1826 when he was given 5s. 0d. in three separate payments. In June 1826 he was given relief at 2s. 0d. a week and in September he was given cash on three occasions 'when wife ill'. With at least five children to look after life cannot have been easy and although the township paid Dr Parkinson £1 13s. 2d. for attending his wife they nevertheless also paid Thomas Mayor £6 10s. 6d. as the fee for valuing James' household goods, presumably before making payment to Dr Parkinson.

However desperate their circumstances the family of James Tomlinson did not have to suffer the fate of that of James Harrison whose wife, in April 1820, received two payments of 4s. 0d. when her husband was in prison. Probably as a result of his time there James Harrison contracted typhus, and from October to December 1821 he received amounts varying from 2s. 0d. to 4s. 0d. 'when ill of Typhus fever'.

In 1826 there was a slump in the handloom weaving trade and in Freckleton representatives from 77 families, out of aprroximately 175, sought and were given some form of Poor Law relief. £554 1s. 4d. was raised through the poor rate, the largest sum ever, and of that amount £396 1s. 5d. was given out in payments. Unfortunately there are no contemporary accounts of events in Freckleton that year but several sundry payments made by the township committee are probably related to efforts made to alleviate the plight of those who had little or no work:

29 April	Thomas Catterall measuring Potatoes	1s.	6d.
22 June	Paid for Cotton Healds etc.	6s.	4d.
7 July	Meeting about dividing London subscription Money	5s.	4d.
10 Oct.	Paid Robt Clifton expences of TA [Thomas Adamson], Edwd Brown etc Distributing Flower [Flour]	6s.	9d.

The vestry relief book for 1831 to 1834 reveals similar stories of hardship and tribulation, particularly for the weavers and labourers who were the main recipients, and some who had once been liable to pay the poor rate found themselves in need of assistance from it. Some idea of the wages then being earned can be obtained from a national survey carried out in 1833. In the vicinity of Kirkham it was said that 'as much as 10s. 0d. a week could be contributed to the family income by the wife and children handloom weaving in summer, and winter bringing in 4s. 0d. of this amount'. However, it was noted that the clergyman respondent for Newton with Scales (Rev. Richard Moore) had adopted a somewhat complacent tone, as the remainder of the 10s. 0d. seems to have been 'available only at harvest times'.[27]

During these final three years of the old Poor Law 58 men and 38 women requested some form of relief and in addition to the provision of financial assistance the township also provided medical aid, as in May 1831 when an agreement was made between Dr Warbrick and themselves to pay 'the Doctor for his Attendance on all the Paupers for one year 9 Pounds.'

Many working families endeavoured to provide for themselves in time of hardship and by 1802 upwards of 74 people were already members of a friendly society. As this also had the effect of relieving the poor rate the paying of club dues was considered so important that the overseers occasionally paid the subscriptions of club members. The name of this early society is unknown but it almost certainly met in one of the local inns and it would appear that it, or a successor organisation, survived into the 1830s, as is revealed by the entries in the relief book relating to Thomas Whiteside:

27 June 1831   Wants his Club dues paying. 1 Year dues 8s. 0d.
                Allowed 4s. 0d. if he will help in the Club.

11 July   1831   Wants his Club dues 15s. 0d. and he has returned the
                4s. 0d. back again that was given him towards his dues.
                To enquire about the Club.

The township committee met every Monday and the following entries in the relief book are typical of the requests made and the assistance given – or refused!

                William Harrison
31 May   1831   Wants a few clothes to go a sailing in.
                Allowed £1.

                Rowland Cornah
17 Oct.   1831   Wants something towards loaming his Potatoes.
                (6 Children). Allowed 3s. 0d.

                Peter Brown
14 Nov.   1831   Wants some relief. Wife poorly and wants a nurse for her.
                Allowed 2s. 0d. for the nurse. Paid for another week.

28 Nov.   1831   Nancy Hall wants 4s. 6d. allowing for attending on Peter
                Brown['s] wife.
                Allowed.

                Margaret Sowerbutts
28 Nov.   1831   Wants 1 Pair of looms at 10s. 0d. to learn her son to
                weave.
                Allowed and to question her more of the matter.

Thomas Towers

3 Sept. 1832 Wants some relief.
Allowed ticket for Workhouse.

Alice Threlfall

27 May 1833 Wants a few things for late Margaret Threlfall['s] children,
a pair of shoes for son and a pair of stockings for
daughter and brats.
Allowed 2s. 0d. extra.

The plight of the families of Peter Brown, Robert Fisher, Joseph Houseman, David Lewtas, Richard Warbrick and Thomas Whiteside was such that they were on almost continuous relief throughout the years 1831 to 1834. It was the cost of providing relief for such families, who were not necessarily feckless but suffering from genuine economic hardship, that was placing an increasing strain on those responsible for paying the poor rate. There is a suggestion that there was a reluctance, or even perhaps inability, by some Freckleton ratepayers to pay their rate, as revealed by a minute passed by the township committee in October 1831:

It is ordered that James Fayre do see the Principal men that owes old arrears of Taxes and if they refuse to pay he is to give orders immediately ... to proceed forthwith with the Arbitration.

In an attempt to resolve this national problem Parliament passed the 1834 Poor Law Amendment Act, under which responsibility for the poor was taken away from the townships and parishes and placed in the hands of Poor Law Unions, controlled by Boards of Guardians. The Act minimised the provision of outdoor relief and made confinement in the workhouse the central element of the new system, whilst at the same time actively discouraging all but the most desperate from seeking admittance. Freckleton became one of twenty three townships in the Fylde Union and in 1844 a new union workhouse was erected in Station Road, Kirkham, being replaced by a new workhouse at Wesham in 1907. This building served as a workhouse until workhouses were abolished in 1945 and is now known as Wesham Park Hospital.

Part V

The Church in Freckleton

CHAPTER 8

The Church of England

The Early Church

How and when Christianity was first brought to Freckleton will never be known. By the time the Angles arrived in the Fylde they may already have been Christians and in the late seventh century St Wilfrid was given lands adjoining the Ribble in order to endow his church at Ripon. A pre-Conquest church almost certainly existed at Kirkham and would have presumably also had contact with the inhabitants of Freckleton.

However, it is not until the Norman Conquest that there are any definite facts regarding the ancient parish of Kirkham, which until the mid-nineteenth century comprised fifteen townships including Freckleton. Shortly after the Conquest the archdiocese of York was divided into territorial archdeaconries and the effective administrator of Kirkham parish from 1190 until 1540 was the archdeacon of Richmond. During this period there is no evidence of any parish clergy in Freckleton and perhaps some of their responsibilities were carried out by the Benedictine monks of Lytham Priory when they visited their Freckleton estate.

Sometime during the medieval period land in the area of the Naze was granted, probably by the Clifton family, to endow their chantry in Kirkham Church. The chantry was dissolved in 1553 and the chantry priest, Thomas Prymbett, given an annual pension of £5. The location of the original chantry land, however, was still remembered a century later and in a conveyance, made in December 1650, between Richard, George and Henry Robinson and William Browne, the land being conveyed was described as 'Two closes in Freckleton, called the naze and the Bank, two acres formerly belonging to the dissolved Chantry of the Blessed Virgin Mary in Kirkham'.[1]

The origins of the two roadside crosses situated in Freckleton at Hall

Cross and opposite Kirkham Prison, known as the Headless Cross, are unknown. The Headless Cross possibly originated as the marker between the townships, or manors, of Freckleton and Kirkham, and presumably at some time the head was either moved or destroyed hence the word 'headless'. The cross at Hall Cross may have served a similar purpose and was restored in 1910 and again in 1989. An alternative use may have been that the sites were used as resting places for funeral corteges taking the dead from Freckleton for burial at Kirkham. Or, indeed, the crosses may have been used for both purposes.

The Church of England

In 1541, following the Reformation, Freckleton became part of the new diocese of Chester. In 1546 the advowson of Kirkham Church was granted to the Dean and Chapter of Christ Church, Oxford and in November 1591 when Christ Church appointed James [2] Sharples as the new vicar he named his father, John [1] Sharples of Freckleton, yeoman, as bondsman. It was the first known occasion that Freckleton men had played a significant role in parish affairs and was indicative of the increasing influence of the Sharples family. In December of the same year the Dean and Chapter granted to John [1] Sharples and Cuthbert [1] his son, the advowson and presentation of the perpetual vicarage of Kirkham for 21 years.

From about 1560 until the early nineteenth century the affairs of the parish were conducted by the select vestry, known as the Thirty Men, which comprised two men from each of the fifteen townships in Kirkham parish. Once elected they held office for life unless they chose to resign and were above the churchwardens whom they appointed. They also acted as guardians of parish property and raised funds for the repair of the church, as in 1606 when they ordered that every township should do its part to enclose the churchyard with freestone, 'as Freckleton had already done'.[2]

Some indication of the religious beliefs prevailing in Freckleton in 1642 can be deduced from the Protestation Oath carried out in that year. In May the previous year members of the House of Commons swore an oath 'to live and die for the true Protestant religion, the liberties and rights of subjects and the priviledge of Parliament'. In January 1642 letters were sent to magistrates in Lancashire requiring them to instruct township officers to arrange the taking of the oath in their own township. In Freckleton the responsibility fell to the constables, Arthur Mureley

Holy Trinity Parish Church. This early photograph of Holy Trinity shows the building as it appeared until the removal of the tower in 1976. The church architect was John Latham who was also responsible for the design of the Preston churches of Christ Church, St Thomas, and St Mary.

and Michael Gualter, and on 1 March 1642 the oath was taken by 75 men and 74 women.[3] Although there is no explanation for his decision only one person, Thomas Hall Jnr, refused to sign. Conversely it is possible that for some the taking of the oath did not necessarily reflect their religious (Protestant) affiliation since, for example, Butler Cowborne was recorded as a convicted (Catholic) recusant in 1671.

Thirty years later the Test Act of 1673 directed that all civil office holders receive sacraments according to the forms of the Church of England and as a consequence George [3] Sharples, as one of his majesty's coroners, presented a certificate to the quarter sessions in July of the same year declaring that on Sunday 29 June 'immediately after divine Service and Sermon [he] did in the Parish Church [of Kirkham] ... receive the Sacrament of the Lords Supper according to the usage of the Church of England'.[4]

As already mentioned parish affairs were controlled by the Thirty Men and their choice of churchwardens was determined by estates in the different townships taken in rotation. In 1758 Henry Grimbaldeston of Lower House Farm was nominated 'for Mr Hornby's Estate in Freckleton'[5] and the same estate was again nominated in 1778 when William Threlfall was named as churchwarden. The growing influence of the Mayor family during the late eighteenth century is evident when in 1788

Edward Mayor was chosen for his estate in Freckleton, and similarly in 1808 when John Mayor was chosen 'for his estate at Ravels [Ravald] in Freckleton'.[6]

There does not seem to have been any attempt by the Church of England during the seventeenth and eighteenth centuries to establish a permanent presence in Freckleton, and throughout the period it was only the Quakers who built a place of worship. For the Anglicans of Freckleton wishing to attend their parish church it required a two and a half mile journey to Kirkham, where several of the leading families paid for pew rents in the church. In 1783 James Goodshaw paid 15s. 0d. for a pew for one year and in 1803 John Mayor paid £3 12s. 0d. for a gallery pew for the term of seven years.

For some families the first Warton church, built in 1722, offered an alternative as revealed by the will of Henry Coulborn, a house carpenter, who on his death in 1780 left his 'Pew or Seat in Warton Chapel to be common to all my children and Grandchildren'.[7] However, the vicar and churchwardens of Kirkham remained entitled to levy a church rate on all owners and occupiers of lands and buildings in the parish, irrespective of the owners' personal beliefs, whenever it was necessary to maintain the fabric of Kirkham church. In 1820 it was ordered that £3,600 be raised in order to take down and rebuild the church, and this was to be raised by instalments of £35 per annum in each of the fifteen townships until the whole was paid. These payments were still being made in Freckleton as late as 1827 when just over £31 was paid by 80 owners or occupiers.

This unsatisfactory and unfair situation continued until the Very Rev. Dr J. J. Webber (vicar of Kirkham, 1813–47) commenced his plans for the division of Kirkham parish. In an undated letter to Christ Church, Oxford, he outlined his aims and also stated that if a chapel was built at Freckleton he intended to unite Warton and Freckleton as a single parish. The building of a chapel was the first stage and the reply dated 12 October 1832 included the following significant sentence: 'Meanwhile if you proceed with Freckleton Chapel as part of this plan, will be ready to find you £100 for it'.[8] In reply Dr Webber confirms that Freckleton Chapel is part of the plan and asks for money, saying he has himself given £100. He adds that he intends to give a certain portion of the receipts of Freckleton to the Rev. G. Wylie (curate of Warton) for doing duty there once a fortnight.

In fact there is evidence that the Rev. George Wylie commenced pastoral duties in Freckleton at this time and in the Freckleton vestry

'Old Parsonage' (75 and 77 Preston Old Road). Formerly one property and originally owned by Robert Mayor, it was purchased by the Church of England in c.1860 when the first resident curate was appointed to Freckleton. It was sold by the church in 1930 when a new vicarage was built on Naze Lane.

relief book there is an entry for 12 November 1832 that reads: 'Rev. George Wylie wants to preach in the barn. £2 0s. 0d. Rent and to put it in Repair'.[9] Unfortunately there is no indication as to the location of the barn that was to be used, but following this rather inauspicious start progress continued and in 1836 Baines recorded that 'A temporary Episcopal Church was erected here about two years ago'.[10]

The year 1837 saw the laying of the foundation stone of the present church and the following notice giving details of the event are taken from an old printed circular which was given to the church by Mr Thomas Parker.

This first stone of a Chapel to be built by subscription and called the Holy Trinity Chapel was laid by Hugh Hornby, the donor of the site, on this 31st day of July A.D. 1837, being the first year of the reign of Her Most Gracious Majesty Queen Victoria.

Signed:
The Very Reverend Jas Webber D.D. – Vicar of Kirkham
Henry Marquis
Richard Knowles
John Pemberton — Wardens of Kirkham
John Knowles
John Latham – Surveyor

Robert Hall, Thomas Catterall, Richard Wall and William Butcher –
Contractors.

There is no known surviving subscription list but presumably the £100
donations promised by both Dr Webber and Christ Church, Oxford,
were made, whilst a further £50 was subscribed by Newton Charity
'towards the building of Freckleton Church on the understanding that
a commodious pew should be reserved for them'.[11] During the ensuing
year the church was completed, and consecrated on 13 June 1838 by Dr
Sumner, the Bishop of Chester.

The building of the church clearly generated considerable interest and
Adam Wright, a member of the Wright family of Kirkham and Freckleton,
enquired in a letter dated 18 April 1838 and written to his sister from
Constantinople where he was a merchant banker: 'What other alterations
are taking place, who builds the Church at Freckleton and what sort of
a building is it'.[12] In fact the church was built of brick and consisted of
a nave and chancel with a western tower and small spire. The architect
was John Latham, the surveyor named in the foundation stone notice.

Although Freckleton now had its own church it served only as a
chapel of ease to Kirkham Church. However in 1845 Dr. Webber wrote
to the Bishop of Chester to seek permission for the separation of Warton
and Freckleton from the 'mother' parish of Kirkham. The Bishop in
turn wrote to the archbishop of York. He represented as follows:

> FRECKLETON. The curacy consists of Freckleton township, the population
> 992, distance from the parish church two or three miles. The church is
> situated in Freckleton and accommodates 300. No house of residence.
> Township of Freckleton has never been legally assigned as a district to the
> said church. The inhabitants being occupiers of pews have repaired to
> Freckleton Church, but there is no legal right to enforce the repairs on
> the inhabitants. No legal right to the exclusive use of a pew or sitting.
> Annual income £25 of which £5 is from pew rents in the church and £20
> gratuitously paid by the Vicar of Kirkham. The townships of Warton,
> Freckleton, Bryning and Kellamere, containing a population of 1597, may
> be advantageously separated from Kirkham.[13]

The submission was granted and on 21 January 1846 Holy Trinity,
Freckleton, became a chapel of ease to Warton Church.

However, despite the change, no resident clergy were appointed to
Freckleton and this no doubt was one of the complaints raised by the
Rev. W. L. Hussey (vicar of Kirkham, 1852–62) who, between 1852 and
1854, wrote three letters to Christ Church, Oxford, saying that the
inhabitants of Freckleton had drawn up a memorial asking to be separated

Rev Edward John Hack. The vicar of Freckleton from 1892 until 1917, who strove continually to improve the well-being of his parishioners. He died at Freckleton and is buried in the churchyard, as is his predecessor the Rev. Walter Scott.

from Warton. The memorial was partially successful and in 1860 the first resident curate, the Rev. G. H. Waterfall, was appointed to Freckleton. In the same year a house in Preston Old Road (now numbered 75 and 77), and formerly owned by the Mayor family, was purchased and this property served as the parsonage house/vicarage until just before it was sold in 1930.

The Rev. G. H. Waterfall remained at Freckleton for only one year and was succeeded by the Rev. Walter Scott, who thirteen years later, on 26 January 1874, became the first vicar of Freckleton when Holy Trinity became the parish church of a separate ecclesiastical parish. The Order in Council, issued at the time, described the church as being 'conveniently placed in or near the centre of the separate benefice ... and affords accommodation for three hundred persons or thereabouts'.

As the earliest surviving minute or vestry book only commences in 1894 little is known about earlier parish activities, or about the individuals who undertook to accept the various church offices such as churchwarden.

The only record of the names of churchwardens prior to 1874 is for the year 1845 when Thomas Green and James Fisher were in office. In view of his active participation in other township affairs it is probable that Thomas Green also took a similar role in church matters. He had married Jane Goodshaw in 1842 and lived adjacent to the church at Holly House. On his death in 1886 the stained glass window on the north wall of the church was installed in his memory.

However, some insight into the church life of the 1860s and 1870s can be obtained from the newspaper report of the death, in 1874, of Robert Lupton, the schoolmaster. The report noted that he was 'ever active in the day and Sunday schools, in tea parties, in evening enter-tainments, in singing classes, in collecting for church and school purposes' and that 'he has obtained for the church new commandments, a new harmonium, had the church painted, beautified, and furnished with heating apparatus'.[14] This was a considerable improvement when com-pared with the comments made by Hewitson when he visited the church in 1872. In that year the building was described as 'exceedingly damp in many parts and singularly cracked in various places. The southern wall and the corners of the building are nearly black with damp and we attribute much of this to the outside ivy'.[15]

The Myres family of Preston and the Naze, also took a keen interest in the progress of the church, and at a sermon preached in 1881 in memory of Alderman John James Myres (who was a member of Preston Corporation from 1842 to 1881) the Rev. Walter Scott described him as 'a cordial helper in every movement that he originated for the use of the parish, and Trinity Church, Freckleton, in its restored condition, affords in several respects evidence of the munificence of the deceased gentleman and the members of his family'.[16] The small stained glass window immediately above the chancel arch was installed in the memory of Alderman Myres and the east window is in memory of his wife.

In 1892 the Rev. Scott died aged 79 and was buried in the north-west corner of the churchyard. He was succeeded by the Rev. Edward John Hack, and some idea of the state of the parish in that year can be ascertained from a letter written by the Rev. Hack to the Bishop of Manchester in 1905.

> When I was appointed here about 13 years ago the place was in a regrettable condition. The Vicars house all but a ruin. Ivy was growing upstairs in the house and the house had to be braced up. About 18 months elapsed before I could reside. The Vicar had grown old and feeble, and was beset by trouble in his family. Dissent flourished. There was a poor church

congregation and a weak Sunday School. Some of the Pews were still privileged. There was no service on Sunday evening. I was obliged to make many little alterations and changes.[17]

Although no doubt a true reflection of the state of the parish in 1892, it makes a sad epitaph and it should be remembered that for 31 years the Rev. Walter Scott devoted his life to the village and its people, firstly as resident curate and then vicar. The newspaper report of his funeral recorded that 'The Church was very full the deceased clergyman being held in great esteem in the neighbourhood'.[18]

The Rev. Hack was vicar from 1892 until 1917 and throughout those years he strove continually to improve the state of the church and the well-being of his parishioners. In 1905 he wrote that 'a series of sales of work has marked my Pastorate'.[19] In 1907 the present organ was installed, with Andrew Carnegie, the American philanthropist, offering to meet half the cost. Money for the other half and other improvements were met by events such as those held in the latter part of 1912 when £20 0s. 0d. was raised at a 'Pound' sale on 2nd October, £4 4s. 1d. at a 'Cob Web Social' on 6 November and £23 5s. 6d. at a 'Cake & Apron' sale on 7 December.

The Rev. Edward John Hack died on 13 May 1917 and was buried at Freckleton. He was succeeded in 1918 by the Rev. F. P. Mansfield, the first vicar to be appointed by the bishop of the diocese following the transfer of the patronage from Christ Church, Oxford, in 1909. The Rev. Mansfield remained until 1920 and was followed by the Rev. W. Preston who was vicar from 1921 until 1922.

In 1922 the Rev. Richard Hayward was appointed. Within a year of his arrival £557 12s. 10d. had been raised towards the building of a new vicarage, and in April 1926 the parochial church council was informed 'that the tender for the building of the new vicarage was let to Messrs Baron of Preston'. At the meeting it was proposed that 'a Memorial Stone to the memory of men who fell in the Great War be laid with a dedication ceremony in the new vicarage'. This building, situated in Naze Lane, served as the vicarage until it was sold in 1980. The present (2000) vicarage is situated in Sunnyside Close.

The Rev. Hayward died at Freckleton in 1929 and was succeeded in 1930 by the Rev. J. W. Broadbent who continued as vicar until 1950. During his twenty years at Freckleton he oversaw the rebuilding of the church tower in 1934 and the installation of electric lighting in the church in 1936. In 1932 the churchyard, resting place of generations of Freckleton families of all denominations, was enlarged for the first time since 1896, but the communal grave of the victims of the 1944 air disaster is sadly the most prominent monument of all. The churchyard was again extended in 2000.

The exterior of the present church is essentially the same building as that begun in 1837, apart from the necessary removal in 1976 of the original tower and its replacement with an 18ft hexagonal bell-cote and gilded cross in 1980. The appearance of the interior was considerably altered in 1993 with the removal of the original wooden box pews and their replacement with modern chairs. The Jacobean pulpit is the church's most prized possession. It was originally made by Robert Weaver in 1633 for Kirkham church at a cost of £10. Prior to its removal to Holy Trinity it had been covered by many coats of whitewash but was carefully restored to its former beauty and now provides a visible link with the mother church which the Anglicans of Freckleton attended over 350 years ago.

Since 1950 Holy Trinity has been served by a further eight vicars (see appendix B) and throughout the church's 163 years' existence they, and their predecessors, have been ably assisted by many lay people. In this century four men have served as churchwarden for twenty or more years: Richard Whittle was a churchwarden on three occasions (1895–1907, 1909 and 1917–25); William Kirby (1929–52); John Threlfall (1939–59); and George Rhodes (1959–90). It is the committed efforts of all such men and women that have enabled the church to survive and provide a continuing service to the present generation.

A view of the interior of Holy Trinity prior to the removal of the box pews in 1993. The Jacobean pulpit was made for Kirkham Church in 1633.

CHAPTER 9

Congregational (Independent) Church

Following the formation of the Lancashire Congregational Union in 1806 the Rev. James Morrow was appointed as minister at Poulton. In May 1812 he moved to Kirkham where a chapel had opened in 1810. Writing in January 1814 he recorded that 'During the summer I preached at Freckleton, a village about three miles hence, once a fortnight on sabbath evenings, many could not get into the little room in which we met'.[1] The Rev. Morrow left Kirkham in 1813 and was succeeded by a Mr Capper who in turn was followed in 1816 by the Rev. Griffiths. The church report of 1817 mentions Freckleton as one of the places where the Rev. Griffiths 'occasionally preached' but after this date there is no further mention of the church until the 'Survey of Dissent', carried out in 1829, recorded that there were twenty Independents in Freckleton.[2] Unfortunately the survey provides no additional information as to who they were or where they met.

However it is almost certain that the Independents held their meetings in Lower Lane at Marsh View Farm (now renamed Quaker House), which in the early nineteenth century was occupied by the Singleton family. In 1817 'a Dwellinghouse and Barn adjoining in the occupation of Edward Singleton' was registered as a place for religious worship of 'Protestant Dissenters'.[3] Edward Singleton does not appear to have had any connection with the Wesleyan Methodist community, then actively establishing itself in the village, and evidence of his early attachment to the Independent cause is provided by the baptism of his daughter Nancy at Kirkham Zion Chapel in 1811.

In 1822 the dwelling house of John Baker (misspelt as Barker) was also licensed for religious worship.[4] Although the particular denomination using the building is neither named nor known it is possible that this building too was being used by the Independents as John Baker, like Edward Singleton, had no apparent connection with any other denomination. After 1829 there is no further mention of the Congregational (Independent) cause in Freckleton and the remaining members presumably either joined with another church or attended the Congregational church in Kirkham.

CHAPTER 10

Wesleyan Methodist Church (Kirkham Road)

The first Methodist society was formed in Bristol by John and Charles Wesley and George Whitefield in 1739, but although John Wesley is known to have preached in Preston on four occasions between 1780 and his death in 1791, progress in establishing Methodism in the Fylde was extremely slow. In 1784 a small band of Methodists met and worshipped in Preston but 'there was not a chapel, or a school, or a ministers house, or a circuit, or a minister in the Fylde country'.[1]

The man credited with forming the first Methodist society in Freckleton was Moses Holden who was born in Bolton in 1777. By 1789 he had moved with his family to Preston where he subsequently joined the Methodist society and eventually became a local preacher. In January 1811 he was persuaded by the Rev. Thomas Jackson, the then superintendent minister of the Preston circuit, to go and preach in the Fylde villages. Moses Holden began his Fylde missionary work on 21 January 1811 when he preached at Little Marton. He recorded in his journal that 'from the time I went down into the Fylde in January until the following Conference I had opened the whole of the Fylde country from Lytham to Pilling, and formed classes in the different villages'.[2] The tour included Freckleton where 'on the occasion of his first visit he began to search about for a place in which to hold his meeting, but none being available he made his way to the smithy at the south-westerly corner of the green, and from the old steps which led to a room over the forge he addressed the small gathering of inhabitants who had assembled'.[3]

However another account records that in August 1810 George Richardson, who would then have been aged only 16, conducted 'the first Wesleyan Sunday School in the district, in the Barn of Park Nook Farm'.[4] As this date is at least five months prior to the first known visit of Moses Holden, and as George Richardson is unlikely to have acted independently at such an early age, then presumably there must have been earlier unrecorded contact with Methodist missionaries that had resulted in the establishment of a Sunday school prior to the visit of Moses Holden in 1811.

Whatever the sequence of events the outcome of the visit made by Moses Holden was the formation of a society comprising twelve members, among whom were James Grayson, George Richardson and Peter Taylor.[5] The choice of Park Nook Farm as the site of the first Sunday school is explained by the fact that James Grayson was the son of Elizabeth Grayson, a widow, who had married Robert Marsden Rigby in 1798 and who, in 1810, was the occupier of Park Nook Farm.[6] It is not known for how long meetings took place at the farm but according to Pilkington 'an arrangement was made to begin preaching services in an old edifice, in which the Quakers occasionally worshipped; and to this building the scholars from Park Nook Farm were transferred'.[7]

However it is clear that church members were also actively seeking a place of their own in which to worship and within three years of the visit of Moses Holden two plots of land, on the site of the existing church, had been obtained. The first plot, containing '85 and one third superficial square yards', was conveyed by Robert Hall, a Freckleton wheelwright, on 4 June 1814, to George Fishwick, a cotton manufacturer who resided at Scorton and the most esteemed Methodist in the Fylde area, and four other trustees for £100. The deed of conveyance further described the site as comprising 'the Cottage Weaving Shop & erections now on – to be shortly converted into a Chapel or Meetinghouse for the Society of the People called Methodists residing in or near Freckleton and by all other desirous to attend divine service there and who shall conduct themselves reverently therein'.[8]

A second and adjacent plot was conveyed jointly by Robert Hall and James Blundell, a Freckleton yeoman, to the same trustees on 10 August 1814.[9] The acquisition of the land, however, appears to have been not without its problems and the report of the death of Ann Hall in 1838, a member whose name was first recorded on the membership list of 1815 and who appears to have been the wife of Robert Hall, records that whilst she promoted the erection of the chapel she also 'prayed long about it, concerning the removal of difficulties in getting title to the ground on which it was built'.[10]

Evidence that there was a chapel in use as early as 1819 is provided by the account book for the years 1818 to 1831 entitled 'Methodist Chapel, Freckleton (in Accompt with Thomas Gaulter, Steward and proprietor in part)'.[11] This book lists the debits and credits of payments made in respect of a building being used as a chapel and the opening entry 'to

Balance on an old Accompt' suggests that it was a continuation of an existing account. In addition to providing the names of those who gave financial assistance the accounts also provide an insight into the work required and the subsequent efforts made, to make the chapel functional, as a selection of entries from the debit account for the years 1818 reveals:

		£	s.	d.
15 March	To an hand brush		1	0
1 April	To Spout hooks & staples 5¾lbs at 4d. per lb		1	11
8 April	To 7ft in board at 4d. per ft		2	4
	To 15½ft of ¾in board at 3½d. per foot		4	6½
	To Nails 1/2. Work of Spouts 4/6		5	8
2 May	To Reparation of Windows		2	0
10 June	To 2lb Brown Paint at 10d. per		1	8
	To 3lb White Paint at 9d. per		2	3
8 August	To 2lb White Paint at 9d. per		1	6
12 August	To Cash for Roughcasting	1	17	0
	To do for Cartage of Materials		7	6
	To do for Ale		4	8

Work on the building continued and as the following four entries from 1819 show, by the end of that year the building appears to have been ready for regular use:

		£	s.	d.
3 Jan.	To Cash for Thatch & Thatching		4	0
25 May	To Brushes & Lime for whiting		2	6
27 Nov.	To an Hearth Stone & Work		3	6
27 Dec.	To Cash for 21ft in board for Kneeling boards		7	0
	To Cash for a shade for a Lamp		1	6

The cost of purchasing and converting this building appears to have been funded primarily by John Leece of Preston a leading local Methodist. In November 1818 there is an entry in the accounts 'To Cash for Int[erest] to Jno Leece £2 10s. 0d.' and these annual payments then continue until 1824. In 1825 John Leece received payments of £4 10s. 0d. for 'Int on £100' and £2 5s. 0d. for 'Int on £50' and from 1826 to 1831 payments were made of £8 2s. 0d. for 'Int on £180' and £2 5s. 0d. for 'Int on £50'.[12] The two local Methodists named as contributors were Thomas Wright and Thomas Gaulter. Thomas Wright, a local shipbuilder, was an active member of the society from its early days, but it is the role played by Thomas Gaulter that is perhaps much underestimated. Adam Wright, in his letters from Constantinople to his sister and nieces, enquires unfailingly about Thomas and his wife and in a letter dated 19 June 1839 says 'I am very glad to hear good accounts of Thomas and Agnes Gaulter and should like to see them again on the old sod'.[13] By February 1840 Agnes had died but Thomas survived a further seven years and died in 1847 aged 82.

In addition to the possible use of the Quaker meeting house, worship prior to the opening of a chapel took place in the homes of the members including George Richardson, who, it is said, was so strongly impressed by the doctrines which Moses Holden expounded that 'he opened his house, a thatched cottage in Preston road, to the Methodists in order that divine service might be celebrated'.[14] This cottage was adjacent to the Coach & Horses Inn, though at the time the cottage was licensed for worship the inn had not been built. In fact when the dwellinghouse was certified, in July 1816, as a place 'for Protestant Dissenters to exercise their religious Worship in',[15] it was still owned by Mary Richardson the mother of George Richardson, and it was not until her death in 1822 that George bought out his brother and sister and became sole owner.

The home of Betty Taylor was also licensed for worship in July 1816. Little is known of Betty Taylor except that as Elizabeth Critchley she had married Peter Taylor in 1772. Peter Taylor died in 1810 and it was their son, born 1775 and also called Peter, who was another original member of the society in Freckleton. In 1817 Betty Taylor is recorded as receiving a weekly payment, usually 1s. 6d., throughout the year out of the poor rate. In addition she was given £2 10s. 0d. as part of her house rent that was due to Mary Richardson'.[16] Both these payments continued until May 1819 when Betty Taylor presumably either died or left the village. The location of the cottage of Betty Taylor is unknown but in view of the fact that she paid rent to Mary Richardson it is possible that she lived in an adjoining dwelling.

The membership and account book of the Garstang Methodist Circuit includes the names of the Freckleton members for the years 1815 to 1817.[17] In 1815 the seventeen members were Edmund Billington, Margaret Billington, Mary Coulburn, Agnes Gaulter, Thomas Gaulter, Ann Hall, Margery Hall, Robert Mare (Mayor), James Parkinson, George Richardson, Mary Richardson, Alice Riley, Laurence Roe, Mary Spencer, Pricilla Spencer, Betty Taylor and Peter Taylor. By 1816 membership had increased to twenty six and in 1817 to forty seven when the leaders were named as James Parkinson, Laurence Roe, Peter Taylor and Thomas

Wright. Freckleton members made Quarter Day payments to Garstang circuit from July 1814 until September 1818 when the society was transferred to the Preston Circuit, and in 1819 Thomas Gaulter and George Richardson were recorded as being 'stewards of the affairs of Methodism in Freckleton and answerable for the same to the Circuit Stewards at Preston'.[18] In 1819 the class leaders were, with the exception of Peter Taylor, the same as those as named in 1817.

By the end of the third decade of the nineteenth century Methodism in Freckleton had become firmly established, a fact supported by the entry in the 1829 'Survey of Dissent' when it was reported that in Freckleton there were 49 Methodists with a chapel,[19] and throughout the 1820s there is evidence of regular payments towards the maintenance of this chapel including items such as:-

			£	s.	d.
6 Feb.	1822	To Cash for Boards for Singing Pew	7	1	
June	1826	To Geo Cooke for Painting etc.	8	3	
June	1827	To Roger Allanson for Lime and Work	9	2	
20 Mar.	1829	To Peter Rawstorn for Thatching and Spelks	12	1	
		To Willm Harrison serving him	3	0	
May	1830	To Robt Richardson repairing Window Shutters	1	2	

The credit entries comprise solely of monies taken in pew rents, which were collected quarterly in February, May, August and November. Amounts ranged from an initial high of £7 7s. 0d. in May 1818 to £4 3s. 0d. in May 1825 and £2 1s. 0d. in May 1831. Although this appears to be a consistent reduction it could be that the early high intake represented extra voluntary contributions in order to raise funds to furbish the chapel.[20] The pew list of 7 May 1831 records eighteen pew holders who paid 1s. 0d. for each person using their pew. There were a further four pews not allocated. Pew number 1 was taken by Thomas Gaulter who paid for himself and three other persons. Robert Mayor and Jonathan Swan each paid for six persons. Other surnames included Brown, Hall, Richardson, Rigby, Spencer, Wright and Wylie.[21]

By 1838 it is clear that a decision had been taken to rebuild the first chapel. Whilst most of the money needed to pay for the new building was no doubt raised by the members themselves they must have been aided considerably by the sum of £175 that was raised in the Preston Circuit during 1838 'for the improvement of Freckleton Chapel'.[22] On

25 March 1840 George Fishwick and the other surviving trustees from 1814, 'being of the opinion that a larger and more convenient Chapel had become necessary', contracted with John Furness and other new trustees for 'the absolute sale to them of the said Chapel or Meeting house at or for the price of £145 being the most money that could be got for the same'.[23]

Rebuilding must have begun prior to 1840 as in October 1839 services were held in the old factory (now the site of the Sports and Social Club) when 18s. 6d. was paid for 'rent of factory used during the rebuilding of the chapel'. The same accounts also record that in February 1840 £4 2s. 2½d. was paid to 'Mr Bedford [the Rev. John Bedford, a Wesleyan Minister] and added to the subscription list for erecting the new chapel.'[24] Soon afterwards the first chapel had been substantially rebuilt, an event recorded by Pilkington who says that 'the thatch was stripped, the walls were raised, the roof was slated, and a gallery put in at one end. The place was made neat and comfortable. — Soon a strong feeling prevailed that a new front to the chapel should be built, and a stone bearing the inscription 'Wesley Chapel' put up'. This was also carried out at a cost of about £80.[25] Further confirmation of these events was provided by Hewitson who, when visiting the chapel in 1872, said 'the erection of a [the first] chapel succeeded the labours of Moses [Holden] and his

Kirkham Road Methodist Church. The third church building on the site: the foundation stones of the present church were laid in 1884 and the building was opened on 9 September 1885. In the eighteenth century a cottage, occupied by the parents of Thomas Willacy, the Freckleton schoolmaster, stood on the site.

colleagues' and added that about 1840 a building, which accommodated 200, 'was erected on the same site'.[26]

At the 1844 quarterly meeting the debt on the chapel was recorded as £230 at 4½%.[27] One of the few receipts from the period is dated 21 May 1851, when George Richardson paid Edward Leece £10 7s. 0d. 'for Interest of money upon the Wesleyan Methodist Chapel Situate in Freckleton for 1 year'.[28] As there are no other known surviving account or minute books covering the period 1848 to 1884 it is not possible to build up a picture of life at the chapel during the mid-nineteenth century, though it was clearly a very active and committed society. When Hewitson visited the chapel in 1872 he described it as having 'a rather genteel exterior; and, as a small village chapel, looks prim and orderly in front' and that 'the building is of neat proportions internally; but it is the dampest chapel we have ever entered; the walls are quite mouldy and black in several places; and on this account the building is completely spoiled in its appearance'. He added that 'the chapel has an average attendance of 150, including scholars; and the general congregation is constituted of a peaceful, thrifty, respectable class of villagers. The chapel serves for a Sunday school, teaching being conducted prior to each service, and the average attendance is about sixty-five'.[29]

In 1877 it was decided to build a new and larger church and by 1883, as a result of collections made Sunday by Sunday in the Sunday school and also at tea meetings, nearly £300 had been raised. In the same year 'after long delay and much negotiation'[30] additional land was obtained from Mr R. Richardson and Mrs Cross Wignall, following which the contract for the building was awarded to the architect Mr D. Grant of Preston. The total cost appears to have been about £1,400 of which £400 had been raised by 1884, with further promises made by 'The Late T. C. Hincksman £100; H. E. Sowerbutts £50; William Wignall £50; and Benjamin Wignall £20'.[31]

On 30 August 1884 the foundation stones of the new church were laid by Mr H. E. Sowerbutts (the owner of Balderstone Mill); Henry Mayor Richardson (grandson of George Richardson); Mr B. Wignall; and Mr W. Wignall, Jnr. The building was completed during the following year and opened on 9 September 1885. The daily administration was the responsibility of the trustees and in October 1885 they decided that pews rents should be 9d., 1s. 0d. and 1s. 3d. They also appointed Joseph Gregson as Chapel Keeper at 5s. 0d. a week, listing his duties as 'lighting and cleaning the chapel, school, and attending to the heating apparatus'.[32] In addition to these duties Joseph Gregson also served as property steward from 1886 until 1902.

In the years immediately following the opening of the new church it became evident that, in order to meet the needs of the increasing congregation, a new (Sunday) school room was also necessary and although this was first proposed in 1891 it was not until 1897 that permission was granted 'on the condition that the entire cost did not exceed the sum of £526'. In September 1898 the new school, accommodating 300 people, was opened and in the following June Messrs B. Wignall, T. C. Wignall and T. Brown were thanked 'for their donation towards clearing the debt off the New School'.[33] From late 1911 to early 1912 the church was closed to allow for alterations in order to install a new organ. In December 1912 it was resolved to accept the tender submitted by Messrs Wadsworth Bros. and the first public recital was held on 16 July 1913. This long standing and still continuing musical tradition was first set by Peter Rawstrone, who from 1855 until his death in 1895 was leader of the choir.

In 1932, as a result of the Uniting Methodist Conference of that year, the Wesleyan and Primitive Methodist communities were brought together, thereby strengthening the case for a resident minister. This was not achieved until 1959 when 'Maida Vale', Lytham Road, was purchased as a manse and the Rev. Stanley Finch was appointed the resident Methodist minister in Freckleton. Since 1960 there have been ten other ministers (see appendix B), though from 1982 the church remained without a resident minister until the present manse in Derwent Close was purchased in 1986.

Throughout the twentieth century the church has continued to play an important role in the community and there are many individuals who have given years of devoted service to its cause. Perhaps the most outstanding name is that of George Wylie Rigby, born at Freckleton in 1858, and who in 1941 was reported to have been a member of the Sunday school for 80 years, of which 63 were as a teacher. Among those still, or recently, associated with the church are families whose surnames – Brown, Hall, Rawstrone, Rigby, Spencer and Swann – were first mentioned in the membership and pew lists of the early nineteenth century, and it is this sense of community and continuity that has enabled the Methodist cause to prosper for almost two centuries.

CHAPTER 11

Primitive Methodist Church (Preston Old Road)

Hugh Bourne, the founder of the Primitive Methodism, began his religious work as a conventional Wesleyan Methodist local preacher. In 1807 Bourne, influenced by the open-air 'camp meetings' so successful in the United States, organised his own at Mow Cop in Staffordshire, but following similar meetings was expelled from the Wesleyan Methodist Connexion in 1808, under the terms of a decision made at the 1807 national conference to condemn and disclaim all connection with camp meetings. It was not, however, until 1812 that Bourne started Primitive Methodism, designed, in his view, to restore Methodism to its primitive simplicity.

There is reference to services in the Primitive cause being held in Freckleton 'as early as 1827',[1] but it was not until twenty years later, when the Rev. Benjamin Whillock decided to visit Freckleton, that Primitive Methodism became permanently established. In a letter sent to officials of the church in 1898 he recalled how one morning in 1847 he walked from Bryning to Freckleton, where he visited a number of homes in the morning to advise people that he intended to hold a short service in the open air during the dinner hour, before the factory hands returned to work.

In describing the event he says 'I got to the side of the little blacksmiths shop – from a grocers shop at the left hand corner of the road going to Kirkham I borrowed a small barrel 12 or 14 inches high; on this I stood – back to the smithy facing Kirkham Road. When I thought the factory hands had taken dinner and were about to return to work I ascended the barrel.'[2] His letter then further describes the short service he conducted and it is not surprising that his principal targets were the factory hands, as the Primitive cause had from its beginnings been associated with the less affluent in society.

Following the meeting the Rev. Whillock began to enquire about the possibility of a meeting place in the village and later recorded that Elizabeth Rawstrone offered the use of her home in Lower Lane and 'did more for my project than all the respectable people were willing or dared to do'.[3] It was in this cottage, which stood on the site of the modern bungalow called 'Bolzano', that services were conducted and the first society formed. On the census of 1841 Betty Rawstorne (sic) was recorded as the wife of Thomas Rawstorne, a wheelwright. By 1851 Thomas had died and Betty was described as a pauper and laundress aged 42. It was their son Peter who by 1881 was the principal shipbuilder in Freckleton.

Tanyard. Originally built as a factory by John Mayor and still known as 'the old factory' into the mid-nineteenth century, it later became a tanyard owned by the Wignall family. It is, however, also remembered as the first meeting place of the Primitive Methodists. It is now the site of the Sports and Social Club.

By early the following year the Rev. Whillock, with the help of John
Webster and William Garlick, prominent local preachers, had rented an
upstairs room of the old factory. The room, entry to which was by a
flight of external stone steps, was fitted out as a mission room and
opened on 5 March 1848, the preacher being the Rev. T. Jobling, then
superintendent minister of the Preston Saul Street circuit. In 1885 Mr
R. Rawsthorne recalled that when the society commenced services in
the building there were 20 male scholars and 35 female scholars. The
building served as the meeting place for the Primitives for the next
fourteen years and gave rise to the perjorative jingle 'Up yon steps I
dare not venture: if I do they'll call me a Ranter'.[4] In 1850 there were
24 members (as opposed to scholars), but this number fell steadily from
1857 until a low of only 9 members were recorded in 1860.

The turning point in the cause of Primitive Methodism came with
the arrival in the village of Henry Hall, who purchased the new [Bal-
derstone] factory in the late 1850s. Henry Hall appears to have been
closely associated with Jonathan Gaukroger and William Sowerbutts, the

Old/New Primitive Methodist churches. The old church (right) opened for worship in
1862 but within twenty years had become too small to accommodate the increasing
congregation. The new church opened in 1892 and had seating for 266. Both buildings
were demolished in 1973 and the site is now occupied by Freckleton Library. (*Courtesy of*
Lancashire Evening Post)

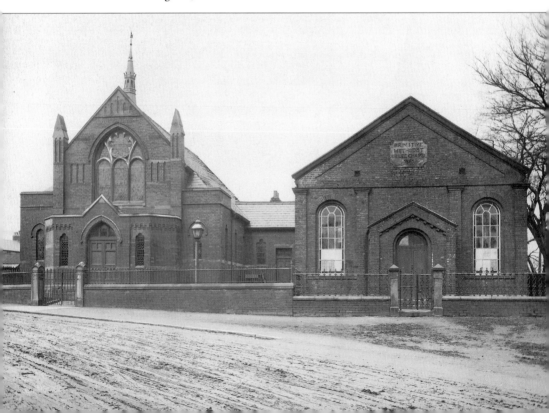

two subsequent owners of the factory, and all three men were involved
with the cause of Primitive Methodism in Preston. It was probably a
combination of their business acumen and religious beliefs, harnessed to
the efforts of the existing Freckleton members that resulted, at a quarterly
meeting held on 17 June 1861, in the motion 'That they have liberty to
build a new Chapel at Freckleton and that the buildings committee be
written to according to rule'.[5]

In August 1861 the following men were approved as suitable to become
trustees for the intended new chapel: Henry Hall, James Hall, Thomas
Flintoff, John Sewell, John Sudell, Rimmer Iddon, Joseph Bamber,
Marsden Rigby, George Norcross, Robert Hall, Marsden Rostern, Robert
Rostern and James Whiteside. At the same meeting the dimensions of
the chapel were agreed, as well as 'the erection of a platform 3 yards
long to be ascended by 3 steps instead of a pulpit', and at the September
meeting it was further agreed that the trustee 'be recommended to have
a Layer of spent lime mixed with sand and gas tar under the foundation
of the intended New Chapel'.[6]

The Jubilee Chapel was built, at a cost of £288, on land known as
Tom's Croft which had been previously owned by the Odd Fellows
(friendly society). The opening took place on 16 March 1862 and opening

New Primitive Methodist Church. A view of the interior probably taken in the
mid-1920s (*Courtesy of* Lancashire Evening Post).

services continued throughout the month. On Monday 24 March a tea-meeting was held attended by 150 persons, after which several 'interesting addresses' were given and presided over by Mr Sowerbutts, who a year earlier had laid one of the foundation stones of the chapel. At a quarterly meeting held in the same month it was agreed that a 'camp meeting' be held at Freckleton in the month of June, also that R. Iddon be society steward.[7] Rimmer Iddon was still society steward when the chapel celebrated its jubilee fifty years later in 1912.

When Hewitson visited the chapel in 1872 he described it as 'made of brick, is compact in form, has a plain interior, and will accommodate about 200 persons'. He added that 'in front of the pulpit there is a square pew, originally intended for the singers; but it did not suit them, and they now occupy an enclosure in the right corner of the building'. The congregation consisted of 'working people – plain, homely men and women'.[8]

Following the opening of the chapel in 1862 society membership increased from 9 to 22 and this latter figure remained fairly consistent until 1877–78 when it soared to between 41 and 50.[9] In the absence of any surviving written records the reason for this sudden increase is not apparent but in November 1880 it was decided to open a fund for the building of a new chapel. Fundraising events were held throughout the following decade, including a three day sale of work in 1884, and by 1891 £395 had been raised. A further £216 was raised on 22 August 1891 when the six memorial stones of the new Chapel were laid by Mr H. E. Sowerbutts (son of William Sowerbutts), Mr Brown Jnr of Blackpool (in place of his father), Mrs Banks (on behalf of Capt. Banks, 'unavoidably absent'), Mr Iddon, Mr H. Hall and Mr Newton Wignall.[10] At this date church membership stood at 55, with 130 teachers and scholars.

Within twelve months the chapel had been completed and the opening service was held on Saturday 18 June 1892. It was described as 'a neat Gothic building of patent brick with stone dressings, having a graceful spire' and was designed by Messrs. Mold of Manchester. Seating 266 persons it was built by the contractor Mr John Gardiner of Kirkham at a cost of approximately £1,400. The old chapel was converted into a Sunday school. Opening services continued throughout June and July by which time £738 had been received towards the total outlay. In 1904–05, when the Rev. W. H. Maxwell was located in the village as a resident minister, the debt was reduced by £200 and in January 1909, during the ministry of the Rev. W. E. Lead, the balance of the debt of £121 10s. 0d. was completely cleared.

Apart from a minute book for the years 1923 to 1966 there are no known surviving twentieth-century records. Consequently there is a void concerning the names of officials and events in chapel life for the last decade of the nineteenth century and early twentieth century. In 1923 Thomas Banks and John Kirby were chapel stewards and they continued in office until 1930 when Henry Allanson took over from John Kirby. Thomas Banks served until 1947, and others whose years in office amounted to eighteen or more years were Henry Rawstrone (1939–59) and Richard Greenwood (1948–66). Chapel members whose deaths were specifically recorded in the minute book on account of their service and devotion were John Banks (1932), William Bamber (1937), Matthew Armstrong (1953) and John Whittle (1966).[11]

During June 1961 centenary celebrations were held to mark the opening of the first chapel and these included several services, including one at the site of the old factory. Chapel services included one with special music by the choir conducted by Mr H. Allanson and one that included a visit by Hesketh Bank Choir, the same choir that had taken part in the opening ceremonies of the new chapel in 1892.

Four years later, however, it was decided to close the chapel and on 18 August 1965 the following resolution was passed:

> It was proposed by Mr W. Banks and seconded by Mr H. Allanson that the trustees in view of the recommendation made by the leaders and members of the Preston Old Road Methodist Chapel that the trustees reluctantly and sadly agree to close the premises of Preston Old Road, and the report of the district commission that services are to dis-continue in these premises as from January 9 1966.[12]

Both the old and new chapels were demolished in 1973 and seven years later the present library was built on the site.

CHAPTER 12

Plymouth Brethren

The name Plymouth Brethren was taken by the followers of John Nelson Darby and originated about 1830 when Darby founded the first 'Society of Believers' at Plymouth. The Brethren believed in baptism and partook of the Lord's Supper every Sunday but repudiated all ecclesiastical organisation and acknowledged no special distinction between clergy and laity.

The Brethren first became established in Freckleton sometime in the 1890s when the occupier of a house on Lytham Road opened his home for Brethren meetings to anyone wishing to join him in worship. The congregation grew steadily in numbers and in 1903 they leased the Quaker Meeting House where the caretaker, Mr Tom Butcher, was an early member. Some idea of the Brethren's numerical strength can be obtained from a letter written in 1905 by the Vicar of Freckleton, the Rev. E Hack, to the Bishop of Manchester:

Plymouth Brethren Meeting House. The Plymouth Brethren first began to meet in Freckleton during the 1890s. By 1905 they were building their first meeting house in Naze Lane. The building continued to be used by the Brethren until it was sold in the 1960s and is now occupied by T. Taylor (Opticians) Ltd.

Your Lordship would not think it likely that the Plymouth Brethren would want to build a Church to hold 150. The fact is this some years ago the Quakers used certain buildings which they afterwards let to the Brethren. The premises have been purchased and are to be given to the Township but the Brethren, nothing daunted, are now building a neat little brick chapel to hold 150.[1]

Shortly afterwards the meeting house in Naze Lane was built by Samuel Rigby, a member who lived in Bush Lane, and in whose ownership the meeting house remained. The building was entered through a small vestibule and there was pine panelling around the lower wall, with brickwork on the upper wall. The seating consisted of wooden forms and in the middle of the house there was an iron stove with flue pipe for heating purposes. Amongst the families associated with the Brethren in Freckleton were Butcher, Hayes, Rawstrone and Worthington, and when Samuel Rigby left Freckleton the meeting house was sold to John Worthington. Worship continued until the early 1960s when the building was sold to T. Taylor (Opticians) Ltd, the present owners of the property.[2]

CHAPTER 13

The Quakers (Society of Friends)

During the quarter century following the visit of George Fox to Lancaster in 1652 Quakerism in the Kirkham district became firmly established and in about 1675 a particularly violent meeting at Freckleton, recorded by Isaac Ashton some years after the event, took place:

> I was with Roger Haydock in a Meeting, where some in office (as was said) with a great company of rude fellows, with great staves, making a noise like madmen, finding him at prayer, had like to have pulled him off his knees, but were something restrained, of which he took no notice. But when he did rise, they laid hold on him, and hurried him away out of the Meeting, with a howling noise, like a company of wolves, that had made a prey upon a lamb. For so he behaved himself: all which did so much touch nor hurt him as to alter his countenance, as I perceived. But after the rude people were gone, Friends continued their meeting: and there being some from several Meetings, we had a good Meeting, for the powers of darkness were driven away, and the enemies blinded.
>
> All this was at Freckleton in the Fylde, where there is now a settled Meeting, and hath been for several years.[1]

In 1676, probably as a result of this meeting, Thomas Tomlinson, Henry Tomlinson and John Townson had, on the order of Edward Rigby, a Preston justice, goods and cattle distrained† to the value of £22 10s. 0d. At the same time Rigby declared that he would 'root the Quakers out of the Hundred where he dwelt, that all the Laws yet made against them were too short, and that he would be the first that would move for a Law to have them tied to and dragged at either an Horse's or Cart's Tail'.[2]

In spite of such threats and intimidations the Quakers persevered and by the late 1680s a small community had been established. One of the earliest members was William Colbron (Coulborne) and in his will, made in 1688, he refers to a deed of feoffment that had already been made in respect of his eldest son Lawrence. Although William Coulborne did not name his property information contained in subsequent wills of the Coulborne, Brown and Brade families indicates that it stood on or near to the present-day Brades Farm. It was almost certainly this property, by then the home of Lawrence Coulborne, that was licensed as a Quaker meeting place in 1689. Two years later the homes of William Blackleach, who married Elizabeth the sister of Lawrence Coulborne, and James Sharples were also licensed as Quaker meeting places.

The establishment of the Quaker community at Freckleton was not to the liking of the Rev. Richard Clegg, vicar of Kirkham. One reason was the potential loss of his parishioners. The other was a fear of loss of income if the Quakers refused to pay their tithes, an ancient obligation to which the Quakers were opposed. In 1691 he appealed to quarter sessions concerning Margaret Coulborne (the wife of Lawrence) in the following terms:

> Also a female preacher we have in Freckleton doth Conventicle from house to house & disquiet her better neighbours in their own houses; viz Richard Ward & the wife of Wm Browne lately seduced, and tells them terminis or effect they must be Quakers or perish: she hath affirmed she hath seen Christ with her eyes and felt him with her hands, with other scurrilous and blasphemous language and she denies (or will not own the resurrection). Also she liveth a scandalous kind of life with one Francis Colbron; having persuaded her Husband Law. Colbron to go to the Gaol, and indeavouring to continue him there, against his inclinations as is reported: upon his default and robbery in non payment of his tithes and offerings'.[3]

In July 1692 Margaret Coulborne was found guilty at the Preston assizes of blasphemy when the court rejected her defence that her words, intended as an explanation of the source of her authority for preaching, had been deliberately misinterpreted. Refusing to pay a fine of ten pounds she was imprisoned at Lancaster Castle where she remained despite Quaker appeals to the vice-chancellor of the Duchy of Lancaster to 'stop proceedings and get this poor woman discharged'. It was only after the Quakers had presented a petition to the Queen (Mary II), who promised 'that she would take care in the Friends case by speaking to the judges that goes that circuit', that Margaret Coulborne was discharged in September 1694. The matter came to a final close in December 1694 when, at the request of the leading Quakers, Margaret Coulborne was requested to send a few lines of acknowledgement to the Queen [who in fact died the same month] for her kindness'.[4]

The prosecution of Margaret Coulborne was not without its effect on her husband Lawrence. In the year that his wife was imprisoned he was reprimanded by the Quakers' Lancaster monthly meeting when two Friends were ordered 'to speak to Lawrence and to exhort him concerning his weakness in paying his tithes and leaving Friends Meetings'. Although events later in his life show that he remained a committed Quaker, at the time of his reprimand Lawrence replied that 'he could not stand against the law'.[5]

Although not all Quakers refused to pay their tithes the Rev. Clegg still considered it necessary on several occasions to seek judgement against those who did refuse. In 1699 James Hall and William Brown refused to pay their great tithe (corn and grain) and the constable of Freckleton was ordered by the justices to levy the sum of 40*s.* 6*d.* against them, by distress or sale of goods or chattels, and make payment to the appropriate authority. In 1710 complaint was made that several persons had for the years 1708 and 1709 neglected or refused to pay their tithes. Among those again summoned was James Hall who was ordered to pay:

for tithe Hay 3 Acres in the year 1709	£0	3*s.*	0*d.*
for his Marriage Dues in the year 1709	£0	6*s.*	8*d.*
& for costs	£0	9*s.*	6*d.*[6]

Evidence of the marriage of James Hall to Margaret Weaver of Clifton in 1709 can be found in the records of the Preston monthly meeting, the same year as their house was licensed as a Quaker Meeting House.[7] In his will dated 29 March 1720 James Hall gave instructions that his 'body be decently Buried with the consent of the People called Quakers only (Relations not to meddle) at the Quakers burying place within Freckleton aforesaid'. In addition to bequests to his wife and children he also left 'eight pounds to my Executors upon demand for said building a meeting house or purchasing land for the same'.[8]

In 1693 the Quakers had attempted to licence a 'Parcel of ground lying in Freckleton called Gwelfolong and intended for a meeting place for an assembly of Quakers... and also a place to bury their dead', but the document submitted to the quarter sessions was noted 'this Court will not record it'.[9] It is unclear whether this was the same site as that later referred to as Twill Furlong and that the spelling is simply a case of the clerk at the quarter sessions being unfamiliar with local names.

However, despite this refusal the Quaker register of marriages, births and burials records three burials at Freckleton during the 1690s, including that of James Sharples who 'died a prisoner at Lancaster Castle'.[10] In addition to the recorded burials Isabel Johnson, who died in 1696, stated in her will that it was 'her desire to be buried in that place called the Quakers Yard in Freckleton'.[11] Quaker burials continued to take place in Freckleton throughout the first two decades of the eighteenth century but it is not until the death of Lawrence Coulborne in 1716 that there is definite evidence of the actual burial site.

In his will Lawrence Coulborne instructed that 'my body to be interred in a certain parcel of ground lying within the said township of Freckleton called Coulborns Yard'.[12] Four years later on 24 February 1720 William Coulborne, son of Lawrence, granted to William Blackleach:

> All that Little parcel of Land as the same was then ditched out of the lower end of one Close of Ground belonging to Wm Coulborn lying within the said Township of Freckleton called by the name of the Twill Furlong'.[13]

As it is unlikely that William Coulborne would have granted land for a burial site other than where his father had been buried in 1716 it can be assumed that Coulborns Yard, otherwise known as Twill Furlong, was the same place that is now known as Quakers Wood. However not all internments took place within the confines of the present wood and thirty-six internments are now recognised as having taken place in nearby fields. By 1758 at least one field was already known as the Burying Yard [14] whilst the tithe map of 1838 names the field adjacent to the wood as the Burying Yard and those opposite as the Higher Burying Yard and the Lower Burying Yard. After the burial in 1810 of William Coulborn (spelt Cowburn in the register), aged 91, no further burials took place until those of Sarah and Joseph Jesper in 1889 and 1890. The last internment was that John Holmes of Preston in 1891. Although Quakers Wood is now somewhat overgrown the gravestone of Joseph and Sarah Jesper can still be seen and the wood itself is managed by local trustees.

To return to the early eighteenth century, it is clear that by 1720 the Quaker community was firmly established and that the need for a permanent meeting house had become pressing. As we have seen, James Hall left money in 1720 towards the building of a meeting house and in 1724 John Turnley, a tailor, left to his executors and fellow Quakers, Cuthbert Sharples and William Brown 'of the foulside [Foldside Farm]', 'ten shillings, upon Trust, that they shall lay it out for the use of the meeting house at their discretion'.[15]

It is, however, William Brown of Foldside Farm who probably joined the Quakers with his father, Butler Browne, sometime in the 1680s, who is the best remembered of all Freckleton Quakers. He was the same William Brown who had had goods and chattels distrained in 1699 for non-payment of his tithe, but despite these hardships his committment to the Quaker cause never wavered. In 1720 he granted, for the sum of three pounds, a portion of a close of land in Freckleton called the 'great Croft' and when he died in 1724 he not only left money for the education of Quaker children but also added a codicil to his will directing that 'they build a stable and little house and that my executors shall be accountable once a year'.[16] Within twelve months a meeting house, the original predecessor of the present Memorial Hall, was built on the Great Croft for the use of the Freckleton Quakers and when the executors of William Brown made out a list of their disbursements they noted that:

> Thomas Ryley has paid £4 13s. 4¾d. for making 15 thousand of brick for building a Stable etc. for the use of friends as appears by a note of particulars.[17]

Members of the Blackleach, Brown, Coulborne, Eccleston, Hall and Sharples families from Freckleton, together with the Lancaster family of Newton with Scales and the Ryley family of Clifton were the locally active Quakers during the eighteenth century and the following extracts of the Freckleton preparative meetings, held in 1761, give some indication of the ways in which the cause was maintained:

> James Hall and John Lancaster to conduct Travelling Friends.

> William Coulborn and James Ryley to see the meeting house and what belongs it Put into Repair.

Quakers Wood. The only visible surviving evidence of the once flourishing Quaker community is their former burial ground situated in Lower Lane. First opened in 1720 the last interment took place in 1891. Quaker burials were not, however, just confined to the present wood and as early as 1758 adjacent fields were known as the 'Burying Yards'.

Joseph Lancaster offers Represent this meeting to the month meeting to be held at Freckleton.[18]

Until the mid-nineteenth century Quaker discipline in regard to marriage was very strict and those who married contrary to the rules were disowned. At a monthly meeting held in Preston in 1779 Isabel Coulborn of Freckleton was accused of marrying 'a Man of another persuasion' which was 'contrary to the advice of her Friends and the well known Rules of our Society'. The meeting decided that they had no option other than to declare their 'Disapprobation' and that they could not have any fellowship with her until 'it may please Divine Wisdom to cause her to see the Error of her ways'.[19] The irony of the decision cannot have been lost on Isabel as only the previous year she herself had been one on the signatories of an identical document concerning the marriage of Elizabeth Ryley of Clifton.

The final quarter of the eighteenth century saw the gradual demise of the Quaker movement in the township, and in 1782 it was decided that 'as the Freckleton is now in a great measure Dropt its agreed that in future our Monthly Meeting should be held in Preston at the time it used to be held there'.[20] Five years later in 1787 Friends from Preston 'tried to revive the interest of the three Friends then constituting it, one of whom was infirm and old and unable to attend, and so the end came'.[21] The last member of the community was William Coulborn, who died in 1810, at the age of ninety-one, and as we saw earlier was interred in the burial ground in Lower Lane.[22]

Although the Quakers retained ownership – in 1790 they paid £2 11s. 10d. for repairs[23] – the history and usage of the meeting house from 1787 to 1870 is somewhat unclear and, as we will see, it appears that in the early nineteenth century it was being leased to the township as a school. In 1809 the Quakers licensed 'a certain house, situated in Freckleton, as a Meeting House ... to exercise their religious worship in',[24] but it is not known whether this was the original meeting house or a private dwelling.

A short-lived revival of the Quaker cause began in 1870 when, through the efforts of Joseph Jesper, a Quaker from Preston, an allowed meeting was set up at Freckleton. In a letter in The (Quaker) Monthly record, published some years later, he recorded that 'there was at that place [Freckleton] a dilapidated old meeting house and stable etc., in such a condition as to be anything but creditable to the owners [the Quakers] ... A Friend from Preston [himself], arranged to pull down the old premises and to erect new, engaging to provide a spacious room for the holding of meetings, as might be required; erecting in the same pile a small occasional residence for himself and family, also a dwelling for the caretakers'.[25] In 1871 John Satterthwaite of Preston registered the new building as a 'Place of Meeting for Religious Worship'.[26]

The revived meeting had an attendance of around fifty and in 1872 Hewitson recorded that 'Service is held in it [the meeting house] once a month, – on a Sunday evening; and there is very fair attendance of all classes.' He added that 'As we passed the place we saw one solitary quakeress, dressed in the everlasting drab of the order, sitting upon the grass in front'.[27] However it was not only the Quakers who benefited from the generosity of Joseph Jesper and in a newspaper article written some years after his death it was recorded that

> 'Jesper', familiarly called, came over [from Preston] to the village once a month and conducted a service. He was an ardent reformer, and was frequently accompanied by Mr Joseph Livesey [the founder of the temperence movement]. Each year Mr Jesper gave a tea to the widows and widowers and a certain number of scholars from the [Sunday?] schools in the village. He was assisted by the late Mr Wm Sowerbutts [of Balderstone

Foldside Farm. The home of William Brown who for over forty years until his death in 1724 was one of the leading Quakers in Freckleton. The farm remained in the ownership of the Brown and, through marriage, the Cookson families until it was demolished in 1966. In this photograph Mrs Bridget Singleton, wife of the then tenant farmer, can be seen together with her five daughters.

The building latterly known as the Hodgson Institute was built by Joseph Jesper in 1870 and replaced the original Quaker Meeting House. In 1904 it was bought by William Segar Hodgson who donated it to the village for recreational and educational purposes. The Memorial Hall now occupies the site. (*Courtesy of* Lancashire Evening Post)

Mill], who was a great friend of his. Tea and oranges were distributed and the treats, which are still remembered by the inhabitants, were greatly enjoyed.[28]

After the death of Joseph Jesper in 1889 meetings would appear to have ceased and by 1903 the meeting house was being leased to the Plymouth Brethren. In 1904, following its purchase by William Segar Hodgson, who presented it to the village for use as a community centre and council chamber, the building became known as the Hodgson Institute. Finally in 1975, almost three hundred years after the first Quaker meetings, this building too was demolished and replaced two years later by the present Memorial Hall.

CHAPTER 14

The Roman Catholic Church

In the years immediately following the Reformation legislation such as the Acts of Uniformity of 1552 and 1559 resulted in strict anti-Catholic laws. However, as elsewhere in much of south and west Lancashire, many of the local gentry refused to conform and became known as recusants or papists, and within the parish of Kirkham families such as Clifton and Westby continued to maintain their own chapels. This strong loyalty to the Catholic faith was particularly exemplified by John Westby of Mowbreck Hall, Kirkham, whose sister Elizabeth had married George Allen, the brother of William Allen, the future cardinal and founder of the seminary at Douai in France, where priests were trained for the English mission. Mowbreck Hall in fact provided a centre for local Catholics until the opening of the chapel at the Willows, Kirkham, in 1809.

The first evidence of Catholic worship in Freckleton is provided by a list of convicted recusants that was compiled in 1671 and which names Butler Cowborne, his wife Ann, John Crompton, then an innkeeper in Freckleton, Ann Browne, wife of William Browne, and Jenett, wife of Richard Holley. Butler Cowborne (the name is variously spelt including the version Colebrand) was baptised at Kirkham in 1618 and was a member of a branch of a family that is said to have included a Sir George Cowburn, a priest who is reported to have died at Freckleton in 1597, whilst in the seventeenth and eighteenth centuries two other members of the Cowborne family were also ordained priests.[1]

There is no record of where this small Catholic community met in the seventeenth century but a map prepared in 1915 notes 'Freckleton Hall' as a former Mass centre and also refers to the hall 'as the seat of the Colbornes'.[2] The map indicates the location of the hall somewhere in the vicinity of Hall Cross but unfortunately no other evidence is provided and as there are no other known documents that refer to any past or present property in the area as Freckleton Hall it is not possible to positively identify the building.

In 1678 Janett Smalley, Anne Browne, Elizabeth Higginson and John Thorneley, a husbandman, were recorded as recusants. Janett Smalley appears to be the same person as Jane Smalley wife of William Smalley, a yeoman, who, before his death in 1682, had instructed that his body be buried in the churchyard at Kirkham. Jane, however, who died in 1685, whilst recognising King James II as Defender of the Faith, committed her soul 'to the merciful hands of almighty God trusting to be saved by the all sufficient merits of Christ Jesus' and requested that she be buried 'In Decent Manner at the discretion of my executors'.[3] One of the apprizers who carried out the inventory of her goods following her decease was Richard Browne, a tailor and husband of Anne Browne one of the other recusants named in 1678.

During the period 1680 to 1770 it is estimated that the Catholic population of Lancashire increased by almost 60 per cent from 16–18,000 to 26,000, some 20 per cent of the county population. In order to determine exact numbers the House of Lords in 1767 ordered a return to be made of papists in every parish, and in the fifteen townships forming Kirkham parish 939 persons were named. In Kirkham the number was 66, in Warton it was 58 but the two extremes were Westby with Plumpton with 436 and Freckleton with just 5 – the family of James Sharples. In 1767 James Sharples was 48 years of age and was described as a miller (at the watermill). He lived with his wife Isabel and their three children and had been resident in Freckleton for nine years. By the time he died in 1789 James had acquired additional land and property in and around the area of Lower Lane and Preston Old Road, all of which he divided amongst his children John, Henry and Mary.

In 1816 John Sharples, a bachelor, made the first of his two wills in which he appointed the Rev. Thomas Sherburn(e) of the Willows Catholic Church and Thomas Adamson, a fellow Freckleton Catholic, his trustees. Whilst his sister, nephews and niece were to be the chief beneficiaries he also bequeathed £10 to 'the Treasurer of The Society for the relief of aged and infirm Catholic Priests in aid of the Fund of that benevolent institution'. In addition he gave £20 to the Rev. Thomas Sherburn(e), 'as a token of my esteem and regard'.[4] Although a later will made in 1830 makes no mention of these specific bequests it is likely that his new executors, his nephew James Sharples and nephew-in-law Henry Singleton, acted in accordance with the wishes made in his earlier 'spiritual' will.

During the first half of the nineteenth century the principal Catholic families in Freckleton were those of Adamson, Houseman and Sharples and in 1829 the Survey of Dissent recorded the number of Roman Catholics in Freckleton as 31. In the second half of the century this community began to grow and, in the view of the clergy, became a particular cause for concern. When in the late 1860s the Rev. John O'Meara updated an earlier church census carried out by the Rev. Frederick Hines of the Willows in about 1857, he noted that 'Freckleton is in a very painful state all owing to Mixed Marriages'.[5] Evidence for his latter remark is to be found throughout the census with comments such as 'Protestant children – nothing' and 'Twice married to a Protestant'.[6]

No doubt the major problem for the Catholic community, both clergy and laity, was the distance between Freckleton and the Willows at Kirkham, and following his appointment to the Willows in 1895 the Rev. Francis Gillow began to say Mass 'in a house by the marsh gates'. This was almost certainly Number 1 Lower Lane which has been described as the 'the meeting place of the Roman Catholics for mass'.[7] In 1915 the property was still occupied by the Misses Battersby, the descendants of Henry Sharples whose daughter Mary had married James Battersby.

In 1898 the Christmas congregation at Freckleton was 60 and in the following year Father Gillow joined with Canon Taylor of Lytham in building a chapel in Warton, on land given by the Clifton estate on a 999 year lease. The chapel, which cost over £500, was funded in part by the Liverpool diocese and was dedicated to the Holy Family. The

Holy Family School Chapel, Freckleton, Nr. Preston.   29829.

Holy Family Roman Catholic Church. Although situated on the Warton side of Lamaleach Brook the church of Holy family has served the Roman Catholic population of Freckleton since it was opened on 30 September 1900.

opening services took place on Sunday, 30 September 1900, when 'a large assembly of the Roman Catholics of Preston, Kirkham, Lytham and other places in the Fylde gathered at Freckleton' to hear Bishop Whiteside of Liverpool preach 'an eloquent sermon'.[8] In the afternoon 'a procession of teachers, scholars, and friends' headed by Freckleton Band walked from the marsh gates through the village to the chapel where Bishop Bilsborrow of Salford preached from the church door so that all could hear.[9]

The chapel continued to be served from the Willows and Lytham until Father Gillow, entirely at his own expense, built and endowed a presbytery,[10] and in 1907 a separate parish was created with the appointment of the Rev. J. Roche as parish priest. Six years later in 1913 Father Roche oversaw the establishment of an all age school which was held in the 'back half' of the church with a wooded partition, withdrawn on a Sunday, dividing the school area from the rest of the church. Prior to this date the nearest Catholic school was that at the Willows, but due to the distance involved it seems unlikely that many Catholic children in Freckleton would have attended there. Evidence that some Catholic children attended Trinity School is provided by an entry in the school log book of 5 June 1913 when it was noted that 'The Roman Catholics have opened a school on the Warton side of Taylors Pool & caused a few withdrawals'.

The Catholic school functioned until about 1953 when it closed and the children went either to Westby, the Willows, or St Peters, Lytham. In 1974 the first phase of a new Holy Family school was officially opened; by August 1976 the second phase had also been completed and the school is now attended by children from both Freckleton and Warton. In 1978 the interior of the church was extensively refurbished when small-paned windows with heavy timber were replaced by slender modern panes; heavy brass light fittings gave way to almost invisible fixtures in the ceiling; and modern pews of Iroko, a teak-like African wood, replaced the original pews. The names of the fifteen parish priests who have had charge of Holy Family since 1907 are listed in appendix B.

Part VI

Education of the Children

CHAPTER 15

Education, 1551–1839

Kirkham Grammar School

The first written mention of the education of children in the parish of Kirkham is dated 1551 when the grammar school at Kirkham received a bequest of 20 shillings from Thomas Clifton of Westby.[1] In 1585 the Thirty Men of Kirkham took on the responsibility of maintaining the schoolhouse and in 1604, in order to provide an endowment fund, raised £10 from each of the 15 townships that formed the parish of Kirkham.[2] The school also benefited from bequests in the wills of Henry Colborn in 1655 and the Rev. James Barker in 1670.

Under the terms of the will of Henry Colborn, a scrivener in London but originally from Kirkham, the school came to be controlled by the Drapers Company of London until 1840 when the trustees of the Rev. James Barker, a former pupil, were given more control on the governing body. Although it was the intention of Henry Colborn that his bequest be used to 'maintain schools and poor people' it is doubtful whether many boys from Freckleton, other than the sons of some of the leading families, received an education at the school until the curriculum was broadened in 1840.

Kirkham Charity School for Girls

It was not until 1760 that a charity school for girls was built in Kirkham.[3] This school was endowed by the purchase of land in Freckleton – the Croft and Bannister Flatt – and twelve marsh gates on Freckleton Marsh, the income from which was to pay a dame to teach the girls.[4] However, despite the endowment land being in Freckleton admission to the school was limited to girls who lived in the town of Kirkham.

The Quaker School

In fact nothing was done for the poorer children of Freckleton until 1724 when the Quaker William Brown left a legacy of £300 on trust for the education of Quaker children. In his will he stated that:

> And I do hereby direct order and appoint that the interest thereof shall for ever hereafter be paid and applied towards the maintainance of a schoolmaster, Appointed by my said Trustees, to instruct and teach, within the said township of Freckleton, all such persons children as are commonly called Quakers coming to him, and belonging to the meeting within the said township of Freckleton, And for want of such a schoolmaster, then to, and for such further or other uses as my said Trustees shall by any note or instrument in writing under my hand, be directed, or for want thereof, as they shall think meet and convenient.[5]

Presumably the school was held at the Quaker meeting house and probably explains the origin of the name of the present School Lane. The only two Quaker schoolmasters whose names are known are William Eccleston and Obediah Cook. In the will of Cuthbert Sharples, a Quaker who died in 1738, William Eccleston was named as an executor and described as 'of Freckleton, Schoolmaster'. Obediah Cook was born about 1725 and served the school at Freckleton for at least two years as in 1752 he acted as a witness to the will of James Goodshaw, a clogger, and in 1754 witnessed the will of William Whalley, a labourer. In his account book dating from 1754 Robert Abbatt, clerk to the Fylde monthly meeting, noted:

4.6mo[nth] 1754   Paid Obed Cook – Jas Cowburn's
                             Interest   £8 8s. 0d.

30.9mo[nth]1754   pd him when he left the School   £3 15s. 6d.

and added that 'Obed Cook left his post as schoolmaster that year'.[6]

The school is next mentioned by Robert Abbatt in 1760 when £1 4s. 0d. was paid to Dame Fisher for 'Teaching 4 poor children belonging to the Town[ship] of Freckleton'.[7] However an entry in the accounts for 1773 records that 'so long as there is no Schoolmaster its agreed that for the future one general account serve for all'.[8] After this date there is no further documentary evidence of the existence of a school at the meeting house, or elsewhere in the village, until 2 August 1803 when an entry in the sundry disbursements book for the township of Freckleton recorded 'To Thos Noblet giving Notice for the men to meet at School. £0 1s. 6d.' [9]

The purpose of this particular meeting was to decide which able-bodied men should be called upon to serve in the militia. As upwards of 100 men would have received notice to attend the 'School' was clearly selected as the most suitable venue. If, as was probable, it was the original Quaker meeting house it suggests that the building, though still owned by the Quakers, was then being used as either a private school or as a school funded by the township following the cessation of regular Quaker meetings in 1796.

Education 1799–1839

During the period from 1799 to 1830 a schoolmaster, Thomas Willacy, appears as executor or witness in sixteen Freckleton wills. The son of Thomas and Mary Willacy (née Breckell) he was born in Freckleton in 1764 and although he served continuously as either the township constable or overseer of the poor from 1794 to 1827 nothing is known of his early life. He does not appear to have married and probably lived with his two unmarried sisters in a cottage which stood on the site of the present Kirkham Road Methodist Church car park. His immaculate handwriting on township documents provides evidence of his own good education.

When he died in 1831 his will was proved by George Richardson, one of the leading Methodists in Freckleton at that time, and whose mother prior to her marriage was Mary Willacy. There is, however, no evidence to suggest that Thomas Willacy was himself a member of the local Methodist society. In the Lancashire Directory of 1828 Thomas Willacy was recorded as a schoolmaster 'Freckleton – boys day'. Unfortunately there is no indication of where the school was held, although the the most obvious venue would be the former Quaker meeting house, an assumption supported by the entry in the 1829 Survey of Dissent which reported that the meeting house was indeed then being used as a school. Whether Thomas Willacy leased this on his own account or whether the township paid him to operate the school is again unknown.

Following the death of Thomas Willacy it would appear that both the Church of England and the Wesleyan Methodist Church endeavored to take over the role of providing education for the village children. The Methodist Sunday school class register book for 1833 lists the names of 69 boys and 68 girls who in addition to Bible and Testament classes also attended Double-spelling book Class, Single-spelling book Class and Alphabet Class.[10] In all there were nineteen classes taught by members of the leading families in the village – presumably without any pay.

Evidence that these classes, and those of the Church of England, were held in the Quaker meeting house is supported by a statement, recorded some years later, 'This [the meeting house] was used for some time [by the Quakers], and then the Church of England and Wesleyans used it as a [Sunday?] school, each body having one end'.[11]

CHAPTER 16

Trinity School/New Memorial School

During the 1830s the population of Freckleton continued to increase until by 1841 there were 108 children, approximately 11 per cent of the population, between the ages of five and nine years. Although nothing is known of the events leading to the decision to build a school it is almost certain that the Rev. George Wylie, curate of Warton, was primarily responsible. Throughout the 1830s he had committed himself to assisting the people of Freckleton and, clearly realising there was a great need for a school, had persuaded the authorities of the Church of England to make the necessary provision. The school was founded under the principles of the National Society for the Education of the Poor in the Principles of the Established Church, who were also among the first contributors. The society was itself founded in 1811 and by 1851 controlled over 17,000 national schools.

The land on which the school was built, now the site of Trinity Close, was conveyed on 4 November 1840 by Mr Hugh Hornby to the Rev.

Trinity School opened in 1839. In 1944 the school was the scene of Freckleton's worst ever disaster when an American bomber crashed onto the building killing 38 children and two teachers. The school was demolished in 1974 and the site is now called Trinity Close. (*Courtesy of* Lancashire Evening Post)

George Wylie and others. This could have been the completion date of the building because the foundation stone of the school, now set into the churchyard wall, is inscribed 'This Stone was laid by the Rev. Geo. Wylie AM, 3 August 1839'. The datestone, which now stands by the entrance of the New Memorial School reads '1839 Trinity School'. According to plans made in 1867 the original school was rectangular in shape.[1] The boys and girls were segregated, each having their own entrance. The east side was the girls school and measured 25ft by 30ft and the boys school on the west side measured 25ft by 20ft. There was also a smaller room, possibly the headmaster's room, jutting out from the main building on the north side, measuring 11ft by 9½ft. The privies were located alongside the south wall of the school yard.

The first schoolmaster appears to have been John Worthington. On the 1841 Census he is recorded as National School Master, aged 20, but as ages were 'rounded down' he could have been slightly older. His private residence next to the school would indicate that the school house had been built at the same time as the school. In 1843 the Rev. George Wylie supported his candidature as assistant overseer at Poulton.[2] However, John Worthington was still the master in 1845 and it may have been that, in order to supplement his income, he combined the role of master with that of assistant overseer.

Some idea of the progress that the school had made within a few years of its opening can be gained from a letter written by the Rev. T. H. Dundas, vicar of Warton (who also had responsibility for Freckleton).[3] The letter, dated 24 July 1845, unfortunately does not name the intended recipient, but the person named Green in the letter was Thomas Green, the Churchwarden. The letter reads:

My Dear Sir,

I would thank you to send me if convenient the subscription which Green kindly promised on the part of Mr Clifton to Freckleton School & pray return him My sincere thanks for his assistance.

You will be glad to hear that the school is getting on almost as well as I could wish it numbers at present between boys and girls within two or three of an hundred.

The Vicar of Preston visited it a few days since & almost promised me assistance from the Diocesan board of education in the Sum of £10 yearly, which is their largest grant, this will raise the income yearly to £35 which with the payment of the children will almost though not quite cover expenses the salaries of Master & Mistress above what the School pays, amounting to £5 above that sum.

I have however the best hopes of its final Success –
with many thanks for your aid

Believe Me
Truly Yours
T. H. Dundas.

As has already been mentioned the number of children in the village
in 1841, aged between 5 and 9 years, was 108. Assuming the ages of the
of the majority of children attending the school in 1845 were of a similar
age range, then the school had achieved a significant attendance figure
within a few years. Not even the required weekly payment seems to
have deterred parents from parting with the few valuable pence necessary
to enable each child to attend.

The names of those who taught at the school during its first twenty
five years are known only from entries in various trade directories.
Thomas Walmsley was master from 1848 until at least 1851 and Isabella
Anderton was mistress in 1848. They appear to have been followed in
1851 by James Bryan and Ann Lewis, and by 1858 Thomas Cumberland
was the master and Agnes Goodshaw the mistress. Agnes Goodshaw,
who was born at Freckleton, was a grand-daughter of James Goodshaw
(of the company Goodshaw & Mayor) and appears to have remained
the mistress until 1863. She had assisted at the school for many years as
revealed by Adam Wright when, in a letter dated 3 August 1848, he
refers to what must have been one of the earliest school outings 'and I
understand the Freckleton children join a train [at Kirkham] that day
and go to Blackpool, Agnes Goodshaw goes with them'.[4] On 2 January
1864 the *Preston Pilot* recorded that the teachers and scholars of Freckleton
Parish Church School held their annual tea party in the school room,
when 100 sat down. After the repast Miss Goodshaw was presented 'with
a beautiful electro-plated copper pot and card case'.[5]

The next known master was Charles Everson, who in January 1864
was also secretary of the Freckleton Relief Committee. From November
1862 to November 1863 this committee had received and distributed
money and goods to the poor during the desperate days of the Cotton
Famine. He must have left Freckleton soon afterwards as in 1865 John
Heron is recorded as National School master. Agnes Hall, the sister of
John Hall the owner of Strike Farm, was mistress in 1864 and 1865.

This lack of continuity of both masters and mistresses was typical and
cannot have been to the advantage of the scholars. In addition it was
not until 1876 that education was made compulsory for the first time

Adam Wright. Born in Freckleton in 1786 he began work in a merchant's office in Manchester. In 1808 he sailed for Malta and in 1819 commenced business as a merchant banker in Constantinople. When writing to his nephew and nieces from Constantinople during the late 1830s and early 1840s he often enquired about local events.

and appointed school attendance officers to ensure the law was carried out. Prior to that date some children did not attend school at all, as typified by George Wylie Rigby, born at Freckleton in 1858, and who in 1941 was reported as saying that 'Beginning to earn his living at the age of 12, he never attended a day school, his only lessons being learned from the local schoolmaster on certain nights a week'.[6]

Fortunately for Trinity School from about 1865 a more stable period began with the appointment of Robert Lupton as master. Born at Burnley he was aged 23 when he came to Freckleton. His sister Hannah acted as school mistress. Robert Lupton was probably the instigator of the negotiations that resulted, on 3 May 1867, in the land on which the school stood being conveyed by Thomas Dyson Hornby and Hugh Frederick Hornby and vested in the the Official Trustee of Charity Lands who directed that the school be used for 'the instruction of children and adults, or children only, of the labouring, manufacturing, and other poorer classes'.[7] In the same year an additional classroom with gallery was added on to the south side of the school.

Evidence that Robert Lupton was held in the highest regard is amply revealed in the following extracts of a newspaper report of his death from scarlet fever in October 1874, and gives us a vivid picture of his achievements:

> When his death was announced to the children in school every child was in tears, and their sobs were most pitiful; so greatly was he loved by them.
>
> Since his coming to Freckleton, Mr Lupton has succeeded in improving both the tone and numbers of the school. His zeal and energy were untiring. In all works of charity, in collecting for widows and orphans – of which there are several in the place – he was the first and foremost.
>
> He has been instrumental in having a new floor, new classrooms, and new desks for his school. The masters residence has been by him greatly improved.[8]

Robert Lupton was succeeded by William Woodhouse Martin who was aged 23 at the time of his appointment. He lived at the School House with his sister Emily, who was school mistress, and by 1881 his niece Kate Noble had joined them as a pupil teacher at the school.

Following the Act of 1876 the school log books commence and from that time up to the present it is possible to obtain detailed information on day to day life at the school.[9] Subjected to regular Government inspection the report of August 1876 provides an insight into the lessons taught and success achieved.

> The School has made very satisfactory progress during the past year. Order is good and the elementary subjects except spelling and composition in the fourth and fifth standards are now fairly accurate. Handwriting however wants care and style and the children should read with more expression

and distinctness. The Class subjects of Grammar, Geography and sewing have been well prepared. Sewing deserves special praise. The accounts should be kept intelligibly. The last report cannot be found and does not seem to have been fully entered in the Log Book'.

The entry in the log book 'Examination of Night School this evening' reveals that by 1878 there was also a Night School, but unfortunately no further information is given. In 1877 the school holidays were Easter Monday, a week at Whitsuntide, two weeks in August, a half day on November 5 and a week at Christmas. Playtime did not figure prominently in the daily routine, as is shown in an entry of 5 September 1877 when it was recorded that 'Allowed the children a few minutes play on the green this afternoon'. Possibly this was to compensate for the range of absences that interrupted the teaching schedule, as the following entries from 1876–77 reveal:

4 July   1876   A few of the children are away this week on account of Kirkham Club.

14 July   1876   All the bigger children away this week, haymaking.

27 April   1877   Some of the winter Scholars are beginning to leave school again.

The weather too affected attendance throughout the year:

16 July   1877   A very wet day. Many of the children away from school on that account.

1 March   1880   Very few little children at school today on account of the snow.

It was, however, the frequent epidemics and illnesses that caused the greatest disruption:

13 April   1877   Whooping [cough] is very bad indeed amongst the children and has reduced the infants average 50 per cent.

4 March   1878   Another of the scholars – Elizabeth Whittle – has died of typhoid fever. Three families are prevented from sending their children to school on account of that disease.

8 Dec.   1879   The measles are very prevalent in the village and the average attendance is greatly reduced.

22 Sept.   1881   Scarlet Fever has broken out in the village and several children are kept at home suffering from it.

Illness was not confined just to the children and when a teacher was absent their place was taken by one of the older and more capable pupils, as happened in May 1877 when 'Michael Coulborn has taught throughout the week in place of Miss Martin'. By May 1881 the classes were arranged so that Mr Martin taught the 1st and 4th Classes (Standards iv, v, vi and i), Miss Martin taught the 2nd Class (Standard iii), Kate Noble taught the 3rd Class (Standard ii) while the Infants were under the care of Elizabeth Richardson, a monitor. However, Mr Martin himself had been absent from November 1880 until March 1881 due to debility following enteric fever and after a further 'long illness' he resigned in October 1882.

In the same month a temporary master, Mr J. N. Herbert, was appointed and he served until 21 December the same year. Frustrated by the conditions he had found his final entry in the log book paints a rather dismal picture:

> I am sorry to say that during the two months I have had charge of this school I have been unable to get pens for the scholars to write with and there has not been, and I could not get, a drop of ink except about a quarter of a penny bottle, which stands on the Masters desk, to mark the registers with, also there is no arithmetic belonging to the school so that every sum has either to be marked before the school commences, or during the lesson, which of course takes up much time, which might be much more beneficially employed.

On the same day the school broke up for a fortnight's holiday and Mr Herbert's final act was to distribute the gifts (toys and dolls) sent the previous day by Mrs Fields of Lytham. The fact that this gift came from a benefactor outside the village is probably due simply to Mrs Fields' response to a request by Mr Herbert, but nevertheless it is also an indication of the underlying poverty present in the village at the time.

Such circumstances cannot have failed to concentrate the minds of Robert Moon of Poulton, William Cookson, T Harrison Myres, Edward Myres, and Richard Cookson of Freckleton who, following the agreement by the Charity Commissioners in August 1882 that the vicar and wardens of Warton should no longer have any role in the running of the school, had assumed full responsibility for the management of Trinity School.[10] Their response was to appoint a master with drive and determination and in James Bramwell they made a wise choice. Born in Preston he was aged 28 when he commenced his duties on 8 January 1883.

Although there is evidence from other school log books that the masters wrote critical notes about the state of the school they had inherited, in order to limit any subsequent personal blame made on them by H. M. Inspectors, it seems obvious that in 1883 Trinity School was in need of much attention. In a detailed first day entry in the log book Mr Bramwell confirmed Mr Herbert's complaints and also commented on the want of desks and the insufficient number of staff. He also made a complete inventory of school material (books and maps). On the following day he noted that 'All work in Arith[metic] Dictation Writing and Geography [has] to be done on slates'.

Within four days of his appointment Mr Bramwell had obtained two quarts of ink from Mr Sowerbutts, the owner of the cotton mill, and had gone one evening to Kirkham but, unable to obtain any penholders, had continued to Preston where he obtained supplies. By 12 January he was able to report 'Exercise books bought up rather readily by the children. Home lessons a new feature here'. By April six desks, two blackboards and two easels had arrived 'after much delay'. Mr Bramwell then turned his attention to acquiring suitable staff and, in August, Miss Miles was appointed assistant mistress at a salary of £30 per annum. However he had great difficulty in persuading able pupils to take up the post of pupil teacher, and in the same month 'The boy Stanley Iddon, who had given the Master to understand he was desirous of becoming a pupil teacher, stated today that his mother wished him to assist at home in the farm work'.

The HMI report of 1883, although not blaming Mr Bramwell, made several adverse comments concerning the level of attainment and expressed concern at the lack of adequate accommodation. The Inspector concluded by recommending the (government) grant but 'with great hesitation'. In July 1883 the number of pupils, including half-timers, was recorded as 228, of which 129 attended all week, but as the Inspector had noted the existing accommodation made perfect order and organisation impossible. The report seems to have had the desired effect as the school managers immediately began fund raising activities and at their meeting in July 1884 'it was resolved to collect the promised subscriptions and to solicit more assistance and to begin building, according to a plan submitted by Mr T. H. Myres, when £120 had been put in the savings Bank, Preston'. A month later the managers resolved 'to accept the tender and plans and that the building should be proceeded with as early as possible'.

Among those who subscribed was Newton Charity (the owners of Lower House Farm) who in September 1884 agreed that 'as Landowners in Freckleton the Trustees are prepared to give a donation of £25 towards the enlargement of the Freckleton School should the same be done at a cost of not less than £200 and the plan be to the satisfaction of the

Trustees'.[11] By 31 October work was almost completed and the master could record 'Workmen again engaged on the New room finishing plastering & whitewashing'.

In order to warm the schoolrooms fires were lit throughout the winter from mid-October onwards, and the parents of the children were asked to contribute towards the cost. In 1887 there was a complaint about the 6*d.* charge and Mr Bramwell noted that whilst most parents paid readily each year there were two or three cases in which the parents refused to pay their share. Such objections would not have been received kindly by Mr Bramwell who, in addition to his endeavours to raise educational standards, also laid great emphasis on discipline and respect. Late attendance and insubordination could result in the child being sent home accompanied by a teacher. In one incident that continued from November 1884 through to February 1885 Mr Bramwell was adamant 'that on every fine day' the children of two particular families 'were to come without stable and shippon dirt about their shoes and trousers'.

However, Mr Bramwell was also very fair, ensuring that no unjust or unnecessary punishments were administered and when in September 1887 Mrs C. Whittle complained of Miss Clayton striking her child Ellen, he entered in the log book 'This is not the first occasion a complaint has been made of this teacher, and the Master has cautioned her respecting striking the children'. Despite this and other incidents Miss Clayton, who had been appointed in December 1885, remained at the school until November 1894. She returned in January 1905 and finally retired in September 1939 aged 72, having taught for a total of 43 years, 7 months. Mr Bramwell's own long term commitment to Freckleton was demonstrated in 1888 when despite a refusal by the school managers (due to lack of funds), for an extension to the School House, he moved to Ivanhoe, Green Lane, where he was recorded on the 1891 census together with his wife, six daughters and two sons.

Another critical HMI report in 1890 resulted in several staff changes and efforts were made to extend the range of subjects taught, and in May 1891 an application for a grant was made to the government's Science and Art Department. Night School opened in November 1890 with an attendance of 50, of whom 21 took an examination the following March, though in what subjects is not recorded. In 1899, the log book records that 'the Committee on Technical Education would make no grant this year towards a Night School or Continuation Class' and the master was advised 'not to trouble about a Class for the coming year'.

However the decision must have been reversed because in October 1900 the HMI 'visited the Evening Continuation Class'.

Under the Elementary Education Act of 1891 a fee grant was made to schools and this enabled the Freckleton managers, in September of that year, to abolish school fees. Up to that date most parents in Freckleton appear to have been able to pay the fee themselves but even a month before the abolition at least two pupils had had to have their fees paid by the Poor Law guardians. Two immediate consequences of the Act are revealed by the log book entry of 24 September when it was recorded that 'Several children under 3 years of age sent to school now it is free, many of the older scholars rather irregular making 7, 8 or 9 attendances instead of 10 as formerly'.

Ill-health continued to affect attendance and each year there are several entries in the log book recording the absence of the children. Other causes were in many instances the same as those encountered by Mr Martin twenty years earlier. Throughout the 1890s, during the months of June/July, there were always several children absent all week, working in the hay fields; in May 1892 Thomas Singleton was reported as being 'employed illegally in a brick yard', and in June 1896 George Helm was 'illegally employed on Freckleton Marsh'.

Even attempts by the attendance officer to improve matters were often thwarted, as on 20 February 1894 when, after cautioning a few irregulars, he received no help from those present when he asked for the names of any children of five years of age not yet attending school. Occasionally the children received an unexpected holiday, as in 1897 when the school was closed from 18 June to 23 June for the celebration of Queen Victoria's Diamond Jubilee.

Improvements to the school during the 1890s included the installation of a hot water heating system used for the first time in January 1892, and new water closets approved in August 1893. Nevertheless, despite all efforts at improvement, the HMI report of 1898 made depressing reading when the inspector stated:

> The rooms are inconvenient, not overclean, badly ventilated and not particularly cheerful. The cloak rooms are inadequate. An additional Class-room would mitigate the inconvenience, though possibly a new Infant school would be a more economical remedy in the end.

In order to remedy the situation the managers once more began fund raising for school improvements and money was obtained by means of appeals and sales of work and in 1901 the school was enlarged at a cost of £400. In both 1901 and 1902 Newton Charity made donations of £10, and by 1905 the Rev. E. J. Hack writing to the Bishop of Manchester was able to report: 'Day Schools. We have spent in recent years about £600 & now we have more than sufficient accommodation.'

Class subjects in 1901 were English grammar and geography for all standards, history from reading lessons in standards iii to vi, elementary subjects – reading, writing & arithmetic – for all in the school. In addition there was drawing for boys; needlework for all girls and also for boys in the infants class, and singing and physical exercises. In 1909 and for several years afterwards the school was visited by Sergeant Major Wright from Fulwood, who inspected the children carrying out their P. E. On his visit in 1913 he expressed himself satisfied that the children knew the exercises but considered that 'more vigour should be put into them'. By 1910 the range in subjects was extended and 15 girls and 9 boys were offered external classes in cookery and woodwork at Kirkham.

Also by 1910, in addition to the occasional 'entertainments' held at the school the children enjoyed longer holidays than had their parents, including from 1908 half day holidays for Empire Day. They were also given a holiday on special occasions, as in 1902 when the school closed for a week in May for the coronation of King Edward VII and for a further week in September for the Preston Guild Merchant. In 1911 a one day holiday was granted for the coronation of King George V, while in 1913 the children were taken to Lytham for the visit of the King and Queen.

In November 1914 James Bramwell resigned as Master. It was an abrupt and sad end to 30 years' service, and was due to an injury to his foot that he had sustained when he fell the previous September, whilst winding the school clock. He was, and still is, the longest serving Freckleton (head) master. The modern day Bramwell Close is named after him in recognition of his service to the village.

He was succeeded by John (Jack) Winchester, who remained as master until 1922. During his eight years at Freckleton Mr Winchester added both swimming and nature study to the school curriculum. It was, however, the effect on the school caused by the events of World War I that required his immediate attention. In late 1915 the school was without heating fuel, and in winter of the same year and for several other winters, school hours were adjusted to comply with the lighting restriction order. Mr Winchester himself had to attend several military medical boards before being considered fit only for sedentary duties.

In October 1916 five boys aged 12 years, in common with children elsewhere, were granted permission to be absent to gather potatoes, a task repeated by other boys and girls in 1917 and 1918. The log books also record the gathering of blackberries which, due to the shortage of fruit, would have been an important supplement to the diet of the children and their parents. In May 1917, at the request of the Lancashire Education Committee, 'the lessons of the week were devised with a view to instruction on Food Economy'.

Also in 1917 a War Savings Committee was formed and 'Socks & Mittens knit by girls for soldier comforts distributed to those whose fathers or brothers were serving in France'. A more unusual war effort is recalled from a log book entry in October the same year: 'Chestnuts collected by children brought to school preparatory to being forwarded to the Director of Propellant Supplies – weight collected about 1 cwt'. It was not possible to celebrate Armistice Day 1918 because the school had been closed since 30 October on the orders of the medical officer and did not re-open until 9 December. A Peace Holiday, however, was held in September 1919.

Throughout the early years of this century the school was often closed due to outbreaks of diphtheria, smallpox, measles and scarlet fever. The regular medical inspections that began in 1913 were evidence of the increasing awareness of the need to combat these potentially fatal diseases. Nevertheless, as late as 1921 the Medical Officer of Health, in his annual report, commented that 'As to Freckleton there has always been a delay owing to parents of children not obtaining medical treatment in time and thus no attention has been given to the first cases until they have been accidentally discovered'. In the same report he also observed that 'there is insufficient ventilation as regards windows, also a deficiency of seating accommodation in this school'.

In 1921 Mr Winchester resigned and was succeeded by Edward Cross Rigby who remained only two years. He in turn was followed by John William Platts who was (head) master until his death in 1939.

During the inter-war years patriotism played a significant role in school life and Armistice Day was commemorated with a service, whilst Empire Day was celebrated with a pageant in which the children themselves participated. In 1928, the school was divided into four houses – 'Balderstone', 'Hillock', 'Marsh' and 'Naze' – each with its own captain, vice-captain and secretary. School outings to London, Liverpool and Chester were undertaken and by 1931 parents were invited to visit the school and see the classes at work. The school premises, however, were definitely no longer adequate and in 1925 Mr Platts attended an inquiry into the need for a new school. However it was not until 1939 that preliminary approaches were made to the Education Authority for its replacement.

Mr Platts, who had been present at school only two days previously, died on 9 February 1939. An entry made in the log book described him as 'A good teacher – a good & kind man – a gentleman'. He was succeeded in July 1939 by Frederick Arthur Billington who within two months of his appointment was having to make arrangements for the arrival of children evacuated from Salford due to the outbreak of World War II. As in World War I the children were encouraged to take an active part in the war effort and during Warship Week in March 1942 the school group raised £1,420, whilst in the Wings for Victory Week in May 1943 the impressive sum of £5,300 was amassed. At Christmas 1943 the American Air Force entertained a total of 178 children over three days at the American Camp.

However, the one single event of World War II that overshadows all others is the tragic day of 23 August 1944 when an American Liberator bomber crashed onto the school. The school had re-assembled only the previous day following a four week summer holiday. On that day the school register recorded 176 local pupils and 14 evacuees; the teaching staff comprised Mr Billington, Miss Healy, Miss Rawcliffe, Mrs Owen, Miss Jenny Hall, a former pupil commencing duties in the Infant Room, and Miss Louisa Hulme from Salford, who had first arrived in Freckleton with the evacuees in September 1940, sharing the Infant class with Miss Hall.

The disaster is described in more detail in chapter 26 but it seems appropriate here to record the words of Mr Billington himself, written in the log book, as being perhaps the most poignant of all:

> At 10.40 a.m. a thunderstorm was at its height, with torrential rain, and almost complete darkness. As a result, an American Liberator Bomber crashed.
>
> The windows of the north room were blown in.
>
> The Infant room was demolished, and enveloped in blazing petrol.
>
> Only seven children and the two teachers were rescued, alive. Thirty four perished immediately. (Both teachers and four children died later.)
>
> The children from the other rooms, all of which were damaged, left the building by means of the door in the boys cloakroom under the supervision of their teachers.
>
> Members of the United States Army Air Force and Civil Defence Units were quickly on the scene.

Immediately following the disaster temporary teaching accommodation was made available in Kirkham Road Methodist schoolroom but by 30 October the school had returned to 'the premises damaged by the plane'.

Whilst the 1944 Education Act had eased the pressure on accommodation with the transfer of children in the 11 to 14 age group to secondary schools, the need for a new school had clearly become a priority. A site in School Lane was made available by Robert Newton Wignall and in due course conveyed to the school managers following its purchase by Lancashire Education Authority. The foundation stone of the New Memorial School was laid by the Rev. J. W. Broadbent on 25 September 1954, and in the same year Phase 1 of the new building began with the provision of three infant classrooms. Phase 2 followed in 1959 with the building of an assembly hall, staff room and school kitchen, and the school was finally completed in 1970 with the addition of four junior classrooms, additional staff and store rooms, and also the laying out of

Church of England New Memorial School. Aptly situated in School Lane, so named after the eighteenth-century Quaker meeting house/school, the foundation stone of the modern Church of England school was laid in 1954, though it was not until 1970 that building was finally completed.

the playing fields. The total cost for three building phases amouted to over £53,000. The original Trinity School was demolished in 1974, although the land on which it had stood was not sold until 1979.

Mr Billington retired as headmaster in 1968 and was succeeded by Mr George Eric Ray until his own retirement in 1983. The present headmaster is Mr Gary Worthy, and the school now (2000) has 220 pupils. Under the requirements of the National Curriculum the four core subjects are English, maths, science and ICT. Foundation subjects are music, art, history, geography, religious education and physical education, whilst extra-curricular activities include various seasonal sports, a badminton club and a choir. In a recent report the school was described as 'a good school and a caring school with many strengths'.

CHAPTER 17

Strike Lane
County Primary School

As early as 1925 there was an organised attempt to persuade the county education authorities to build a council school, and following a petition by ratepayers in March of that year the parish council voted 6 to 2 in favour of an undenominational school. However, by the following July the county council replied that in view of the heavy building programme they were unable to make any recommendation as regards a council school in the village.

In fact it was not until 1965, when Strike Lane County Primary School was built as a replacement for the Kirkham RAF County Primary School, that there was another school in the village. The school was designed in three phases between 1965 and 1970.[1] The first phase included two junior classrooms, two infant classrooms, staff accommodation, kitchen and assembly hall, and opened on 26 August 1965, with 114 children on the roll. The staff consisted of Mrs Doris Bryan (the headmistress), Mr Marsh, Mrs Ludlow and Mrs Henderson (full time teachers), and Mrs Bursa who taught part time in the mornings. In addition to those from the village other children came from the RAF quarters and the prison officers' quarters.

Almost immediately there were problems with overcrowding, and in October 1965 extra classes had to be formed in the assembly hall, due to an increase in numbers created by the children of Army families who were beginning to occupy the former RAF quarters. To overcome the problem a second building phase began in 1968, which included two further junior classrooms and additional service areas, and was followed immediately by Phase 3 with another infants classroom and also an infants play area. On 11 March 1970 the school was officially opened by the Rt Hon. the Lord Rhodes, the Lord Lieutenant of Lancashire.

Mrs Bryan retired as headmistress in 1977, after having served 23 years, first at Kirkham RAF School and then at Strike Lane. She was succeeded by Mr Roy Bracegirdle who retired in 1997 and who in turn was succeeded by Mr Lee Pimlott, the present headmaster. At present (2000)

Strike Lane School. Although there had been attempts to build a council school as early as 1925 the first phase of the present school was not begun until 1965. Built in three phases it was officially opened by the then Lord Lieutenant of Lancashire in March 1970.

206 pupils attend the school. In addition to the National Curriculum subjects extra-curricular school activities include seasonal sports, a choir, chess, a computer club and a gardening club. The school also provides music tuition for violin, flute, guitar and clarinet.

Part VII

The Marsh

CHAPTER 18

Marsh Gates and Marsh Owners

In 1972 the *West Lancashire Evening Gazette* published an article about the Freckleton Marsh Owners and asked four questions: Who are the Freckleton Marsh Owners? What land do they own? Why do they own it? How long have they owned it? In fact the answers to these questions are contained in the many surviving documents that record the decisions made and the work carried out by past and present beast/marsh gate owners during the past 300 years.

The allocation of 'gates' for the purpose of common grazing on the marsh probably originated in medieval times and was determined by the number of oxgangs of enclosed land associated with each farmstead. An oxgang varied in size from township to township and although there does not appear to be any record of its measurement in Freckleton, at nearby Kirkham in 1705 it was equivalent to 16 acres. One of the problems with this method of allocation however was that as more land in the township became enclosed the number of oxgangs, and consequently the number of gates, would have increased, with the result that the marsh was liable to have become overstocked. To remedy such a situation a lower stint† for every oxgang of land would have been agreed at either the manorial court or township meeting.

The first reference to the right of pasture on stinted lands in Freckleton occurs in an indenture dated 12 May 1580 between James Anderton of Clayton and James Sharples of Freckleton of the one part, and Will(ia)m Cowburne of Freckleton of the other part when:

> In consideration of the sum of £14 alienated, Bargained and sold to William Cowburne The one half of such and so much herbage and common of pasture in and through all the commons waste grounds and Stinted Lands in Freckleton aforesaid now lying abroad and occupied in common or

used as Stinted pasture or common by the tenants or Inhabitants of Freckleton ...[1]

The first known reference to a 'Cowe grase' is in a lease dated 1601 when, for the sum of £6, Richard Harrison granted Thomas Freckleton half one acre of moor and 'one Cow graze upon the common marsh in Freckleton' for the term of one hundred years, the yearly rent being two shillings and also 'one Day Shearing yearly in the time of harvest'.[2] In another part of the same indenture the term 'cowe grase' is used to describe the right of common pasture for one cow on the marsh, though in most later deeds and documents the term cattle or beast gate is used.

It would seem, therefore, that by the seventeenth century the leasing, and perhaps selling, of cattle gates on the marsh had become established practice. However, perhaps due to disputes over pasturage rights and illegal attempts at ownership caused by disruptions during the Civil War and subsequent Commonwealth period, it was decided in 1670 to draw up a new constitution for the governing of the marsh. Because of its historical importance the constitution is reproduced in full in appendix C and as can be seen it was very detailed and clearly recognised the need for a communal approach to ensure a fair distribution of grazing land for the farmers within the township.[3]

The primary function of the elected marshmen, whose role progressively evolved into that of modern marsh managers, was the day to day administration of the marsh gates on behalf of their fellow marsh gate owners. One of their responsibilities was to appoint the herdsman, later known as a marsh tenter, who lived at the Dungeon,† a name that survived until this century as the name of a row of cottages just to the south of the *Ship Inn*. From this high vantage point the herdsman would have had a commanding view over the marsh enabling him to maintain a regular watch over the livestock and to carry out his duties which were not dissimilar to that of a medieval pinder.

By another order of 1670 the marshmen had power to impound any livestock trespassing on the marsh and 'not restore the said Goods to the owners thereof without payment for every Beast so impounded 4*d.*, for every Mare or Gelding 8*d.*, for every sheep 2*d.*, and every Goose 1*d.*'[4] Furthermore for every sum 'so due and forfeited – the said Marshman at their discretion hath hereby power to distribute amongst the poor of the said Township of Freckleton and not otherwise'.

Further ordinances were agreed in 1671 but it would appear that not every marsh gate owner was prepared to comply with them. On 15

January 1673 the Chancery Court of the County Palatine at Lancaster sat in judgement on a case concerning the byelaws of Freckleton township, brought by George *[3]* Sharples and others landowners in Freckleton against Thomas Tomblinson who, it appears, although 'an owner of lands and tenements within the said township' had attempted to put livestock onto the marsh contrary to the ordinances and had consequently had them impounded.[5]

In their submission the petitioners claimed that 'within the said ancient Township there is a parcel of ground called Freckleton Marsh adjoining to the said side which hath been used and reused for the time whereof the memory of man is not to the contrary as a Stinted comon of pasture for the inhabitants and owners and possessors of lands and tenements within the Township of Freckleton'. In their judgement the vice-chancellor and attorney-general of the Palatinate confirmed the byelaws of Freckleton until the majority of the inhabitants decided otherwise.

By the end of the seventeenth century the gate system was clearly established and from that time 'beast gates' or 'cattle gates' are often mentioned in Freckleton wills, usually in the form of a bequest to a member of the family. Sometimes it was a spinster or widow as in 1692 when Cat(he)rine Singl(e)ton stated, 'And whereas Grace Waide of Freckleton oweth me for one marsh gate four years the sum of one shilling and sixpence a year and one shilling of Lent money being in all 7 shillings owing to me by the said Grace Waide I give the same to the said Edward & Ann Sharples'.[6]

In 1746 a Bill of Complaint was brought by 22 proprietors of land in Freckleton against Thomas Grimbaldeston, the then tenant farmer at Lower House Farm. The basis of the complaint was that Grimbaldeston had been taking the rich soil, sand and slitch (slutch) from the marsh in order to spread onto and improve his own lands. Whilst the outcome of the case is not known the information supplied by Mr Shawe, solicitor to Edmund Starkie, a Preston barrister acting for the petitioners, provides a detailed account (see appendix D) of the then prevailing customs whilst re-iterating the rights of the marsh gate owners. Mr Shawe added that the removal of the soil was beneficial only for those marsh gate owners whose lands were adjacent to the marsh and thereby to the disadvantage of those whose lands lay at a distance from the marsh. He concluded by saying that he believed that a Court of Equity would restrain the carrying of soil and 'deem a satisfaction for the damage already sustained'.[7]

In his answer to the bill of complaint Thomas Grimbaldeston defended vigorously his right to remove soil from the marsh and his arguments provide not only additional information about how the marsh was being used and administered in 1746 but also tells us that at this date it was separated and divided from the inclosed lands in the village 'by fences and ditches'. It was his contention that the marsh had been used not only as a stinted pasture but also as a piece of waste ground where the owners got soil, clay and earth for manuring and improving their lands and 'also Dug and got Sods for the covering their buildings upon the several inclosed Lands or for covering their Brick Killns where they made brick to be used in buildings upon such ancient inclosed grounds and to Dig and get Clay and Sand for repair of their ways and buildings'.[8]

It also appears from his 'Answer' that in both summer and winter cattle and horses were turned out onto the marsh. Sheep however were only allowed to be put out in winter and one of Thomas Grimbaldeston's complaints was that, since the issue of the bill of complaint against him, the other marshowners had directed that no sheep were to be turned out. This he claimed was contrary to 'ancient usage and Custom'. Just as with present-day practice the dates of the turning out of livestock were strictly adhered to, and in order to better the summer pasturage, no cattle were put out between 25 March and the second Saturday in May when the summer pasturage began. The summer pasturage continued until 15 August 'being the Summer Fair at Preston'. After 15 August the winter pasturage began and continued to 25 March.

The strength of feelings between Thomas Grimbaldeston and the other marsh gate owners had clearly simmered for some time, and it may be that certain of the more influential owners were adopting a somewhat arbitrary approach. This is hinted at when Thomas Grimbaldeston comments that 'some of them are – grown to such a pitch of extravagance in the exercise of their pretended power'.

Conversely his own first loyalty would have been to the trustees of Newton Charity, whose primary purpose when they purchased Lower House Farm would have been to maximise their profits from the farm for the benefit of the Newton Blue School.

The earliest known list of gate owners dates from 1734, when 22 named individuals were recorded as owning a combined total of 118½ gates.[9] However, a note at the end of the document states that 'The number of gates upon Freckleton marsh and in the hands of the persons named Above Written – 230 & one half'. The reason for the combined allocation of 118½ being less than the 230½ quoted at the end of the document is unclear, unless only the lesser number of gates had actually been used for grazing that year. An 'Account of Marsh grass & by whom'[10] shows that in 1763 the marsh was overstocked as thirty six marsh gate owners allocated out 248½ gates. The majority of these gates were occupied either by the owners themselves or other Freckleton residents, but at least two other individuals drove their beast(s) some distance in order to take advantage of the valuable grazing afforded by the marsh. Nan(n)y Wilson from Heyhouses (in Lytham parish) leased one of the seven gates owned by James Coulborn, and from the same parish ... Winstanley of 'Cominsid' (Commonside] leased a gate from Mr Langton.

From 1796 the number of gates owned is consistently recorded as 230½ and this figure is again confirmed in an 1867 document prepared on behalf of the marsh gate owners when they were involved in a dispute about the land that had been reclaimed by the the Ribble Navigation Company:

> The number of Cattle Gates has from time immemorial remained 230½ but the number of cattle to be depastured on each gate has been from time to time varied as the pasturage served ... For upwards of a century and to the present time the stinted marsh has been held and enjoyed in the same number of cattle gates [gates commonly sold to purchasers in fee simple]. There is no Lord of the Manor and until the present time no claim has ever been made to the Soil of the Marshes by any person other than the owners of the Cattle Gates.[11]

However, before the dispute between the marsh gate owners and the Ribble Navigation Company can be fully understood it is necessary to look at the events that occured in previous centuries in relation to the reclamation, and protection, of the marsh from the River Ribble. It is probable that part of the upper stinted marsh had been reclaimed by the fourteenth century as the several fields called the Hannings,† lying adjacent to Lower House Farm and which would originally have been part of the marsh, were specifically referred to as 'the haynyng meadow' in a deposition, made in 1427, concerning a dispute between the lord of Freckleton and the lord of Newton.[12] However, the absence of any substantial embankment meant that much of the remainder of the lower marsh ground would still have been covered at each high spring tide. In 1673 there is a reference to the 'tempestuous waves' which sometimes formed new ground or alternatively took some part away 'so that the said Marsh is larger or less'.[13]

In 1735 a dispute arose between the gate owners of Freckleton and those of Newton as to the bounds and usual way and passage of the

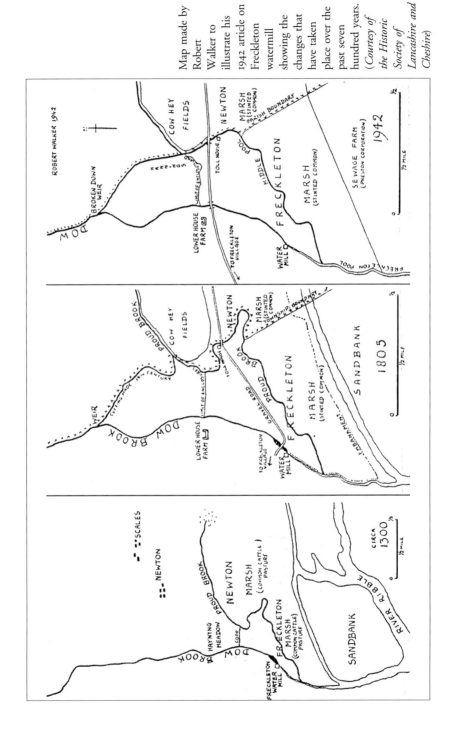

Map made by Robert Walker to illustrate his 1942 article on Freckleton watermill showing the changes that have taken place over the past seven hundred years. (*Courtesy of the Historic Society of Lancashire and Cheshire*)

marshes.[14] The dispute was referred to an independent umpire whose decision appears to have been accepted by both parties, as within thirty years marsh gate owners from both townships co-operated by building and joining embankments on their respective marshes. As a result of these eighteenth-century embankments, which still survive, the land north of the embankment became known as the 'Inner Marsh' whilst the remainder of the marsh on the river side was known as the 'Outer Marsh'.

The embankments alone, however, could not arrest the water flowing onto the marsh from the stream now known as Middle Pool, but which was then the tidal River Proud (or Proud Brook), which flowed into Freckleton Pool (now alternatively known as the River Dow or Dow Brook). Accordingly it was decided to build a floodgate or clow (also called a clough) on the site of the surviving but now defunct Clow just below the Ship Inn. An agreement was made in June 1765 between 'Robert Smalley, Henry Grimbaldeston and Henry Sharples all of Freckleton superinteders of a Wear or wears to be maid in Order to support or keep up the Bank or Copp now standing upon Freckleton Marsh'.[15]

According to Walker 'The difficulty of erecting the clow at the junction of the tidal Middle Pool and Freckleton Pool was overcome in a rather ingenious manner. Excavations and building operations were commenced on dry land a few yards south of the original point of the Middle Pool's entry into Freckleton Pool. When the clow was completed a new channel was cut to bring the Middle Pool through the clow doors, and a shorter cutting was made to allow the water to flow from the clow into Freckleton Pool. The old mouth of the Middle Pool was filled in and an embankment raised to keep out the tide'.[16]

In 1812 a further agreement was made between the marsh gate owners of Freckleton and those of Newton to rebuild the clow, as according to the opening words of the agreement 'the Clough which lately stood in the Pool or Arm of the River Ribble opposite the Public House called Bunkers Hill Freckleton – has by a great Inundation been lately washed down and destroyed'.[17] The rebuilding was considered necessary for the protection of the two marshes from the high tides flowing out of the River Ribble, and it was further agreed that Freckleton should meet 'three full fourth parts of the costs' and Newton the remaining fourth part. Thomas Hornby of Kirkham, John Mayor and Thomas Mayor the Elder, of Freckleton. and Henry Cook of Clifton were appointed to direct, superintend and manage the reconstuction.

The cost of the rebuilding based on the number of gates owned was incurred by the marsh gate owners. A township minute book of 1812 lists the names of the 41 Freckleton gate owners whose three fourths contribution amounted to £530 3s. 0d. Single gate owner such as John Higham and Cuthbert Kirkham had to pay £2 6s. 0d., whilst Thomas Hornby with 53 gates was required to contribute £121 18s. 0d.[18]

It was, however, not only the gate owners of Freckleton and Newton who were anxious to control the unruly River Ribble but also the owners of other lands bordering it, and in 1805 a company was formed for improving its navigation. In 1806 a Parliamentary Act was passed that enabled work to commence to keep the Ribble within fixed bounds, and during the next thirty two years the company built a number of cauls† for the purpose of training the river channel from Preston to a point beyond Freckleton.

In 1838 an Act of Parliament authorised the formation of a second Ribble Navigation Company which in due course completed the canalisation of the river and in so doing created new land alongside the riverside banks. As mentioned earlier in this chapter, it was with this second company that the Freckleton marsh gate owners became embroiled in a series of disputes. In a report circulated to the company shareholders in 1850 the company's engineer, in referring to Freckleton marsh, stated that the grass line in Freckleton and Newton was (now) about half a mile distant from the low water channel, and that the additional green marsh averaged about a quarter of a mile in width. He added that the highest parts of the new marshes on both sides of the river including Freckleton:

> are now partially covered with vegetation, [but] are still from 2 to 4 feet below the out-marshes, which were existing at the commencement of your works – the uninterrupted flow of the tide over these lands twice in 24 hours, is gradually raising the whole; up to a certain point of elevation, the deposit is very great and the rise proportionately quick, afterwards the rise is more slow, but the silt which is deposited upon the highest parts of the land, is much superior in quality to what is left upon the lower, the one being mostly sand, the other a very powerful manure. The perpendicular height of embankments which would vary according to the present level of the sites from 12 to 15 feet, every foot which can be saved in height in these embankments, will effectuate a saving in cost from £300 to £400 per mile. For these reasons, I do not think it would be wise to exclude the tide from these lands for some time to come'.[19]

From 1854 frequent negotiations took place between the marsh gate owners and the navigation company concerning the reclaimed land and the old out-marsh. Although the navigation company did not dispute the marsh gate owners' right to the out-marsh, no provision had been made in the 1838 Act of Parliament for fencing off the out-marsh from the reclaimed land, and it was this matter that was the cause of most of the friction between the two parties.

In April 1864 the marsh gate owners agreed that the navigation company be allowed to form an embankment on the south and west sides of the reclaimed land, and also be allowed to tie their new embankment into the old cop belonging to the marsh gate owners on the west and east sides. At the same meeting it was further resolved that the marsh gate owners should request the company to fence off their land in front of the old out-marsh and at a subsequent meeting with the company this was agreed.

This conciliatory offer was broken in May 1866, however, when the company erected a railing at the foot of the eighteenth-century Cop and took absolute possession of the whole of the old out-marsh. In addition the company then proceeded, throughout 1867, to embank the reclaimed land. The marsh gate owners once more sought legal advice and obtained from their QC the following opinion:

> I am of opinion that if the Marsh owners can prove the Old out Marsh which is in dispute was above the line of High Water of medium tides before the high water mark was altered by artificial works or if they can prove that they & their predecessors have as far back as living memory goes depastured the grass thereon they will make out their title against the Ribble Navigation Company.[20]

Following an agreement made earlier in the year the dispute was finally settled on 20 August 1868 when an award was made that was essentially in favour of the marsh gate owners, although each party had to pay its own costs. The company was instructed to fence off and divide the reclaimed land from the old out-marsh at their own expense in accordance with the boundary lines determined by an independent arbitrator. In addition the company had to pay the gate owners £74 for damage caused by 'ploughing and breaking up part of Freckleton Out Marsh and removing sods and herbage therefrom and cutting the grass therefrom and making holes therein and erecting Railings thereon'.

At the end of three fractious and expensive decades of dealings with the navigation company the marsh gate owners were able to direct their attention to other matters and at a meeting held in 1869 it was proposed that steps be taken to enclose Freckleton marsh. Although the resolution was passed it was a far from unaminous decision, and based on the gates held by those present the voting was 92½ to 46. Application was then made to the Inclosure Commissioners for England and Wales but at their suggestion it was not carried any further. A further application made approximately ten years later likewise failed and the marsh continued to remain stinted pasture.

The oldest surviving minute book of the Freckleton marsh gate owners [21] commences in the year 1842 and ends in 1922. The minutes record the decisions taken at the annual meetings of the owners and reflect a diverse range of matters, including the appointment of cattle tenters, the prevention of trespass by cattle between Freckleton and Newton marshes, the leaking of the clow doors, and correspondence with public and private organisations.

When Henry Rawsthorne was appointed marsh tenter in 1848 he was required to sign an agreement which read as follows:

> I Hen[r]y Rawsthorne engage to tend freckleton Marsh according to the directions of the Marshmen both Summer and Winter at the following Wages viz 22 First Summer weeks at 8*s. od.* per week and the next 7 weeks at 4*s. od.* per week and the remaining part of the year for 11*s. od.*
>
> To bring Wm Harrisons Hy Marquiss' & Cuthb[ert] Adamsons milch cows to the north side of Preston Road.
>
> Not to gather any Dung off the Marsh except from the Road the Bridges and outside the Cops and also to keep the Thistles etc. well mown down.

Claims were sometimes made against the marsh gate owners when livestock strayed from the marsh, as in 1902 when they disclaimed any liability in respect of a claim for £12 made against them by a Mr Singleton in lieu of a stirk that had either strayed or had been stolen from the marsh. In 1909 when the owners were presented with a bill for 10*s. od.* from Mrs Rawstrone of Clitheroes Lane, in respect of damages to a garden wall caused by colts which had strayed from the marsh, payment was agreed subject 'to the production of a receipt showing actual costs incurred repairing the wall'.

Regular expenditure was incurred by the need for repairs to the clow, which as already mentioned was rebuilt in 1812. In 1904 attention was drawn to the leaky condition of the clow doors which was claimed to be the cause of occasional flooding on Newton Marsh, and in 1906 the committee appointed to attend to the matter was allowed to spend 'a sum not exceeding one third of the cost of repairing the doors'. The contract for the work was given to James Halsall of Newton and his bill amounted to £19 7*s. 8d.* It had clearly been a more demanding task than anticipated as on the bottom of the bill Mr Halsall wrote to Mr Peat, who had arranged for the work to be done, in the following terms:

> I should be very glad if you could manage to get me a little more for the above work as I lost a little over Three pound, as you know what a job it was bailing water out everyday through bottom of the Culverts being over 3ft lower than bottom of the Pool & I am sure that they have got a very satisfactory job, & has had a good test.

Mr Halsall appears to have been successful in his appeal and at their 1908 meeting the Freckleton marsh gate owners agreed to pay £8 as a third share of the account 'for the repairs of the flood gate including Messrs Wilson and Peat's charges'.

This 1845 edition of the Ordnance Survey map clearly shows how the estuary looked before the canalisation of the river created new land along the riverside banks. (*Courtesy of Ordnance Survey*)

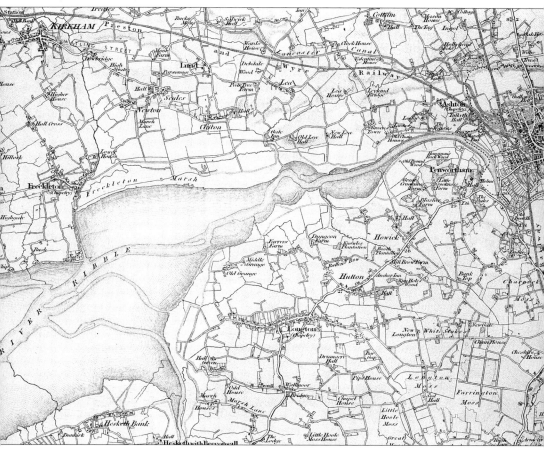

In 1936 Lancashire County Council advised the marsh gate owners
that unless the condition of the Middle Pool and Dow Brook was
improved and repairs made to the clow the Council would carry out
the work themselves and charge the marsh gate owners accordingly. The
clow was finally abandoned as a floodgate following the severe floods
of 1977, when the River Authority built a new culvert just to the south of
the clow, and at the same time the adjacent embankments were raised
three feet in height.

Only in times of national emergency have the marsh gate owners been
made subject to decisions taken outside their control, as in November
1917 when a special meeting was called to consider steps to be taken
following notice from the Lancashire War Agricultural Committee for
putting the marsh under arable cultivation. During the meeting a Mr
Taylor, on behalf of the War Agricultural Committee, spoke of the
seriousness of the food problem and the desire of his committee to have
as much land as possible put under the plough. A month later the marsh
gate owners were informed that they were required to plough up 60
acres of marshland, but before any ploughing took place the scheme
was abandoned in March 1918.

This, however, was not the case during World War II and in 1942
the Lancashire Agricultural Committee advised the marsh gate owners
of both Freckleton and Newton that the marsh would be requisitioned
in order to meet Government demands, and by the following year wheat
was being grown on 350 acres of former marshland. The marsh was not
de-requisitioned until 1952 and since then the gates have been let on a
yearly basis, with their letting price being decided at the annual meetings
of the marsh gate owners.

It is at these annual meetings where, throughout the past 330 years,
the marsh gate owners have endeavoured to maintain their ancient rights
first articulated in the agreement of 1670. The last major challenge to
their rights occurred as recently as 1972 when Lancashire County Council
registered the marsh as common land under the Commons Registration
Act of 1965 and it was this action which prompted the newspaper article
referred to at the beginning of the chapter. It took a further eight years
before Lancashire County Council finally withdrew their application and
the rights of the marsh gate owners were once more confirmed.

CHAPTER 19

Marsh Road

Despite its potential hazards and its users requiring an intimate knowledge of the numerous creeks and gullies that intersected the area, there is evidence that a road across Freckleton, Newton and Clifton marshes to Lea was already in regular use by the end of the seventeenth century. On 21 March 1699 Thomas Clifton of Lytham, who owned Clifton Marsh, leased to William Campbell, a sailor of Lytham, the toll of Clifton Marsh on the following terms:

> And if it shall happen at any Time during the said Term – that – Thomas Clifton – shall be stopped or hindered from passing and repassing over either of those two Marshes called Newton Marsh and Freckleton Marsh ... or ... be forced or made to pay for the same, then William Campbell – shall not Permit or suffer any of the inhabitants in Newton or Freckleton ... to pass or repass over the said Clifton Marsh till restitution be made ...[1]

The lease was renewed in 1719 and further evidence of the existence of the road is provided by a document which records the monies spent during the years 1691 to 1726 on the repair, maintenance or rebuilding of the bridges and platts and entitled 'A True & perfect Accompt [Account] of what moneys the township of Freckleton hath laid forth in repairing the bridges & other the ways over Freckleton Marsh since the year 1690'.[2] Names such as Proud Bridge, Killn Bridge, 'new' Bridge, 'stone platt' and platt over Robins Pool are now virtually unknown but to our seventeenth- and eighteenth-century contemporaries they would have been familiar locations.

Proud Bridge obviously spanned the stream called Proud Brook (now Middle Pool) possibly near to the site of the Toll House, where there is still a bridge over Middle Pool. The site of Killn Bridge cannot now be pinpointed with absolute certainty but it almost certainly spanned Dow Brook at or near the present marsh entrance and was so named after the new watermill and kiln built in 1609. The building of a bridge 'over the damm' in 1691 could also refer to Killn Bridge. Remains of another stone platt that once spanned the Dow Brook below Lower House Farm still survive. The platt at Robins Pool probably spanned the stream by Taylors Pool where it empties into the River Ribble by British Aerospace and where there is now a modern footbridge.

Altogether the amount laid out from 1691 to 1726 totalled £40 10s. 8d. and although in some years there was no expenditure it is clear that in most years a continuous battle was waged with the elements to ensure that the ways remained passable. Repairs to Proud Bridge were necessary in no less than fifteen years from 1697 to 1722, and in 1721 an entry in the account records 'laying proude bridge againe being taken downe by the water'. In addition to the regular repair work other tasks included 'skouring Platts'; 'paveing a Callsey'; 'rampering' and 'gravelling'. The largest single amount laid out was £8 0s. 0d. in 1717 for 'building a bridge over the Pools betwixt the higher & under Marshes'.

By 1781 tolls were being collected on the then marsh road, as is shown by the following clause to the agreement made that year between the Clifton and de Hoghton families concerning the construction of the toll road from Lea Gate to Kirkham:

> Provided further that if the Road leading over Newton and Freckleton Marshes ... which is now used shall at any time during the said term ... be stopped or the tolls now taken there shall be increased ... that then ... Thomas Clifton ... shall have full power to prevent ... all of the Land-owners and inhabitants of the said Townships of Newton with Scales and Freckleton from passing through the said Toll Bar to be erected [at Lea]'.[3]

By this date it would seem that the township had ceased to maintain the road and responsibility for it had passed to the marsh gate owners. In the absence of any contemporary township books it is not clear why or when this occurred but in the late eighteenth century, presumably following the opening of the toll road to Kirkham, the Clifton family entered into negotiations with the marsh gate owners of Freckleton and Newton concerning the making of a permanent route over their marshes.

A copy of the original articles for the regulations was entered in a marsh gate owners minute book of c.1844 and noted 'A copy of a document found in the Possession of Edward Singleton relating to the Road over Clifton, Newton and Freckleton marshes'.[4] Because of their relevance and interest the first 12 articles are reproduced in full in appendix E. The remaining 4 articles concern matters of general admin-istration. Joseph Hornby and John Mayor were the persons nominated to act on behalf of Freckleton.

The articles were probably written shortly after 1799 as article 4 refers to the road over Freckleton marsh being already made, and the earliest known account book, entitled 'New Road over Freckleton Marsh – A/C

Book',[5] commences 6 April 1799. From that date until 5 January 1800 a total of £137 2s. 8d. was expended on a wide variety of materials, and work such as carting, loading and discharging gravel, use of flat (boat) for gravel, levelling of gravel, and other sundry tasks including that of the collection of subscriptions. Money was raised by subscription in Freckleton, Warton, Bryning and Lytham but the largest amount (£77 13s. 2d.) was by assessment at 2s. 0d. in the pound levied on the Freckleton marsh gate owners.[6]

By March 1804 the new (or remade) road over Newton marsh had also been completed at a cost of £327 5s. 5d. with subscriptions coming from Freckleton, Warton, Mr Clifton, Lytham, Preston, Blackburn, Walton-le-Dale and the Earl of Derby, but with no apparent financial contribution from Newton. Freckleton was the largest contributor with £134 18s. 6d. but what is even more notable is the contribution of £57 5s. 0d., or 17½% of the final cost, made by various members of the Mayor family.[7] This indication of their readiness to pay for more reliable access to market centres such as Preston and beyond is reinforced by an entry in the accounts for 1812, 'To J Mayors Arrear for finishing Building And Newton Marsh Road in 1806 – £23 13s. 0d.'[8] implying that John Mayor had also loaned money for the road to be completed.

The route of this 'new' road commenced just beyond the toll house at Lea Gate and then followed the approximate line of the present road from Three Nooks until it reached the site of the former Lancashire County Council depot. Passing behind Marsh Garage, where there was a gate (of which a gatestoop still survives), it then took a course just to the south of the present main road until it reached the Toll House, otherwise known as Halfpenny Hall. Thereafter it continued westwards until it reached the final gate at Preston (Old) Road where it rejoined the public highway. In 1844 its dimensions were recorded as: 'Length over Freckleton Marsh 914 yards; Length over Newton Marsh 1,273 yards; Length over Clifton Marsh 1,894 yards'.[9]

The considerable advantages for travellers in terms of a shorter journey and an improved travelling time were obvious from the outset and in 1805 the committee proudly noted the following fact in their minute book:[10]

From Freckleton [Water] Mill to Preston Cross through Kirkham 11¼ miles 15 roods;

From Ditto to Ditto over the marshes 7½ miles;

Difference betwixt going thro Kirkham & over the marshes 3¾ miles 15 roods.

Construction of the original toll house, on the site of the present 'Toll House', was completed during 1804–05 and the following three entries extracted from the account book provide examples of work carried out:[11]

29 Jan.   1804 To Jno Mayor 1 Day with Cart at Toll House

                                                  £0   4s.   6d.

28 July   1804 To Jonathan Allansons 1st Bill for House £4   0s.   3d.

28 Dec.   1804 Thatching etc Building   £0   7s.   3d.

The first tollkeeper was John Hall who combined the role with that of marsh tenter for Newton Marsh, and in October 1804 was paid £9 16s. 0d. for 14 weeks tenting. When the livestock were taken off the marsh the weekly summer rate of 14s. 0d. per week reduced to only 5s. 0d. per week for the autumn and winter, and on 28 December John Hall received just £2 15s. 0d. for a further 11 weeks 'Tenting Gate'. This lesser rate then continued until May 1805 when livestock returned and the rate resumed at 14s. 0d. per week. John Hall remained as tollkeeper until 1808 when John Benson was appointed, to be followed in 1828 by James Carter who continued until 1858 when the existing mode of collecting tolls and payment of the tollkeeper was discontinued. A toll board was obtained in 1805 to display the amounts charged and although there is no record of any attempted robbery on the then isolated toll house it was considered necessary in November 1810 to pay William Harrison £1 11s. 6d. 'for a gun for the House'.

The road required regular maintenance, as entries in the surviving account books reveal. Gravel for the top surface was taken by cart to the marsh road where it was the responsibility of the marsh tenter to keep the road surface level, and for such work John Benson was paid 2s. 0d. a day in 1817. The gravel came from (Warton) Brows and Lytham, and was sent by flat to Freckleton Pool where in August 1821 Richard Spencer and others were paid £0 19s. 6d. for discharging 78 tons of gravel from the flats *Alice* and *Darling*. The amount represents a rate of 3d. per ton and was in fact a reduction of 1d. per ton when compared with the rate paid the previous year. In 1839 the minute book records that 'The gravel to be had as usual from the liberties of Thos Clifton Esq Lytham who will make no charge for the same provided that the stones be broken and properly applyed'. Despite its exposed situation every effort was made to keep the road open and on 16 February 1828 nine men were paid 1s. 6d. each for 'Shifting Snow'.[12]

A coach service, from Preston to Blackpool by way of Freckleton, is

The line of the old marsh road can still be traced from the marsh entrance gate in Preston Old Road. Turning left after the still surviving bridge over the Dow Brook the road took a straight course to the Toll House, thereafter continuing across Newton marsh.

said to have been started in 1781 'and in 1816 a regular coach-run was established'.[13] The coach operators are not named but according to *Pigots Directory* of 1821 the *Vice-Chancellor* left Preston every morning in the summer months arriving at the Clifton Arms, Lytham, by 11.30 a.m., and the *Neptune*, also from Preston, called at the same inn at 3.30 p.m. Unfortunately the actual route from Preston to Lytham is not given but presumably some if not all of the journeys would have been across the toll road. James Mayor and Henry Cook who, when declared bankrupt in 1830, were described as coach proprietors of Freckleton and Preston, may also have provided a service between the two locations.

There is no record of the volume of traffic using the road but tolls collected in 1804–05 are recorded as 'Amount of 1st Years Tolls – £47 11s. 3d.' increasing the following year to £59 7s. 6d. Between 1822 to 1825 there seems to have been a decline, as in the latter year John Benson was given an allowance of £15 'for three bad years'. This apparent downturn, however, did not deter the Hornby family from opening the appropriately named Coach and Horses Inn in 1824–25, presumably in anticipation of an increase in traffic. By 1833 the amount of tolls collected had risen to £133 17s. 0d., but during the 1850s there was a further decline until by 1858 only £67 6s. 3½d. was taken. This considerable reduction in income was caused, at least in part, by competition from the railways, with the result that the stagecoaches and other 'through' traffic to Lytham stopped using the marsh road, leaving Freckleton once more without a regular public transport service, apart from carriers who plied their trade to Preston.

At a special meeting of the trustees held on 10 September 1858 it was unanimously resolved that the then mode of collecting tolls be discontinued and that the tolls be advertised for let by public tender. The entire expense of keeping the road over the three marshes 'in proper and satisfactory repair' was to be defrayed by the person taking the tolls, although they did have the 'advantage' of the Toll House rent free.[14] The successful applicant was Charles Fisher from Newton who offered to pay a yearly rent of £15 for the right of collecting the tolls. He was appointed for a period of seven years but only six months later on 16 March 1859 the trustees again met and resolved 'that Charles Fisher have notice to quit his house and to cease collecting tolls ... in two weeks'. The reason for this summary dismissal is not recorded but clearly it related to a matter completely unacceptable to the trustees.

Charles Fisher was succeeded by Joseph Gregson who remained toll collector until 1872. He was followed by Joseph Rawsthorn whose appointment for five years was at a yearly rent of £10. However, within a year the trustees were of the opinion that the roads were in a very unsatisfactory state of repair and Joseph Rawsthorn was requested to immediately put the road into 'a thoroughly good state of repair', otherwise the trustees would take the necessary steps to enforce the terms of his agreement. Working relations between Joseph Rawsthorn and the trustees were clearly never easy and, no doubt, the seemingly extraordinary increase of the yearly rent to £90 in 1874 did not help matters. Whatever the reasons in August 1876 he was given notice to quit at the end of the year, being replaced by John Whittle who remained until 1885.

During the final years of the nineteenth century tolls were collected by George Taylor (1885–92) and Robert Dobson (1892–1900). Following the resignation of Robert Dobson no less than twenty three persons applied for the post of toll collector, the successful applicant being Joseph Whiteside, the owner of Ravald House Farm. In order to obtain the post, however, Joseph Whiteside had to agree to pay a yearly rent of £165 for five years, which when renewed for a further five years in 1905 increased to £270.

In 1895 the trustees decided to replace the old toll house, though the decision seems to have been taken more in response to the state of the existing building rather than in anticipation of the advent of the modern motor age. The contract for building the new toll house was given to John Haslam and as the twenty page specification for the new building

The original toll house was built in 1804–5 and in November 1810 it was considered necessary to pay 'for a gun for the House'. It was replaced by the present building in 1895 and tolls were collected until the road was taken over by Lancashire County Council on 31 December 1923.

required him to 'take down existing cottage, remove all old foundations' [15] all evidence of the old toll house was destroyed. In order to meet John Haslam's tender of £277 14*s.* 0*d.* the trustees agreed to apply for £250 from the Prudential Assurance Company, repayable by 30 yearly instalments of principal and interest.

In 1896 motor vehicles with pneumatic tyres were admitted to public roads and by 1904 damage 'by Motorists' to the toll gates was being reported. As a consequence the trustees resolved in 1905 to purchase oil lamps for all three gates. It was further agreed that Joseph Whiteside was to provide the oil and be responsible for seeing that the lamps were 'properly lighted'.

Dissatisfaction with the state of the road was reflected in a letter received in 1907 from the North East Lancashire Automobile Club in which they enquired whether the trustees would be prepared to place the road under the control of the Fylde Rural District Council. In reply the trustees pointed out that the cost of abandonment of the toll bar, fencing off the

road and providing a water supply to the toll house would be at least
£2,000, and in addition a capital sum would have to be provided for
maintaining the sea wall near the Pool. They concluded their reply,
somewhat wryly, by saying that they would be glad to know 'whether
the Automobile Club would be prepared to pay the cost of the works'.
In May 1911 similar correspondence took place with the Lancashire Automobile Club, who again complained about the bad state of the road and
stated that 'unless some satisfactory arrangement was come to with regard
to the tolls and repair of the road the members would cease to use the
road'. On this occasion the trustees replied 'that no increase in the tolls
for pleasure Motors had been made. The price had always been 6*d.* return
same day. Whiteside, the late Tollkeeper had charged a reduced price of
4*d.* entirely on his own responsibility'. This was not the first time that
Joseph Whiteside had been accused of charging a reduced toll. In December 1910 the trustees had written to him to say they had been advised
that 'he had induced heavy traffic to pass over the Roads by a reduction
in charges'. At a further meeting five days later they introduced the
following amended charges for vehicles using the road:

Steam, Petrol or Electric Motor Lurry, Van	2*s.* o*d.*
Each Trailer attached to above	1*s.* o*d.*
Lurry or Van with 4 wheels & 4 horses with width of	
wheels less than 3 inches	3*s.* o*d.*
" " " exceeding 3 inches	1*s.* 8*d.*

In November 1912 Fylde Rural District Council asked the trustees
upon what terms and conditions the trustees would be willing to consent
to the abolition of tolls and handing the road over to the council. At
a meeting of the marsh gate owners held the following January it was
proposed that the road be handed over to Fylde RDC subject to
satisfactory terms being agreed but, presumably due to the outbreak of
World War 1, no action was subsequently taken. In May 1914 the trustees
paid Mr J. H. Maxwell £148 10*s.* 7*d.* 'for repairing and Tar spraying
the Marsh Road', but despite these attempts to maintain the road the
annual income continued to decline. In October 1918 George Sudell,
who had become tollkeeper in 1910, was paying a rent of £300. He
reported to the trustees that in 1917 his gross takings had been £343 but
from January to October 1918 he had taken only £223. Not surprisingly
he did not re-apply for the post and in December 1918 John Dewhurst
became the last person to be appointed tollkeeper, for which he was
required to pay an annual rent of £400.

However in the years immediately following the end of World War I Lancashire County Council began a programme of road mending and by 1922 had made plans for a new road across Clifton, Newton and Freckleton marshes, quite independent of the Marsh Road which by then was in 'a state of complete disrepair'. At a meeting held that year the trustees were advised by Mr Whinnerah, acting for Mr Clifton, that 'he was strongly of opinion that the Marsh Owners ought to be moving in the matter, or he was afraid they would be too late and the [new] Marsh road would be scrapped'.

In 1923 Lancashire County Council announced that it was to spend £71,955 on improvements (a new road) to the marsh road, and that it was arranging for the abolition of toll charges. At the same time Mr Clifton voluntarily relinquished his interest in the toll house and the building passed into the joint ownership of the Freckleton and Newton marsh gate owners. In the circumstances the trustees, acting on behalf of the marsh gate owners, began negotiations with the County Council concerning compensation for loss of the toll. These were completed during the next two years and the final entry in the trustees minute book dated 16 July 1924 reads: 'As and from the 31 December 1923 the Marsh Roads were taken over by the Lancashire County Council and the duties of the Trustees came to an end'.[16]

Exit Gate onto Preston Old Road. Taken just prior to the closure of the road this photograph is noted 'End of the old road across the marsh showing the awkward turn approaching Freckleton village'. The sign at the marsh exit is directing traffic to Whittle's Garage. (*Courtesy of* Lancashire Evening Post)

CHAPTER 20

Watermill and Windmills

Medieval Mills

The first reference to a mill in the township occurs in 1199 when Roger de Freckleton granted to Richard de Freckleton ¹⁄₁₆ of a mill and a fishery.[1] Watermills had been in use since Roman times, whereas it was not until around 1180 that wind-powered wooden post/peg mills began to be built, and it is therefore probable that this early mill stood by the Dow Brook on or near the site of the watermill which operated there until about 1922.

The next mention of a mill in the township is in a deed dated sometime prior to 1290 in which:

> James son [of] Roger de Eccleston grants to Sir Adam de Hoghton half of his inheritance from Marjory widow of Gilbert de Meols namely the fourth part of a messuage and 4 bovates and half of two mills in Freckleton, saving to the grantor 'hoperfre and tolfre' without multure, of his own corn in those mills.[2]

The privilege of 'hopper free and toll free' meant that the miller, on receiving the corn sent by Sir Adam de Hoghton, would have had to completely clear his mill hopper of any existing corn. He would then have had to grind the corn and deliver the resulting flour to Sir Adam before refilling the hopper and grinding the corn sent by other villagers. In addition Sir Adam was not required to make any payment to the miller unless he chose to make a courtesy payment, nor could the miller take for himself a proportion (multure) of the flour produced.

There are three further records relating to the existence of mills in the township during the later medieval period: in 1325–26 Gilbert de Singleton was said to have 'held a house, twelve acres of land and a mill';[3] in 1382–83 when Ralph de Freckleton is recorded as having 'mills';[4] and in 1395 John de Cottam obtained a mill and an oxgang of land from Nicholas and Ellen Croft.[5] However, neither the location nor motive power of any of these mills is known, though presumably one of them was the already mentioned watermill.

Windmills

The first mention of a windmill in Freckleton occurs in 1565 when Henry Robinson, the elder, stated in his will that seven years after his death his sons William and Thomas were to have his 'new windie mill' and his son Richard was to have his 'old windie mill'.[6] These would have been peg and/or post mills, since modern windmills, such as the present building at Lytham, were not built until about 1750. It is almost certain that one if not both windmills occupied a site in the small field, just to the south of Lower House Farm, known in 1781 as Mill Hill and on the 1838 Tithe map as Mill Hey, but which was intersected by the opening of the present marsh road in 1926.

In 1621 John *[1]* Sharples leased 'a dwelling house … commonly called Henry Robinson's house to John Clitheroe of Freckleton, miller'. The location of this house is not known but was possibly in the vicinity of Lower House, because when he was writing in about 1623, John *[1]* Sharples refers to the fact that the Sharples family were by that date in possession of the former Robinson estate. It is possible that the Sharples family had purchased the Robinson estate as early as 1580, as in that year, when they sold a quantity of pasture land to Ellen Cowburne, they obtained a covenant from her 'neither to erect nor build any houses or edifices upon the said tenement [one to which Ellen was co-heiress] nearer to the windmill of the said John Sharples in Freckleton than the houses of the said tenement now stand, nor plant trees nor any other thing in any part of the said tenement which shall be prejudicial to John Sharples concerning the windmill or shall stop from the windmill the wind which might drive the same'.[7]

As we saw in chapter 4, by the early eighteenth century the Sharples estate was being managed by Richard Harrison who, on 20 October 1701, advised George *[4]* Sharples that 'Yesterday a messenger from Freckleton gave me an account that a spar is failed at the wind mill, and I have ordered a new one to be fixed'. The following month he was reporting that 'another Spar is wanting to the Windmill besides what I mentioned before'. He also refers to the new stone and jack ropes that were installed in the watermill when it was decided that the 'old stone rope is to be made use of at the Windmill whilst it will doe any service there, which may be for some time whilst there is a light stone'.[8]

The final mention of the windmill is in 1715 when George *[4]* Sharples gave instructions to sell his Lower House estate including 'one windy corn mill'. Nothing is known of the subsequent history of the mill nor when it fell into disuse, and it could be that following the purchase of Lower House in 1719 by Newton Charity the new trustees decided that the windmill should be demolished.

Watermill

About the year 1427 William Huddleston married Joan, daughter of Ralph de Freckleton, and became the new lord of Freckleton. Included in his new acquisitions was a watermill which probably occupied the same site as the watermill granted to Richard de Freckleton in 1199. As a result of his new acquistion William Huddleston became involved in the previously mentioned dispute with the lord of the manor of Newton concerning the watering of cattle on the marsh. Forty years later, in 1467–68, Richard Hodylston (Huddleston) and his wife Isabell appointed an attorney to take possession of a watermill in the lordship of Freckleton, and in 1496 when the Huddleston estate was sold to the Earl of Derby the watermill was no doubt included in the transaction. The fact that the Huddleston watermill documents, referred to in a seventeenth-century deed as 'Divers old deeds declaring the right of the Lords of Freckleton to the stream of the water mill & concerning the fishing in the Water of Ribble', were found amongst the papers of the Sharples family, who were lessees of the watermill under the Earl of Derby, also reinforces this conclusion.

There is no further mention of the watermill until 8 April 1609 when Arthur Sharples obtained from William, Earl of Derby:

> One parcel of the waste or common of Freckleton near unto a place commonly called the outland hill in Freckleton aforesaid or in and upon any other place near unto the Marsh called Freckleton Marsh fit and sufficient to erect and build a water corn mill or mills under one Roof thereupon together with the stream and water course falling and usually running between Newton and Freckleton to serve the said mill or mills together with the full and free liberty to make and erect or cause to be made and erected any further fences dam or dams floodgate or floodgates or other necessary works for the serving of the said mill or mills ... And also a parcel of the waste aforesaid for the erecting of a house to be a kiln and other rooms necessary and fit for the use of the said mill or mills.[9]

The building had been completed by 1615 as it was referred to in the memorandum compiled at the time of the marriage of John *[2]* Sharples

Possibly the site of the watermill granted to Richard de Freckleton in 1199. The history of the watermill that stood on Dow brook near to the marsh gate entrance can be followed from 1609 until it ceased production in 1922. The remains of the then decayed building were finally demolished in 1968.

to Anne Nowell. In the memorandum Roger Nowell, the father of Anne, refers to the 'water mill he [John *[1]* Sharples] holds by lease from the Earl of Derby for three lives'. Roger Nowell added that he understood that the watermill and the windmill 'do generally yeald 200 mets [measures] of multure yearly which I do estimate to the value of £30 per annum'.[10] In 1619 Arthur Sharples granted the profits of the 'water corne mill and kilne' to his son John *[2]* in consideration of John clearing his father's debts which amounted to £103.

During the remainder of the seventeenth century the Sharples family continued to lease the mill from the earls of Derby, but only occasionally is it possible to identify the actual miller, though even then it cannot be certain whether he was miller of the watermill or windmill or indeed of both. In his will dated 1688 William Colborn, a yeoman, appointed Robert Sidgreaves, his son in law, as one of his executors. In the document produced when the will was proved Robert Sidgreaves was described as 'Miller of Freckleton'.[11]

As already mentioned, when the Sharples estate passed to George *[4]* Sharples it was managed by his cousin Richard Harrison and from June 1700 to December 1701 an increasingly acrimonious correspondence took place between the two men concerning the cost of the extensive repairs necessary to make the watermill operational.[12] On 17 June 1700 Richard Harrison wrote:

> I got the water-mill view'd by an old experienc'd Millwright, shaft & wheel must be gotten to the ground, so I must forthwith send about wood. The fellow I had look at the Water-mill is one that has left work, not acquainted with any to be employ'd, so I suppose deliver'd his judgement fairly.

On 28 February 1701 he wrote:

> I have ordered the buying [of] 2,000 brick for your Water Mill & Arms for water-wheel to be season'd and made ready, they tell me Bucket-boards & starts may be got in your ground.

There then followed a series of letters written on behalf of Richard Harrison by John Alston, schoolmaster at Poulton, who acted as his secretary. On 20 October 1701 George *[4]* was advised that:

> The Mill now very near finishing but yet there is wanting a Sack rope which I am told will be very chargeable. I intend to get the mill viewed by some other expert workman, and shall take care that Edward Swartbreck [the tenant of Lower House Farm] send you his Accounts that you may be satisfied of the whole charge ...

On 3 November 1701 George *[4]* was informed that:

> I [Richard Harrison] have got the work at the Mill viewed by a very honest understanding man who tells me it is very well done, and that the charge is not extravagant considering how much it was out of order.

It seems clear that at this time George *[4]* was questioning both the cost of repairs to the watermill and the loss of revenue whilst repairs were taking place and that he had written to Richard Harison accordingly, as on 14 November 1701 Richard Harrison replied:

> I admire you should expect an account of the profit of the mills whilst they were managed by Edward Swartbreck whereas if you remember he paid you some money when you was in the Country, and the rest which was about £3 I am sure I gave you account how it was disposed of, at or before the time they were lett to Coulburne who hath them at present.

Clearly annoyed by the unappreciative attitude of George *[4]*, Richard Harrison wrote personally on 20 November 1701. Before raising the subject of the water mill he explained that 'I have scarce written any thing myself since I had the Fit which the physcians say was Apoplectick nor had I written now but for yours of the 10th instant fill'd with wonder at the charge of the water-mill'. He then continued:

> I do as much admire at you as you do at the charge ... You ordered the doing of it in as good a manner as if you had contracted a new Lease.
>
> There was one to attend the workmen daily to see they did not loiter, more timber had been used but that some was got out of your own ground.
>
> All your amazement proceeds from your being unacquainted with taking down old water-mills and building them anew and that several do say which have experience.
>
> I have ridden for you and spent many a shilling I never charged upon you, and now in effect requited with most severe censures as to your Water-mill.

The final letter in this series of exchanges was dated 9 December 1701 and written by John Alston who, after introducing himself, informed George *[4]* that he had kept the accounts of the watermill. He continued:

> I am satisfied you have no just reason to think of any extravagant charges therein, for I have heard several sufficient persons say that the work is done well and reasonably (all disadvantages considered) and besides 'tis said that had the Out South End Wall been brought up with brick instead of wood (which saved a considerable charge) the last violent storm would have brought it down again and that is what makes the mill wrights Bill extend so much to your admiration but Mr Harrison is very sorry to think you should be so much disatisfied with his management, he has this day discharged most of the workmen out of George Easthams Martinmas rent, and intends to give you Account of the remainder as soon as all is paid off.

As the Sharples family were only lessees of the watermill it was not included in the sale of Lower House estate in 1719 but remained in the ownership of the Earl of Derby. The names of the lessees are then unknown until 1767 when, as we saw in chapter 14, James Sharples, the head of the only Catholic family in Freckleton, was described as a miller. It is unclear whether this family were a junior line of the Sharples of Lower House or a completely unconnected family that had moved into the township, but their arrival began a family association with the watermill that was to last over one hundred years.

Some twenty years after he became the miller James Sharples found himself in dispute with the Freckleton and Newton marsh gate owners, and in an undated and incomplete draft document (but which must have been prepared sometime prior to 1782 because in that year Robert

Smalley of Freckleton, one of the parties named in the agreement, died)
James Sharples was accused of having:

> lately erected a Stone clough or damn on the East Side of a certain Water
> Course lying between the Townships of Newton and Freckleton aforesaid
> called Dawbridge [sic] Brook and hath raised the same to a much greater
> Height than it formerly stood the better to work a certain Water corn
> Mill in Freckleton aforesaid whereof he is Tennant whereby the Water is
> confined in the said Brook and prevented from running its usual course
> and frequently overflows the lands lying contiguous to the said Brook And
> the Owners and Occupiers of such Lands thereby sustain great Loss and
> Damage And by reason of the said Clough or Damn being so raised and
> erected a certain other Water Course [i.e. Proud Brook] branching from
> the said first mentioned Brook and running from thence to Newton Marsh
> is in a great measure stopped up and obstructed by which means the
> Cattle kept upon the Marshes of Newton and Freckleton aforesaid have
> been and yet are deprived of wholesome Water necessary for their sustenance
> and Nourishment.[13]

As there is no subsequent mention of the matter being pursued by the
marsh gate owners it would seem that James Sharples was allowed to
operate the mill after some compromise had been reached. The concern
expressed by the marsh gate owners had, however, no doubt been shared
by their predecessors, and throughout all the years that the mill was in
operation the flooding of the fields adjoining Dow Brook, presumably
caused by the damning of the waters, must have been a constant problem.
At the quarter sessions held in 1675 it was ordered that the Dow Brook
be scoured 'to the width of ten foot at the least',[14] whilst in 1747[15] and
again in 1752[16] several land occupiers in both Freckleton and Newton
were ordered, at the Penwortham baronial court, to 'open Scowre and
Drain' their respective parts of the Dow Brook.

In his will of 1789 James Sharples gave to his eldest son John 'The
house wherein I now Dwell together with my Water Mill and Kiln all
situate and lying in Freckleton Held by lease for Three Lives under the
Earl of Derby'.[17] When John himself made his will in 1828 he gave to
his nephews James and Thomas Sharples 'all that Kiln, Water Corn
Mill, Mill race, Mill Dam, going geer and appurtenances situate in
Freckleton in my own occupation being the residue of the premises held
by me under the said lease from the Earl of Derby'.[18]

As a consequence of this bequest and by an indenture dated 21
December 1829, Edward Earl of Derby demised to James and Thomas
Sharples of Freckleton, millers, for the lives of 'the said James Sharples

Another view of the watermill (left) and the mill house, taken from the marsh looking across towards Preston Old Road. (*Courtesy of Lancashire Record Office – DDNw Box 4*)

aged 37 years, and of Thomas Sharples aged 30 years, and of Thomas (whose mother Mary was the sister of James and Thomas) son of the late James Battersby of Clifton, Farmer aged 18 years a messuage with a water Corn Mill, Drying Kiln, and two Mill Dams 'now in the occupation of James Sharples and Thomas Sharples'.[19]

In 1850, after it had been in his family's possession for 354 years, the Earl of Derby sold the watermill to Thomas and John Talbot Clifton of Lytham Hall. The Sharples family, however, continued to lease the mill and on the 1851 census James Sharples is described as miller and proprietor of land, Thomas Sharples as miller and landowner, and Thomas Battersby as miller journeyman. By 1861 the Sharples brothers seemed to be concentrating on their farming interests and Thomas Battersby is named as the corn miller, as he was again in 1871. When on 24 June 1882 the lease was surrendered to the trustees of Thomas Henry Clifton one of the surrending parties was Edward Smith, whose wife Agnes was the daughter of James Sharples.

On 13 September 1882 the trustees of Newton Charity purchased the watermill from Mrs Clifton of Lytham Hall for £350, the sole 'object of the purchase being to benefit the property of the Charity [Lower

House Farm] which now sustained damage by reason of the water not being able to get off properly'. At the time of the purchase the watermill was still occupied by Thomas Battersby but by February 1883 the mill and cottage were let for £22 on a yearly tenancy to Christopher Dobson, thus ending 124 years of continuous occupation by members of the Sharples and, through marriage, the Battersby families.

During the 1880s there was a succession of tenants but by then the overriding problem was that the Dow Brook had become the main sewage outlet from Kirkham. In 1889 Dr Winn, Medical Officer of Health, reported that 'from Lower House Farm to the Marsh Gates at Freckleton the stench was intolerable, and he would ask the Board [the Rural Sanitary Authority] to bear in mind the constant presence in this locality of a large supply of water with an equally large quantity of sewage must prove a source of danger to the inhabitants in the immediate neighbourhood'.[20]

At a meeting of the Rural Sanitary Authority in the same year the representative from Newton Charity hinted at legal action in order to compel the sanitary authorities 'to cease fouling the waters'. Freckleton marsh gate owners were also clearly unhappy at the then prevailing situation and at their meeting in August 1890 resolved to 'purchase the Mill and Dam from the Newton Charity if they are able to sell the same for the sum of £350. The Mill to be done away with on receiving £100 from the Kirkham & Wesham Sewage Committee'.[21]

At a further meeting in December the Freckleton marsh gate owners confirmed their intention to purchase, but added that it be subject 'to the Marsh Owners being only called upon to cleanse out the watercourse for ordinary agricultural drainage so far as is co-extensive with the Marsh owners property', and that they could not bind themselves 'as to no sewage in the stream this being a matter for the Kirkham & Wesham Sewage Committee'.[22]

On 25 February 1891 the trustees of Newton Charity resolved to 'sell to the Freckleton Marsh owners the mill and dam at Freckleton for the sum of £350 on the distinct understanding that the dam in the main stream be removed and that any sewage obstruction to the stream be removed and done away with, that the dam at the Mill be removed and that the stream be cleansed to its original depth so as to afford sufficient outfall for the draining of the abutting agricultural lands to a depth of from 3 to 4 feet but that the Marsh owners be not called upon to build any new structural works nor be allowed to construct any works so as to impede the free flow of water in the stream and that no sewage be allowed to go into the stream'.[23]

Robert Walker and Percy Hall, of the [Blackpool and] Fylde Historical Society, removing the support stone for the main cog wheel from the then derelict watermill in about 1942. After being in the custody of the society for over half a century the support stone was returned to Freckleton in 2000 and now forms the centrepiece of the flower bed adjacent to the marsh entrance in Preston Old Road.

Following its purchase by the Freckleton marsh gate owners the watermill was leased to Richard Spencer at an annual rental of £45. The watermill appears to have continued to operate at full capacity until the mid-1920s but thereafter it fell into a state of decay and was eventually demolished in 1968. Some years prior to its demolition one of the stone supports of the main cog wheel was removed and taken to the Grundy House Museum, Blackpool, before being removed again to the garden of a cottage in Layton. The significance of figures '1433' carved on the stone is not known but is unlikely to be a contemporary date. However, apart from one or two millstones, the stone is the most important surviving link with the ancient watermill and, following its return to the village in 2000, now forms the centrepiece of the flower bed situated by the marsh gate not far from the site of the actual watermill.

Part VIII

Trade and Industry

CHAPTER 21

Agriculture

Medieval Farming

It is not known what use was made of the land in Freckleton before and during the Roman period, but with the arrival of the Angles the township fields would have begun to take on the appearance they were to retain for the next seven or eight hundred years. By the thirteenth century the township was probably surrounded by common open fields organised on a form of arable farming known as infield/outfield. Under this ancient method of farming the 'infield', that is land nearest the settlement, was continuously cultivated and relied for its fertility on regular applications of manure, while the 'outfield' was periodically cropped to exhaustion before being returned to pasture. Land utilisation in the Kirkham district at this time has been described in the following terms:

> In these vills the whole of the arable territory was divided into strips varying in size from a quarter to one acre, and these lands or seillons [selions] were grouped in the fields of the vill commomly called the townfields. Each particular aggregation of strips constituted a furlong known by a special designation, and the furlongs in their turn made up the fields, generally described from their situation.[1]

> Each householder or owner of a toft was alloted strips of lands within the fields. The amount of room required to turn a team of oxen at the end of a furrow regulated the width of each strip thus the arable was ploughed in long rectangular strips called lands or seillons. Short straight plough sections that fitted into the seillon system of each furlong were called butts or half butts. In order to gain access to each system of seillons there were headlands the last strips to be ploughed; these linked up with the outrakes from the fields to the village.[2]

In this vill [Freckleton] we again have evidence of the division of arable land into small strips or seillons grouped into furlongs.[3]

During survey work carried out in the 1980s by Lancaster University Archaeology Unit surviving patterns of this medieval ridge and furrow farming were identified in the vicinity of Lower House Farm and Strike Farm.

By the mid-fourteenth century there is evidence that farms were beginning to exist as separate units. A culture was a large unit of cultivation, generally known by its own name, that could include the tenant's homestead, and the reference in the 1332 rental of Thomas, Earl of Lancaster, to 'a culture called Roaker in Freckleton' perhaps suggests that by this date Raker Farm had already have become such a unit. The same rental also contains two references to oxgangs of land which, as we have already seen, appears to have been the measurement that determined the number of cattle each farm was allowed to graze on the marsh. At or about this same period strips were probably being consolidated into 'old earths' or small enclosed fields, and as late as 1804 two fields forming part of the Hall Cross House (Grimbaldestons) estate were still known as the nearer Old Earth and the further Old Earth.[4]

Farming in Tudor and Stuart Freckleton

From the mid-fifteenth century enclosure of open arable land, meadow and pasture began to create the privately owned hedged fields still to be seen today. Some of these newly created fields can still be identified by the names by which they became known, particularly those having the word 'hey', denoting an enclosure, as part of their name. Conversely, Mean Meadow (the word 'mean' meaning shared) situated adjacent to the Dow Brook was still a shared field until the last half of the twentieth century, even though there was no visible division within the field.

An illustration of the farming conditions in Freckleton in the mid-sixteenth century is provided by the inventory to the will of Lawrence Cowburn who died in 1563. At his death he possessed eight oxen, nine 'kine' (milk cows), two bullocks and two 'quyes' (female calves), four 'twinters' (beasts that had lived through two winters), and three calves. He also owned four ewes and four lambs. His crops included wheat, barley, beans and peas.[5] In 1605 another Lawrence Cowbourne farmed fifteen acres of arable, fifteen acres of pasture and ten acres of meadow, and in 1617 William Brown had twelve acres of arable, two acres of pasture and one acre of meadow.[6] By this time a class of dealer, known as a badger, had arisen, whose economic function was that of 'linking up the producers of a surplus in one locality with consumers in a district which was not self-sufficing'.[7] The badger went from farm to farm with pack animals to carry the grain he purchased and in 1601 Lawrence Cowburne was licensed, at the quarter sessions, as a badger and Edward Freckleton was licensed as a maltman. Richard Butler and Gregory Freckleton acted as the sureties for both men.[8]

An analysis of fifty-one inventories available at the Lancashire Record Office for the years from 1657 to 1718 confirms that both pastoral and arable farming continued throughout the period. Of the forty three 'farmers' whose occupation was stated one was described as a gentleman, twenty three as yeoman, eight as husbandman, eight as widow, two as linen webster, and one as tailor. With two exceptions the number of cattle each individual owned ranged from one to twenty, though for forty two the number was from one to eleven.

The chief crops were oats followed by barley and wheat, and forty inventories mention either stores of grain or refer to growing corn. Some of the barley grown was probably reduced to malt and used for brewing ale, and in 1718 goods in the brewhouse at Lower House Farm were valued at £3 5s. 0d. Peas and beans were also a field crop rather than a garden crop. Oxen were probably used for ploughing until the late seventeenth century and the Lancashire Longhorn – a black beast with a white tip to its tail – formed the basis of the cattle herds until the eighteenth century.

As might be expected the largest herd recorded was that of the George *[3]* Sharples, gentleman. At the time of his death in 1691, his 'goods at the Higher House' included ten bullocks, one 'seg' (a castrated bull), thirteen cows/heifers, eight twinters, nine spring calves and six sucking calves with a total value of £79. The value of his crops totalled £29 5s. 0d. and included oats in the garner, value £13, wheat at £8 and wheat upon the ground at £6, and beans and peas at £1 5s. 0d. His horses, mares and colts were valued at £20 and he also had two hogs, value £2 8s. 0d., and some poultry, value 3s. 0d.

Henry Freckleton, a yeoman, also had an above average number of cattle and in 1663 he owned three kine, two oxen, one bull, three calves, four bullocks, one heifer and two ox stirks. More typical, however, were George Marcer in 1661 with four cows and a calf, Elizabeth Freckleton in 1684 with four kine, four calves, one bullock and two heifers, and Lawrence Webster in 1706 with two cows, two stirks, four twinters and a calf. The only inventory that provides any insight about the different breeds that were favoured by the early eighteenth-century farmer in Freckleton is that of Lawrence Coulborne, who in 1716, in addition to a twinter heifer, a stirk, and two weaning calves, had one red cow, value £4, one black cow, value £3, a branded cow, value £3, and a little black cow, value £3. The reason why most farmers had beasts in various stages of growth is probably explained by the fact that for every beast slaughtered in the autumn it required five others to maintain the breeding stock of the herd.

There are also eight references to cheese presses and in 1657 Lawrence Coulbron had 'one stone for a Cheese press', whilst the press owned by William Smalley in 1685 was probably the same one recorded in the inventory of Jane, his widow, three years later. Among the more unexpected items were the 'swarm of bees', value 6s. 8d., and honey, value 2s. 0d., that appear on the inventory of James Hall in 1670.

Forty one inventories mention horses and in 1657 Lawrence Coulbron owned a total of nine horses and colts, including a blind mare. Most farmers had two or three horses and in 1693 Robert Hall owned two with a value of £11, whilst Richard Browne, who died in 1709, also had two horses, but these were valued at only £1. Sheep are mentioned in eighteen inventories with numbers ranging from the one ewe owned by Margaret Browne in 1688, to the twelve (a large flock for the Fylde) of Ralph Freckleton in 1678 and which were valued at £4. Swine are mentioned in twenty-five inventories, with   bers varying between one and three, as in the case of Edward Sharples whose one swine was valued at £1 5s. 0d. in 1717. Poultry/hens and geese are recorded in approximately one third of all inventories, and in those of Lawrence Coulbron (1657), Henry Freckleton (1663) and Richard Harrison (1675) there is specific mention of turkeys.

Of the crops, both oats and barley predominate, though only in two inventories is the actual acreage recorded. These acres will have been customary Lancashire acres which, as mentioned in chapter 2, were larger than modern statute acres, and were usually eight yards to the rood as against the statute measure of five and a half yards. In 1667 Henry Robinson had two acres of beans, two acres of barley and five acres of oats under cultivation with a total value of £20, and in 1674 Dorothy Browne had four acres of oats, value £13, and two acres of barley, value £7 6s. 8d. Three years earlier Dorothy Browne had leased from George [3] Sharples three closes in various parts of the township containing six acres of land, known as the Stony Lane, the Middle Hey and the Bank.

In 1685 Jane Smalley had barley at Preston as well as at home and also had corn growing. Nineteen inventories refer to either 'corn growing', 'corn of the ground' or 'wheat growing', whilst in 1693 John Kirkham had 'wheat to thresh' to the value of £11 – almost a quarter of the value of the entire inventory. Similarly in 1717 Edward Sharples had 'barley threshen and to thresh, twenty motts [about forty bushels] more of barley at the kill[ne], oats threshen and to thresh, wheat threshen, wheat growing on the ground', all of which was valued at £18 19*s*. 4*d*. In addition he had eight load of groats, value £6, and beans, value 13*s*. 4*d*.

Perhaps an indication of the increase in crop production in Freckleton during the late seventeenth century can be detected in the instructions given by William Brown to his executors in 1683. In his will he named his farm as 'Gaulters Tenement' which he held under a ninety nine year lease from George *[3]* Sharples dated 15 February 1682. Although the farm cannot be positively identified the field names mentioned within the lease suggest that it might have been Hall Cross House (later Grimbaldestons). The lease also included a covenant that bound William Brown 'before the end of four years next after the date thereof to erect and build four bays or Mousteads of building in and upon the premises', and it suggests that a significant increase in the amount of space needed for storage had become necessary.

At the time of making his will William Brown had already built one bay but he instructed his executors that if George *[3]* Sharples would not release the covenant then Alice, his wife, 'at her own personal cost build one bay thereof and enjoy the same', and that his brother George 'be at the cost of building the other two bays'. The inventory to his will also records that William Brown owed John Ga(u)lter, after whom the tenement or farm was presumably then named, the sum of £14.[9]

Farming tools and equipment were also listed in inventories. Sometimes the apprizers compiling the inventory combined items together and, as in the case of William Brown, recorded 'carts and wheels and all the husbandry gear – £3'. A more detailed inventory was that of Richard Harrison who in 1675 had one hay cart, two turf carts, two muck carts, four ploughs, two harrows and other husbandry gear, all of which were valued at £4 2*s*. 8*d*. In addition he also had forks, spades, pitchforks, riddles, scuttles and flails valued at a further 14*s*. 0*d*. Elizabeth Freckleton, in 1684, had carts and wheels, ploughs and harrows, horse gear and cart ropes, two stone troughs and one grindle stone, an axe, one hook, and one spade all of which had a total value of £4 9*s*. 6*d*.

In the inventory of Jane Smalley in 1685 there is a specific mention of a marl cart. This cart, and no doubt some of the carts mentioned in other inventories, would have been used for the carting and spreading of marl, and as early as 1520 there are reports that marling had doubled the value of lands in Lancashire. Marl is a soft, soapy earth found 18 inches to several feet below the surface and its value around Freckleton lay in the fact that when spread like manure its slow effervescence action would have gradually opened up the particles of clay soil, and enriched the earth for up to twenty years. Many of the 'pits' still to be seen in the township fields probably date from the days when marl was extracted.

Eighteenth-century Farming

By the middle of the eighteenth century the largest estates were probably those centered on Foldside Farm, the two Hall Cross estates, Higher House, Lower House, Naze House, Raker House and Park Nook. At this period both Foldside Farm and Park Nook were owned by branches of the Brown family. Hall Cross House (Grimbaldestons) was presumably the farm purchased by William Shaw from the estate of George [4] Sharples in 1719. William Shaw possibly also owned the farm known just as Hall Cross, which faced Hillock Lane. Higher House, following its sale by the Sharples family, appears to have passed through several ownerships, and by 1769 was owned by John Hawksworth, a London silk mercer,[10] although probably leased by the Shaw family. The owner of Naze House is unknown though the land tax returns point to it being the Coulborne family. Raker House was owned by the Freckleton family and had probably been in their possession prior to this period for some time. By 1747 Ravald House was owned by Nicholas Parker of Chancery Lane, London, and this estate subsequently passed to his nephew Robert Escolme, and then to Robert Escolme's cousin John Ravald after whom the farm is still known.[11]

The one estate about which there is ample documentary information is Lower House. Following its purchase by trustees of John Hornby (Newton Charity) in 1719 Thomas Grimbaldeston and his son Henry became the tenants, and in 1726, under the terms of the lease, most of the building 'except one bay at the south end of that part called the Hall'[12] was taken down and rebuilt. An undated but contemporary document shows that Thomas and Henry Grimbaldeston farmed forty two acres of freehold land and eighteen acres of leasehold land together with seventeen beast gate on Freckleton marsh.[13] These sixty acres were made up of nineteen fields, varying in size from one (customary) acre to five acres, together with a further five acres of crofts and orchards

around the house. Thomas Grimbaldeston would appear to have continued to farm at Lower House until the bill of complaint, described
in chapter 18, was brought against him in 1752.

An analysis of a further thirty six inventories covering the years 1719
to 1782 provides confirmation that, in general, farming practices evident
in the latter half of the previous century continued largely unchanged.
One notable addition to the traditional crops of oats, wheat, barley, peas
and beans was the potato. Lancashire was the first English county in
which the potato was grown and its first mention in Freckleton occurs
in the inventories of Richard Baine in 1724 and Robert Sanderson in
1727.

The largest herd of cattle was owned by John Hall, a husbandman
who, when he died in 1750, had fourteen beasts with a total value of
£33 17s. 6d., an amount that represented one third of the value of his
inventory. In addition to grass and corn 'upon the ground' he also had
a cheese press and fifty two cheeses. When his brother Thomas, a tanner,
died in 1758 his inventory was valued at £343 3s. 0d., an amount that
included leather, hides and bark at £65 and 'nine wooze [?] pitts' with

LANCASHIRE COW.

In 1795 Holt, in his *General View of the Agriculture of the County of Lancashire*, wrote that
'The Lancashire long-horned cattle are known all over the kingdom, and found in almost
every part of the county, the prime stock of which is bred in Fylde, whither the
purchasers from different parts of the kingdom have usually resorted, but applications
have not of late been so frequent as formerly.'

a value of £180. It is not known where Thomas carried out his tanning work, nor is it known what, if any, complementary arrangements the brothers had between themselves. Perhaps John traded in cattle in order to obtain milk for his cheeses, and sold his dry cattle to his brother, who may also have bought the dry cattle of other farmers in the township.

In 1779 a Dr Bowers conducted a survey on behalf of Christ Church, Oxford, on the valuation of tithes in the parish of Kirkham. In the course of his survey Dr Bowers visited the farms or smallholdings of twenty one tenant farmers in Freckleton who collectively had seventy two acres of oats and peas, fifty acres of wheat and twenty three acres of barley and beans under the plough with a further fifty seven acres fallow for wheat. In his comments on Freckleton he noted:

> No large holdings, judging by the corn acreage, except William Threlfall's [Lower House] 30 acres at 8yards. 21 tithe payers. Considerable quantities of wheat as well as oats, barley roughly half that of wheat, quality of the corn on the poor side. Apart from the holding of Threlfall about 10 farms had 10 to 20 acres of corn, the rest only small holdings.[14]

Although he named James Goodshaw as tithe 'tenant' it is unclear from Dr Bowers, report whether there was still a tithe barn in the township. If there was then the only clue to its possible location is contained in a deed of 1639 in which John *[2]* Sharples agreed to 'confirm and allow to George Marcer the Tythe Barn Croft and all that parcel of land belonging to John Sharples lying at the west end of a parcel of land belonging to George Marcer called the Stryke'.[15]

The poor quality of the corn referred to by Dr Bowers was almost certainly due to the farming practices described and criticised by John Holt in 1795. In his agricultural survey of Lancashire he remarked that 'in the Fylde, which, from its fertility, has been called the Granary of the county, the soil has been still worse abused. Certain fields have been kept under cultivation, it is asserted, for more than a century, without intermission.'[16] Later in the same survey he concluded that 'neither marle nor lime produces any good effects upon the exhausted lands of the Fylde, which have undergone the centennial ordeal. Upon these occasions the farm-yard dung seems to be principally wanted, to restore the oily part extracted by such succession of exhausting crops ...'[17]

Nineteenth-century Farming

An awareness of the need to restore and improve the land is evident, however, in the seven year lease, granted by the trustees of Newton Charity, to Thomas Fair of Lower House Farm on 1 December 1816. The seven year lease was a relatively new form of agreement, being an attempt by landowners to direct their tenant's farming methods, and one of the requirements in the lease granted to Thomas Fair was that 'all the Muck Manure Dung and Soil which yearly during the said term shall be produced – from the said Premises shall and will lay spread and bestow in an Husbandman like Manner upon the Lands and Grounds belonging to the said Premises'.[18]

In 1838 the tithe survey recorded 514 acres of arable land, 404 acres of meadow and 582 acres of pasture in the township, but from the 1840s there was a long and steady decrease in arable farming, with grassland increasing. Evidence of attempts to improve the breeding stock of dairy herds can be detected in the January 1864 newspaper report announcing the sale of the farming stock of John Watson of Raker, which in addition to twelve Spring calving Cows also included 'one bull stirk, and one heifer calf both of Hector and Sheriff's blood'.[19]

In 1875 the average farm size in England was 58.54 acres; in Lancashire it was 33.74 acres and 80% of the county's holdings were under 50 acres. In Freckleton the 1881 census records twenty eight farms, of which five were over 100 acres and a further three had an acreage of between fifty one and one hundred. The largest farm was Grange Farm, with an area of 551 acres, built on the land reclaimed by the Ribble Navigation Company. It was originally taken in 1866 by the Preston Farming Company on a twenty one year lease and the first farmer appears to have been George McQueen who was born in Scotland. In 1873 it was sub-let to William Allsup, for the remainder of the term at a rent of £1,653 4s. 6d. per year and in 1883 it was recorded that 'under Mr Allsup, this farm, with all its outbuildings, has become one of the best agricultural holdings in the country'.[20]

There were four other farmers with holdings of one hundred or more acres: Benjamin Raby farming 200 acres at Higher House; Richard Mason farming 160 acres at Lower House; Sarah Cartmell farming 106 acres at Hall Cross (Grimbaldestons); and John Crossfield with 100 acres at Naze Mount. John Hall farmed sixty two acres at Strike Farm and of the smaller farms Anthony Parker farmed twenty three acres at Naze House, while John Eastham farmed twenty one acres at Ravald House, the same number as Henry Fowler at Bottoms Farm.

Twentieth-century Farming

During the twentieth century there was a steady decline in the number of working farms. As early as 1926 it was being noted that 'the number of men employed on the farms is not 25% of what it was thirty years ago'.[21] Dairy farming with pigs and poultry formed the basis of the larger farms in the 1920s and 1930s, and all farms used to make cheeses as no viable market was available for excess milk. Each farm had its own cheese presses and drainer and cheese production took place on a regular basis; for example, at Bottoms Farm two cheeses of approximately 28lbs were made daily.[22] The finished product was taken to Preston cheese market every month where it was placed on straw on the ground before being sold. Cheese production gradually declined following the establishment of the Milk Marketing Board in 1933, which was a lifesaver to the small dairy farmer as the Board not only collected the milk but also guaranteed a price.[23]

It was, however, the development of the poultry industry that was the principal agricultural feature of the inter war years. This industry effectively began in 1910 when William Segar Hodgson made a gift of twenty six acres of land in Pool (Bush) Lane and as the result of an idea made by John Cardwell, 'who can thus claim to be the father of the industry',[24] the parish council decided to sub-let twenty three acres into plots for use as poultry allotments. In 1926 the parish council rented another field of seven and a half acres which provided a further eight allotments, and by 1927 the number of laying hens kept by these thirty tenants was estimated at 6000. A similar number were kept by the general farmers which, together with the 29,000 kept by the small-holders, meant that the total stock amounted to some 41,000 laying hens producing over four million eggs in one year. Land for the keeping of poultry continued to be in demand and in 1932 the parish council decided to write to several landowners in the village to see if they would sell or rent land for the purpose of poultry farming.[25]

During World War II land in the township was compulsory purchased and every farm was required to put a percentage to arable production, principally wheat and oats. Although at the onset of the twenty first century the number of working farms in the township was less than ten, modern farming practices have resulted in the establishment of pedigree cattle herds at both Lower House Farm and Naze Farm. At Lower House Farm, which when purchased by Newton Charity in 1719 comprised sixty acres, the acreage has increased threefold to 200 acres, and since 1966 an accredited herd of Friesian dairy cattle, all bred on the farm, has been increased from two hundred and fifty to almost four hundred.[26] It is on lands which still retain evidence of the ridge and furrow farming of a 1000 years ago that these cattle are now grazed.

Lower House Farm, 2000. Since 1966 an accredited herd of Friesian dairy cattle, all bred at the farm, has been increased from two hundred and fifty to almost four hundred.

Gattle Gate Sale, 1882. From at least the late seventeenth century cattle (marsh) gates have been bought and sold, and bequeathed in wills. The practice continues to the present day and there is still an annual marsh gate owners' meeting.

CATTLE GATES.

FRECKLETON MARSH.

TO BE SOLD

BY AUCTION, BY

MR. ROBERT CROSS,

At the house of the Coach and Horses Inn, in Freckleton, near Kirkham, on

TUESDAY, 16TH DAY OF SEPTEMBER, 1884

At Three o'clock in the Afternoon prompt, subject to the printed public Conditions of Sale of the Preston Law Society, and the Vendors' special conditions.

LOT 1. TWO

CATTLE OR BEAST GATES

ON FRECKLETON MARSH.

LOT 2.

Two other Beast or Cattle Gates.

LOT 3.

Two other Beast or Cattle Gates.

LOT 4.

Two other Beast or Cattle Gates.

LOT 5.

Two other Beast or Cattle Gates.

For further information apply to the AUCTIONEER, Kirkham; or to

Messrs. TURNER and SON,

Solicitors, Fox Street, Preston.

EDWARD AMBLER and SON, Printers, 186, Lancaster Road, Preston.

CHAPTER 22

Linen and Cotton

The Tudor and Stuart Period

From the growing of flax to the production of coarse linen the linen trade was an important part of the domestic industry in Freckleton from at least the sixteenth century. Evidence of the production of cloth in the township is contained in the inventory of Lawrence Cowburn which records that when he died in 1563 he left three pecks of linseed and linen yarn, together with fourteen yards of white cloth (linen) and twenty yards of canvas cloth.[1]

Some idea of the extent of the trade that had already been established by the early seventeenth century can be gained from the evidence of John Sharples of Ribby who, in 1609, petitioned the vice chancellor of the County Palatine of Lancaster.[2] In his petition John Sharples stated that he, together with Lawrence Cowborne of Freckleton and Richard Sharples of Heapey, had agreed four years earlier to trade and travel together 'by buying and selling of linnencloth and other wares and merchandizes', and to divide their credits equally between themselves.

John Sharples, however, considered that he had been cheated of his share of the profits, justifying his complaint by stating that because Richard Sharples had the most experience in buying and selling linen cloth 'the said stocks, with the increase thereof which was gained by two journies which your suppliant & the said Lawrence Cowborne made to London, being five marks (a mark was worth 13s. 4d.) a journey, was all delivered to the said Richard Sharples. Sithence which time, the said Richard Sharples hath made divers & sundry journies to London, & hath gained there by great sums of money'. He further stated that despite requesting 'in very gentle and courteous manner' his share of the profits both Richard Sharples and Lawrence Cowborne not only delayed 'with many fair words' but appeared to have no intention of making any payment. In the circumstances John Sharples requested the vice chancellor to issue a subpoena ordering either or both Richard Sharples and Lawrence Cowborne to appear in court to answer the charge against them.

Although the outcome of the case is not known it nevertheless does appear to provide evidence of locally produced linen being sold on the

London market. If this was so, presumably the linen was transported by packhorse. In the will of (a third) Lawrence Coulbron, who died in 1657, there is mention of 'wantoes' (ropes for tying items onto a packhorse), five yards of cloth and both flax and canvas yarn. The inventory of Richard Harrison, who died in 1675, also listed wantoes, whilst the inventory of William Harrison, who died the same year, includes a collar of bells which presumably was for placing around the neck of the leading pack horse.

Both flax and hemp were grown by the farmers in the township and in a deed dated 1659 one of the Strike fields was called the Blue Strike, presumably obtaining its name from the blue of the flax flower grown there. The inventory to the will of Henry Robinson in 1667 records 'hemp growing on the ground', whilst the inventory of William Brown in 1724 records 'flax on the ground'. Harvested in late July the flax was pulled up by its root and, in order to soften the tough outside of the stem, was first *retted* by being soaked in pools of slow running water for up to two weeks before being spread out to dry in the sun for four or five days.

A similar process was also carried out with hemp, used in the production of coarser cloths and in ropemaking, which again needed the fibres to be released from the hard woody stem. When dry the flax was taken to be broken, or heckled, a process that involved beating the fibrous woody stem using various methods including 'scutching'. Finally a heckle was used to separate and clean the fibres before combing and carding them into alignment ready for the spinner, who drew and twisted the fibres using a spindle or spinning wheel. Only after washing and bleaching could the finished yarn be passed to the weaver.

Between the years 1657 and 1726 there are references to textiles in some forty one Freckleton inventories. Amongst those who either relied upon or supplemented their income from the linen trade were Agnes Brown, a widow who died in 1661, and whose inventory included linen, spinning wheel, hemp and a heckle, whilst William Brown in 1694 left weaving gear and linen. The earliest will in which the testator is specifically described as a linen webster (weaver) is Henry Meareley (Muerley) who died in 1680. He left just £12 4s. 7d., including £1 0s. 6d. for 'loomes and gear', whilst 10s. 11d. was 'owing to him of work'. The inventory totalled £12 4s. 7d., of which £11 15s. 8d. was noted 'debts and funeral expences'.[3]

In 1658 John Freckleton bequeathed a pair of looms to his nephew Andrew Freckleton, adding that it was his will and mind that Agnes, his wife, 'shall maintain and bring up ye said Andrew at the trade of a linen webster until he shall attain the full age of eighteen years'. Provided Andrew was prepared to be governed by Agnes and Henry Robinson and John Sharples he was to have 'meat drink lodging and apparrell' during his apprenticeship.[4] As we saw earlier Andrew made the most of the opportunity given him by his uncle and when he died in 1709 he was one of the wealthiest men in Freckleton.

One of the last inventories to provide evidence of domestic textile production is that of John Hall who, on his death in 1750 left, in addition to his other household goods, cattle and crops, two spinning wheels, twenty two yards of cloth, fifteen hasps of yarn and fifteen pounds of flax.

The Flax Industry, 1700–1800, and the Mayor Family

From the mid-seventeenth century there was a growing demand for sailcloth due to the increased number of British-built ships. In 1712 the government imposed a duty on imported sailcloth and following further legislation in 1736 all English ships were required to carry a full set of English-made sails. In Kirkham, where there was a population skilled in flax dressing, groups of merchants such as the Hornby, Shepherd, Langton and Birley families had found it increasingly profitable, by the middle of the eighteenth century, to import flax from the Baltic and put it out to the local flax dressers, spinners and weavers for the manufacture of coarse linen canvas suitable for sailcloth. Whilst the development and progress of the flax industry in Kirkham is well documented its origins in Freckleton are more difficult to identify.

In the Kirkham marriage registers from 1755 to 1767 only two Freckleton men were described as flax dressers, namely Ishmael Salisbury, and Edward Mayor, who married Jane Sharples of Wharles in 1764. Edward was the son of Thomas Mayor and Ann Swarbreck and was baptised in 1736. On the evidence of the recurring use of the same first names it would seem that the ancestors of the branch of the Mayor family that was to become so prominent in Freckleton had been settled in the township of Hutton since at least the early seventeenth century. Their association with Freckleton appears to have begun when Thomas Mayor married Ann Swarbreck, the daughter of Edward Swarbreck, the last tenant at Lower House Farm before its sale, by the Sharples family, to Newton Charity.

By the end of the eighteenth century the Mayor family were the pre-eminent family in Freckleton and, although the absence of any

The Mayor family first appear in township records in the early eighteenth century. By the end of the century the families of John Mayor and Edward Mayor were arguably the most influential in Freckleton and were to remain so until the mid-nineteenth century. This abridged family tree shows the relationship between those most involved with township affairs.

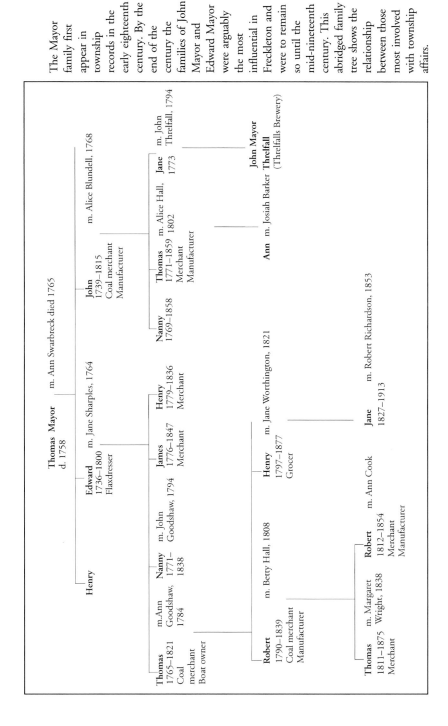

Thomas **Mayor**   m. Ann Swarbreck died 1765
d. 1758

Henry

Edward   m. Jane Sharples, 1764
1736–1800
Flaxdresser

John   m. Alice Blundell, 1768
1739–1815
Coal merchant
Manufacturer

Thomas   m.Ann Goodshaw, 1784
1765–1821
Coal merchant
Boat owner

Nanny   m. John Goodshaw, 1794
1771–1838

James
1776–1847
Merchant

Henry
1779–1836
Merchant

Nanny
1769–1858

Thomas   m. Alice Hall, 1802
1771–1859
Merchant
Manufacturer

Jane   m. John Threlfall, 1794
1773

Ann   m. Josiah Barker Threlfall
(Threlfalls Brewery)

John Mayor

Robert   m. Betty Hall, 1808
1790–1839
Coal merchant
Manufacturer

Henry   m. Jane Worthington, 1821
1797–1877
Grocer

Robert   m. Ann Cook
1812–1854
Merchant
Manufacturer

Jane   m. Robert Richardson, 1853
1827–1913

Thomas   m. Margaret Wright, 1838
1811–1875
Merchant

known family or business papers makes it difficult to follow their commercial progress, the foundations of their success seem to have been already laid by as early as 1748. In that year Henry Mayor, brother of Edward, took a 78 year lease on a property in Freckleton called Lorimers where his father Thomas was already the occupant. Due to a lack of continuity in the deeds this property cannot now be positively identified but it almost certainly stood on the site of Mount House in Preston Old Road. In 1787 John Mayor, another brother of Henry and Edward, is named as the occupant of Lorimers[5] and in the 1830 Township Survey[6] the property is described as 'New House on Lorimers' in the joint ownership of (the late) John, Thomas and Nanny Mayor. It is probable that the initials IM (I = J), which form part of the 1793 datestone still visible on the rear wall of Mount House, relate to the year in which John Mayor rebuilt the property.

Edward Mayor died in 1800. In his will, where he describes himself as a yeoman, he refers to his two dwellinghouses, together with a third held in common with his brother John, but unfortunately does not name or indicate the location of any of them. Apart from a reference to (weaving) shops being attached to one of these properties there is no other mention in his will of anything to do with the linen trade, and consequently it is not possible to determine the role he played in helping to establish the commercial success of the family, of which his brother John was the dominant force.

John Mayor & Co.

John Mayor was born 1738–39 and at the time of his marriage to Alice Blundel of Croston in 1768 he was described as a husbandman. It is probable that he began to trade by acting as a middleman or putter out to the handloom weavers, who then returned the finished cloth to him to be marketed. In addition to 'Lorimers' he may also have owned or leased other premises in Freckleton, but if so it is not until 1788 that there is any evidence of where these were situated.

In that year John Mayor purchased from William Coulborn six messuages off Kirkham Road in the area now known as Spring Gardens but in the nineteenth century known as Bedlam. Perhaps of greater significance is that the deed of conveyance refers to an earlier deed, now lost, that described the six messuages as formerly being 'All that Messuage or dwelling house with the Baukhouse Barn Cottage Shops and other Outbuildings'.[7] The presence of a baukhouse (bowkhouse) where

In 1788 John Mayor purchased from William Coulborn six messuages off Kirkham Road in the area now known as Spring Gardens, but formerly known as Bedlam. From information contained in the property deeds there is evidence of linen production and of a bowkhouse where bleaching would have taken place.

bleaching would take place and (weaving) shops implies that linen weaving was already being carried out on the site and the noise generated by the various processes is presumably the reason why the area became known as Bedlam. These properties remained in the ownership of the Mayor family until the family bankruptcy of 1830.

The first flax factory in Freckleton was almost certainly the building which stood on the site of the present Sports & Social Club, in Preston Old Road. Although it is not possible to positively identify the original owner, evidence again points to it being John Mayor, who probably commenced production there sometime at the end of the eighteenth century or beginning of the nineteenth century. Throughout most of the nineteenth century the building was invariably called the old factory to distinguish it from the new factory (later named Balderstone Mill) which was built sometime prior to 1830. In that year production was still being carried on at the old factory, as the township survey[8] records 'Factory and Heckling shop' and 'New Factory & Starchhouse' both of which were owned by (the late) John, Thomas & Nanny Mayor. Even in 1868, despite no longer being used for either linen or cotton manufacture, the compilers of the township valuation still described it as 'the Old Factory'.

As we will see in the next chapter John Mayor also had commercial interests in the local coal trade and was part owner in at least seven vessels built at Freckleton between 1786 and 1810, in which sailcloth and sacking made by his company was trans-shipped to Liverpool. It is possible that John Mayor had contracts for sailcloth with the Royal Navy, as did the Kirkham company of Langton Birley, but the absence of documentation means this assumption cannot be confirmed. As we saw earlier, in addition to his shipping interests John Mayor had also been involved in the remaking of the marsh road, and the Commercial Directory of Preston published in 1815 records that John Mayor & Son, Sail Cloth Manufacturers of Freckleton 'come to the Castle Inn [Market Place] Preston every Saturday'.

On his death in 1815 he gave all his messuages in Freckleton to his son Thomas, with the exception of his dwellinghouse named as 'Rigby's' (now the site of Rigby Close and named after the family who resided there in the early eighteenth century) which he rebuilt in 1805, and left to his daughter Nanny. He had presumably removed from Lorimers in 1805 and it then appears to have been occupied by his son, Thomas. Amongst other bequests in his will there is a legacy of £1,500 to his daughter Jane, the wife of John Threlfall of Liverpool, whose son John Mayor Threlfall was to become the driving force behind the establishment of Threlfalls Brewery, which in due course became part of Whitbread plc. John Mayor named his son Thomas as one of his executors, but it is his choice of his two other executors that is perhaps the most significant; in naming Thomas and William Hornby of Kirkham (who traded with their brother as J. T. & W. Hornby) he had clearly become closely associated with two of the most influential and successful sailcloth manufacturers in the district.

After his death the company continued to trade under the name of John Mayor & Co. and as late as 1821 was still importing flax from the Baltic.[9] The company continued to operate until 1830 when Thomas Mayor was declared bankrupt following his inability to repay a £2,000 loan taken out in 1825 and, as we will see shortly, the Mayor family interests were purchased by Robert Mayor the son of Thomas' cousin.

Sailcloth and Sacking Manufacture

In 1824–25, in addition to the company of John Mayor Son & Co., four other men were recorded as sailcloth manufacturers in Freckleton:

John Baker, James Mayor, Thomas Mayor, and George Segar, together with John Harrison who was described as a sailmaker.[10]

John Baker was a book-keeper to the Goodshaw family. In 1823 he built Stanley House in Preston Old Road (the property is discussed in more detail in chapter 24), and although clearly a successful man nothing more is known of his involvement in sailcloth manufacture. He died in 1825, aged 32. James Mayor was the son of Edward Mayor and it is unclear why he and Thomas are listed separately. It implies that they owned their own companies in addition to the company of John Mayor & Son which Thomas, and possibly James (his cousin), had inherited. It is, however, more likely that their names appear in the directory as 'individuals' and there can be no doubt of their close business association as both men were declared bankrupt in 1830.

The flax warehouse of George (Whiteside) Segar was situated in Higher (Kirkham) Road at Hall Cross, and in addition to their Freckleton interests 'Messrs Segar & Co. also had a manufactory for sacking and sailcloth'[11] in Kirkham. George Segar built and resided at Freckleton Cottage near to his Freckleton warehouse and on his death in 1834 gave

Cottages, Kirkham Road. Originally one dwelling it was not divided into four cottages until the 1840s. In 1841 it was occupied by Joseph Stuart, a sacking weaver, his wife and five children. The date of the photograph is not known but the family standing outside (the then) 52 Kirkham Road may have been that of Richard Porter who resided there in 1910. The cottages were demolished c.1964 when the present bungalow, Ash Nook, was built on the site.

Old Cottages, Freckleton.

two cottages and weaving shops in Freckleton to his sister, Ann Hodgson. It was from this family that William Segar Hodgson, one of Freckleton's most generous benefactors, was descended. In addition, although not listed in the directory, John Birley of Kirkham also owned cottages and weaving shops in Strike Lane which he had purchased from the Langton family in 1803, and which in 1841 were still occupied by sacking weavers.

The employment opportunities created by the need for such large quantities of sailcloth and sacking resulted in a rapid increase in the population of Freckleton during the early nineteenth century. By 1841 the new factory was providing increasing levels of employment, but even so there were still 75 sacking handloom weavers, together with 12 sack makers and 18 cotton handloom weavers, at work in the village. In 1851 there were 107 individuals earning their living as handloom weavers, of whom fifty five were engaged in the production of sacking, fifty in weaving cotton, one combining sacking and cotton and one producing canvas. As part of the 1861 Freckleton census is missing it is not possible to obtain an exact picture but there were still at least twenty three handloom weavers at work in the village, although by 1871 not one remained.

Ropemaking

Although it is possible that small scale ropemaking had been carried out earlier, the development of the industry in Freckleton no doubt coincided with the commencement of commercial shipbuilding in the late eighteenth century. As we saw earlier in this chapter hemp was being grown in the township as early as the mid-seventeenth century but it is not until 1799, when James Tomlinson was apprenticed to John Whittle, a local twinespinner and heckler, that there is any suggestion of the trade of ropemaking. The first men who can be specifically identified as ropemakers are James Grayson, Peter Rigby and Marsden Rigby, the stepson and two sons of Robert Marsden Rigby, who were so described on the 1823 militia list. As we saw in chapter 10 Robert Marsden Rigby, then a widower and originally from the parish of Ormskirk, married Elizabeth Grayson (formerly Tomlinson), a widow, in 1798. On the occasion of his first marriage in 1789 he was described as a ropemaker and he clearly brought his ropemaking expertise to Freckleton and taught his sons and stepson their trade.

Ropers were usually self employed and worked with other family members. The ropemaking process involved the 'roper' walking backwards

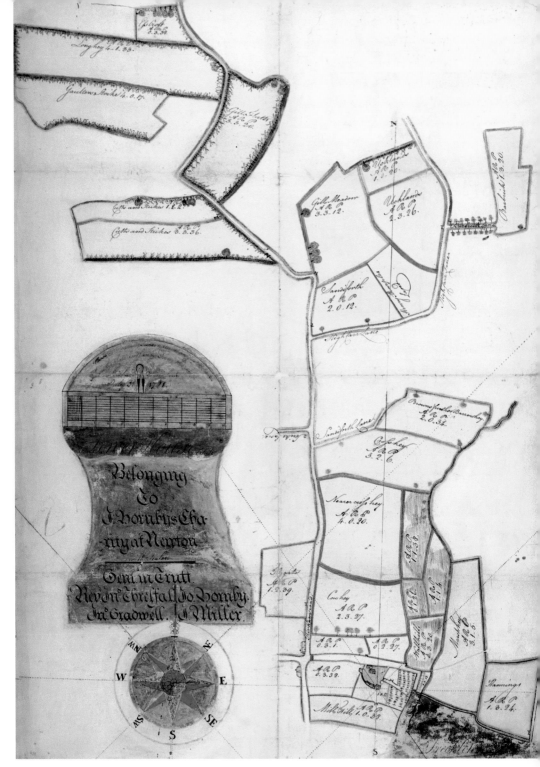

PLATE I. A map of Lower House estate made by the then schoolmaster of Newton School, for which he received £2 2s. 0d. Several of the field names will have been known to earlier generations of farmers. Note that Higher Carr Lane has now been corruupted to 'the eeka' (the high carr).

(Courtesy of Lancashire Record Office – DDNw, Box 20)

PLATE 2. Of all the vessels built at Freckleton it is perhaps the *Welcome*, an 188-foot, three-masted round-sterned schooner, launched in 1885, that is now the most fondly remembered.

PLATE 3. The opening of Wesleyan Methodist Church. This photograph is noted on the reverse 'Opening of the Present Chapel' and presumably was therefore taken in September 1885. Among those present were members of the Brown, Coulborn, Hall, Rawstrone, Rigby and Wignall families.

PLATE 4. Mount House (94 Preston Old Road). The datestone set in the building suggests that it was rebuilt in 1793. It is, however, almost certainly the site of the dwelling known in the eighteenth century as 'Lorimers' and occupied in the early seventeenth century by members of the Freckleton family.

PLATE 5. The Headless Cross marked part of the course of the northern boundary with Kirkham.

PLATE 6. Grove House. The owner and occupant in 1838 was Robert Mayor who at the time was the principal employer in the township and owner of the new [Balderstone] factory. During the next fifty years the Mayor family retained their interest in the property and in 1184 the house was conveyed to Annie Wignall (née Wright), the grand-daughter of Robert Mayor. Grove House remained in the ownership of the Wignall family until 1995.

PLATE 7. Ravald House. On 18 November 1598 William, earl of Derby leased to Richard Harrison an estate in Freckleton. The grandson of Richard Harrison sold the estate in 1675 and in 1756 it passed, through inheritance, to John Ravald, the younger son of a Preston grocer.

PLATE 8. The support stone for the main cog wheel from the watermill which now forms the centrepiece of the flower bed adjacent to the marsh gate entrance.

PLATE 9 (*right*). The first mention of a friendly society in Freckleton occurs in 1803. However, nothing is known about it or its successors until a tent [society] of the Independent Order of Rechabites was formed in 1873/74. There are still individual members of the society residing in Freckleton.

PLATE 10. Freckleton Brass Band, 1997. Following the appointment of Paul Dalton as the resident principal conductor the band has achieved considerable success and in 1997–98 were National First Section Champions.

The ropewalk of Henry James Hall. The location is now the garden of 54a Preston Old Road.

down the rope walk, which may have been several hundred feet long, paying out the fibres with one hand from a supply carried round his waist and supporting the yarn with the other. At the start of the ropewalk a machine was rotated by hand twisting the various fibres into strands and the strands into rope. The location of at least five rope walks in Freckleton are known. The four shown on the 1898 Ordnance Survey Map were: (1) west from Park Nook Farm through the surviving stile on Naze Lane and following the route of present day Green Lane towards Further Ends Farm; (2) north of Park Nook Farm leading towards present-day Summit Drive; (3) east from the rear of the Coach & Horses almost to Croft Butts Lane; (4) running parallel to Croft Butts Lane and present-day

Ropemaking. Hemp was being grown in the township as early as the mid-seventeenth century but it was probably the establishment of the port in the mid-eighteenth century that generated even greater demand for rope. The trade survived until the early twentieth century. In this picture we see Henry James Hall (right), together with one of his employees, at the machine which spun the various fibres into strands and then into rope.

Green Lane. A further ropewalk is known to have existed in what is now the front garden of 54a Preston Old Road.

In 1841 James Grayson was still working as a roper and living at Park Nook Farm where his mother Betty Rigby was head of the household. Present with them was William Councill who was a ropers apprentice. Peter, Marsden and Thomas Rigby, although no longer at Park Nook Farm, were still continuing their father's trade. William Coulburn in Bunker Street was another roper, as were Henry, George and John Hall. Ten years later approximately twenty five men were at work in the industry, with brothers Peter and Thomas Rigby between them employing ten men and two apprentices. In addition Robert and Thomas Mayor were also described as rope manufacturers but whether they contracted out their work or had their own ropewalk is not clear. Wheel turning was an essential part of ropemaking and where the sons of ropers often learnt their skills; in 1851 John and Henry, the sons of William Coulburn, aged ten and eight respectively, were both described as wheel turners.

By 1881, however, the decline of the ropemaking industry was evident and only eight ropemakers, one twinespinner and one wheel turner were recorded in the census of that year. By 1898 only John Coulburn, Thomas Seed, Robert Hall and William Henry Hall, whose son Henry James Hall recalled rope being taken across the River Ribble on a hand cart to sell to Tarleton farmers as cow ties,[12] were named as rope or twine makers.[13] John Coulburn was resident at Park Nook Farm from where almost a century earlier the Grayson and Rigby families had also plied their trade. By the early twentieth century the demand for locally produced rope had all but ended and ropemaking finally ceased as a trade in Freckleton.

The New Factory/Balderstone Mill

The first reference to the factory that was initially known as the new factory, but which was later named Balderstone Mill, is in the Lancashire Directory for 1828. In its brief description of Freckleton the directory notes that 'The large sacking and sailcloth manufactory of Messrs Mayor & Co. is in this township'. Exactly when and by whom the factory was built is not known, but as in 1830 the premises are recorded as being in the ownership of the (the late) John, Thomas and Nanny Mayor it is almost certain that the builder was John Mayor. When Thomas was declared bankrupt his estate was put up for sale at public auction and in 1832 Robert Mayor became the purchaser of 'various properties'.

Although there was no specific reference to the sacking and sailcloth manufactory it seems certain that new factory was one of the properties purchased by Robert, as in his will dated 1839 he gave 'all my flax spinning Mill or factory and close of Land called Long Raker or Brickfield on part of which the said Mill is erected situate in Freckleton together with the buildings steam engine going gear fixtures machinery and utensils'[14] to Elizabeth, his wife, Edward, his brother, and Thomas and Robert, his sons. The census of 1841 gives the occupation of both the sons as linen manufacturer, though as subsequent events reveal it was Robert who was to be the driving force.

In 1851 Thomas was named as a sail and sacking manufacturer, whilst Robert was described as a sail cloth manufacturer and depot owner, employing 105 men, 40 women, 30 boys and 26 girls. It is doubtful as to whether all these people were employed in the new factory because in the same year the Mannex Directory noted: 'There is likewise in Freckleton an extensive sailcloth, sacking, and rope manufactory belonging to

STATEMENT OF

Money Received and Distributed to the Poor, by the Freckleton Relief Committee, in the Year 1862 and 1863.

1862,	*Payments.*	£.	s.	d.
Novr. 26th,	Relief to 164 Cases, ...	6	3	0
Decr. 3rd,	Do. 206 do.	8	5	3
	Expenses, ...		11	0
Decr. 10th.	Relief to 236 Cases, ...	11	18	6
	Expenses, ...		12	6
Decr. 17th,	Relief to 223 Cases, ...	14	0	6½
... 23rd,	Do. 251 do.	55	8	2
.... 31st,	Do. 259 do.	16	6	10
1863.				
Jany. 2nd,	Bills for Clothing.	32	13	8
.... 7th,	Relief to 294 Cases, ...	18	18	0
... 9th,	Paid for 23 pairs of Clogs,	2	8	3
... 14th,	Relief to 291 Cases, ...	19	6	8
.... 21st,	Do. 266 do.	18	0	7
.... 28th,	Do. 263 do	15	15	7
	Paid for Clogs, ...	8	2	10
	Expenses, ...		8	6
Feby. 4th,	Relief to 242 Cases, ...	14	10	2½
.... 11th,	Do. 191 do. ...	10	17	6¼
... 18th,	Do, 167 do. ...	8	5	0½
	Paid for Clogs, ...	4	8	5
	Expenses, ...	3	7	1½
.... 25th,	Relief to 143 Cases, ...	6	19	3
	Flour, ...		13	2
	Expenses, ...		3	9
March 4th,	Relief to 83 Cases	3	9	2
	Flour, ...		14	2
.... 11th,	Relief to 92 Cases, ...	4	1	1
.... 18th,	Do. 93 do.	3	15	7
.... 25th,	Do. 95 do.	4	0	6
April 1st,	Expenses, ...	3	4	10
	New South Wales Grant, to use of School,	6	0	0
.... 1st,	Relief to 82 Cases, ...	3	7	4
Novr. 18th,	Do. 67 do.	9	4	0
.... 25th,	Do. 87 do. ...	9	0	0
	Expenses, ...		14	6
Decr. 2nd,	Relief to 85 Cases, ...	7	3	8
... 9th,	Do. 75 do.	5	16	6
	Expenses, ...	1	17	0
.... 16th,	Relief to 52 Cases, ...	4	12	6
... 23rd,	Do. 60 do, ...	5	10	6
.... 30th,	Do. 61 do.	3	17	4
	Expenses, ... 14 3; Stamps, &c. .... 5 0; Printing Statement, ... 8 0	1	7	3
	In Treasurer's Hands, £ 2 1 9; In Preston Bank,.. ... 3 6 0	5	7	9
	TOTAL,..	£ 361	8	0½

1862,	*Receipts.*	£.	s.	d.
Novr. 26th,	Local Subscriptions.	4	19	6
.... 26th,	Miss Otter, ...	5	0	0
Decr. 3rd,	Miss Lemon, ...	2	0	0
.... 3rd,	Miss Hornby, ...	2	0	0
.... 4th	Colonel Clifton, ...	5	0	0
.... 4th,	Manchester Cen. Commit.	40	0	0
.... 6th,	E. C. Milne, Esq.	10	0	0
.... 8th,	Mansion House, ...	50	0	0
.... 17th,	Manchester Cen. Commit,	20	0	0
.... 17th,	T. Shawe, Esq.	1	0	0
.... 17th,	Mr Crossfield, ...	1	1	0
.... 23rd,	Mansion House, ...	50	0	0
.... 23rd,	Christmas Dinner for Poor,	10	0	0
.... 25th,	Manchester Cen Commit.	40	0	0
1863,				
Jany. 19th,	Mansion House, ...	50	0	0
Feby. 9th,	Grant for School, from New South Wales Fund	6	0	0
.... 12th,	Concert at Lytham, per Mrs. Milne,	30	4	0
.... 12th,	966 lbs Flour, Sold to the Poor,	5	7	6
Mar. 18th,	996 lbs Flour, Sold to the Poor,	5	7	2
.... 30th,	107¼ Bacon, Do.	1	15	8
.... 30th,	28 lbs Biscuits, ...		7	0
April 30th,	554½ Flour, ...	3	1	7
	Note.—For the last few Weeks Relief was granted partly from the Funds, and the rest in Flour, amounting to	6	4	7½
Novr. 29th,	Miss Hornby, ...	2	0	0
.... 30th,	Mansion House, ...	10	0	0
	TOTAL,..	361	8	0½

☞ *The Committee Discontinued giving Relief in April, 1863, and Resumed it in November.*

Mem.

1862,

Decr. 17th, Two Packages of Clothing from the Lord Mayor's Committee.
Do. Two Packages of Clothing from Repton, (per Rev. Walter Scott)
... 31st. Three Packages of Clothing from the Lord Mayor's Committee.

1863,

Feby. 13th, Three Barrels of Flour from the Mansion Cen. Committee, (thro. George Griswold)
.... 25th, Ten Do Do. Do. Do.
Do. A Parcel of Children's beautiful Clothes from Hayton Park, Prescot, (per Rev. Walter Scott.)
.... 28th, Three Barrels of Flour and one Box of Bacon from "New York Cen. Relief Committee."

WALTER SCOTT, ... Chairman.
JOHN WATSON, ... Treasurer.
CHARLES EVERSON, .. Secretary.

January 8th, 1864

E. WILLIAMSON, PRINTER, FYLDE OFFICE, POULTON STREET, KIRKHAM.

Sometime between 1858 and 1861 Henry Hall of Preston bought the 'new' factory. Within a few years, however, the operatives found themselves in desperate circumstances due to the effects of the Lancashire cotton famine. This contemporary poster shows how money received from relief commitees was distributed amongst the unemployed. (*Courtesy of Lancashire Record Office – DDX 1482/20*)

Balderstone Mill – 1892. When the Mayor family built the factory in the 1820s, for the manufacture of sacking and sailcloth, the building was known as the 'new' factory. It did not acquire the name Balderstone until after its purchase by William Sowerbutts in 1866. This pen and ink drawing was made by Edwin Beattie, the Preston artist, in 1892. (*Courtesy of Lancashire Evening Post*)

Messrs Thomas & Robert Mayor of the firm Robert Mayor & Sons, at which 120 hands are constantly employed. The works are put in motion by steam power equal to that of 25 horses'.

In 1854 Robert died at the relatively young age of 42. In his will, made the previous year, he describes his flax spinning mill, owned jointly with his brother Thomas, in the same manner as had his father only fifteen years earlier, adding that his half share was to be first offered for sale to his brother, but if the offer was declined the half share was to form part of his residuary estate. The absence of any relevant documents covering the years 1854 to 1861 prevents a full understanding of events during that period but it would seem that shortly after the proving of Robert's will in 1858 the new factory was sold to Henry Hall of Preston.

The 1861 census records Henry Hall living in Bunker Street, together with his wife Elizabeth (née Norcross), his son James and daughter in law Alice (née Flintoff). Henry Hall, who had been born at Ribchester in 1817, was described as a cotton manufacturer, employing 40 men.

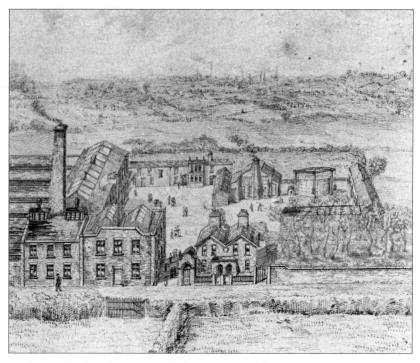

Detail from drawing of Balderstone Mill, as seen on previous page.

Also living in Bunker Street were Thomas Flintoff, a cotton manufacturer, and George Norcross, born at Ribchester, an overlooker at the cotton mill. It would appear therefore that the new factory had been purchased by Henry Hall sometime between 1858 and 1861, possibly with Thomas Flintoff as a junior partner. The change of ownership seems to have resulted in a change to cotton production and the 1861 census return records both cotton weavers and factory cotton weavers, but there are no entries for linen weavers.

It was, however, a particularly inopportune time to have invested in a cotton mill as by 1862 Lancashire was in the throes of the cotton famine, brought about by earlier over production and the American Civil War, when the import of raw cotton from the Southern States ceased. By November 1862 it was reported that:

> The distress has become so great, in consequence of the low wages of the operatives, in the little town of Freckleton, that it has been found necessary to form a committee, in order that they may, by their united exertions, endeavour to mitigate that distress. The committee met on Wednesday

evening last; investigated, for the first time, thirty six cases, comprising 152 individuals, and assisted them to the amount of £5 14s. 0d.; but as the committee, after affording this relief, have but £9 5s. 6d. in hand, they ask for the assisstance of the benevolent public to help them forward in their good work.

Donations, we are informed, will be thankfully received by the Rev. Walter Scott, Mr John Watson, or Mr Everson, Freckleton'.[15]

On 13 December 1862 it was reported that:

The Distress at Freckleton continues. The local relief committee have had a liberal response to their appeal, having received, in addition to local subscriptions, £50 from the Mansion House Committee, and £40 from the Manchester Relief Committee. The subscriptions raised in the neighbourhood amount to about £29. The committee have on their books upwards of 200 persons [the population of Freckleton in 1861 was 879], whom they relieve at the rate of 9½d. per head per week.[16]

Two and a half weeks later a more comforting note was sounded when it was reported that:

The Freckleton funds have so much increased from grants from the Mansion House Committee, from the Manchester Central Fund, and from local donations, that the committee were enabled to distribute more liberally to the poor, on Tuesday last, than they have before done. They gave relief to 251 individuals, at a cost of £12 11s. 4d.; also a Christmas dinner, at a cost of £9 3s. 5½d.; and three cwt of coals to each family, at a cost of £5 5s. 7½d., amounting in the whole to £27.

The committee intend also distributing this week a hundred blankets, at a cost of £27 1s. 8d. together with clothing, etc., kindly sent by the Bridewell Committee.

The chairman, last week, divided amongst the poor the contents of four packages, sent to him from the same source, together with three bales sent from private friends.[17]

A statement prepared by by the Freckleton Relief Committee shows that from November 1862 to November 1863 £361 8s. 0½d. was received from both individuals and relief committees, principally from the (London) Mansion House appeal which donated £160, and the Manchester Central Committee which donated £100. Other donations included £30 4s. 0d. from a 'Concert at Lytham per Mrs Milne'; 'A parcel of Children's beautiful Clothes from Hayton Park, Prescot, per Rev. Walter Scott'; and 'Three Barrels of Flour and one Box of Bacon from New York Central Relief Committee'.[18]

Relief was distributed to a maximum 294 'cases' on 7 January 1863, thereafter gradually reducing to 82 'cases' by 1 April. During April it was noted that 'For the last few Weeks relief was granted partly from Funds and the rest in Flour'. Relief was then discontinued until 18 November when 82 'cases' were assisted and the last entry on 30 December 1863 records that relief was given to 61 'cases'.

There is no mention of the role played by Henry Hall during these desperate days and it appears that he had to seek financial assistance in order to retain ownership of his factory. His problems were compounded in January 1864 when his son James died aged only 24, and in April the same year, possibly under pressure from the Preston Banking Co., the mortgagees, he sold the factory to Jonathan Gaukrodger. Henry Hall continued to live in Freckleton until his death in 1895 and for many years was the owner of the shop in Bunker Street, adjacent to the Coal Hill.

Jonathan Gaukrodger owned the new factory for only two years and in 1866 he sold to William Sowerbutts and his son Henry Eli Sowerbutts. An account of the sale made some thirteen years later records that 'the mill which contained 160 looms was, we believe, bought as an investment

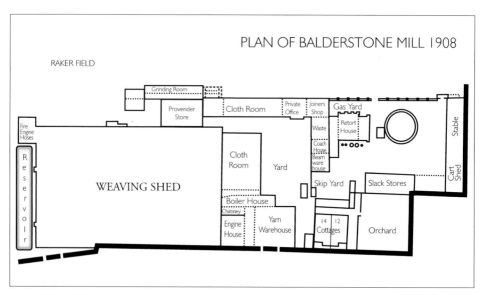

The only known surviving plan of Balderstone Mill showing the layout of the building at the time of its purchase by John Bibby. The plan forms part of the property deeds of 32 Lytham Road, one of the two surviving houses formerly attached to the mill, and this is an example of historical information contained in modern deeds. It also reinforces the importance of retaining 'old' deeds, containing as they often do a wealth of detail that would otherwise be lost forever.

One of the many Freckleton weavers employed at Balderstone mill over a period of 160 years, Lizzie Halsall was photographed at her loom sometime in the early twentieth century.

with all its assets and liabilities; and Messrs Sowerbutts entered upon possession within 24 hours of its purchase'.[19] It was probably at this time that the factory acquired the name of Balderstone Mill, from the village where William Sowerbutts had been born in 1807. By 1874 the factory employed 240 hands, and in September that year the previous light pressure engine was replaced by a pair of compound condensing engines of about 150 horse power, which resulted in a saving of about 20% in fuel per week. The engines were 'christened' *Bessie* and *Ellen* at a ceremony which included the Mayor of Preston amongst the dignatories. On arrival at Freckleton they 'found the mill hands and many of the inhabitants in holiday attire and the village assuming all the appearance of a festival'.[20]

Shortly before his death in 1879 William Sowerbutts oversaw completion of a third extension to Balderstone Mill, which by this date contained 500 looms, providing employment for '350 persons'.[21] His personal impact on Freckleton had been considerable and on his death in December 1879 the mill hands requested that they be allowed to attend the funeral service in Preston and:

A view of Balderstone mill looking along Lytham Road. On the left, located behind the fencing, was the mill lodge.

About 250 of the hands and residents came over and assembled near the residence of the deceased'. — The cortege left for the cemetery shortly after eleven o'clock. First came the hands, who walked in couples, and who were attired in mourning ...' [22]

After the service lunch was provided in Lune Street (Preston) Schoolroom during which a Mr Whittle (almost certainly Richard Whittle who had been born at Freckleton in 1815), proposed that a vote of condolence be sent to the family of William Sowerbutts. His remarks provide a rare insight of nineteenth-century mill life at Freckleton as seen through the eyes of an employee.

... Mr Sowerbutts was the best master that had entered Freckleton for the last 65 years. He [Mr Whittle] had worked in Freckleton for 3s. 3d. per week; but now there were many females amongst them who earned 23s. and 24s. a week. Such was their respect for their departed master that they would not have considered it too much to follow him even so far as Manchester to show their respect to his memory. Their late employer had ever shown an interest in them, and had oftimes attended to the wants of the needy in Freckleton and elsewhere'.[23]

In 1881 approximately 232 Freckleton residents were employed at Balderstone Mill. These included the mill manager William Fortune, aged 41, six overlookers, two mechanics, an engineer and 186 weavers, of whom 142 were female and 44 male. The 142 female weavers included one aged under twelve, forty one aged between twelve and seventeen, and sixty five aged between eighteen and twenty five, of whom only eight were married. The 44 male weavers included two aged under twelve, fourteen aged between twelve and fourteen, and five aged fifteen to seventeen. Two female weavers, including one widow, and three male weavers, including one widower, were aged between fifty one and fifty five.

Also employed were two loomers, three tapers/sizers, one cloth binder, one cloth looker, fourteen cotton winders, one cotton drawer, six cotton warpers, one heald knitter, two joiners, one labourer, three warehouse staff and one clerk.

The enlightened attitude set by William Sowerbutts was continued

Throughout all the years Balderstone mill was in operation it was usually referred to as 'the factory' and this tradition prevailed until its final closure in 1980. (*Courtesy of Lancashire Evening Post*)

by his son Henry Eli and in 1886, on the occasion of his election as first president of Freckleton Polling District Liberal Association, he declared that 'he also wished it to be understood that as an employer of labour in the village he would not allow any coercion or undue influence to be exercised by anyone in his employ but for every man to vote as he thought best'.[24]

There is, however, an almost total absence of information about actual mill life and working conditions in the last quarter of the nineteenth century, and it is only extracts from the Trinity School log books that provide the occasional detail.

26 June 1885   Several half-timers attending morning and afternoon during Thursday and Friday owing to a part of the works at the Mill being stopped.

7 Oct. 1886   Several children have lately obtained half time certificates under pretence of working at the Mill but have either not attended the Mill or only occasionally done so. Many children seen playing in the streets during School hours.

10 Feb. 1896   Last Thursday owing to a strong smell of gas in the Schoolroom the Master saw the Mill Manager with reference to the cause and found that it arose from the emptying of a tank at the Mill gas works.

19 Feb. 1897   Owing to the Cotton Factory here working short time and lack of other employment several families have left the village.

21 May 1897   Two boys in Standard vi absent because of the stoppage at the Mill here.

The mill continued to be owned and operated by Henry Eli Sowerbutts, until his own death in 1901. Shortly afterwards Balderstone Mill was sold by Henry Reginald Sowerbutts to James William Liver and John Bibby for £8,000. In 1908 John Bibby bought out his partners share for £3,000, thus becoming sole owner. At that time the mill was described as comprising of 'Weaving Shed; Reservoir; Fire Engine House; Provender Store; Cloth Rooms; Offices; Joiners Shop; Gasometer; Retort House; Coach House; Stables; Cart Shed; Cottages; Boiler House; Engine House; Yarn Warehouse and other buildings erected thereon and known as Balderstone Mill and Raker Field and also the Engines; Boiler and fixed machinery'.[25]

The working relationship between the new employer and his employees, whilst never attaining the level achieved by William Sowerbutts, seems in general to have been harmonious and the only serious industrial dispute of note was that in January 1912 when there was a ten day lock-out.[26] This was probably the occasion when wages were cut and the weavers held a meeting on 'Bonney's Field' in School Lane, with those who talked about joining a trade union being refused access to the mill the following day.[27]

Some aspects of early twentieth-century mill life were recalled by Lena Butcher, who started work at the mill in 1912 as a twelve year old half-time tenter or weavers helper. At thirteen she commenced full-time and had to be at the mill for a 6 a.m. start. There was a brief pause at 8 a.m. when the weavers had breakfast beside their looms, an hour's break for dinner, and work finished at 5.30 p.m.[28] Other employees recall that after completing time as a tenter a weaver would begin to operate two looms increasing to three or four as they gained experience.[29] During the 1920s wages varied between £1 10s. 0d. and £2 0s. 0d. per week dependent on whether twills or velvets were being woven,[30] but if there was a flaw in the weaving 6d. was taken from the weaver's wage.[31] If the cut-looker felt the action warranted it he could make the weaver buy the whole cut of cloth, although 'whenever that happened people in the village would help the unfortunate weaver by buying a piece of the faulty cloth from her to ease the financial strain'.[32]

In November and December 1927, when the mill was closed, it was reported that 250 workpeople had to 'tramp' to Kirkham three times a week to sign on at the Ministry of Labour. The parish council enquired whether the workforce could sign on locally but were told that 'owing to certain irregularities of the Firm, the privilidges which they once enjoyed would never be granted to the Firm again and the heads of the Firm knew why the people had to walk to Kirkham'. Three years later the workforce were still having to go to Kirkham, the only concession being that arrangements had been made 'for the applicants of Freckleton to sign twice a week Wednesday and Friday during such period as the weather conditions may warrant'.[33] At sometime during the 1930s depression, when the mill was open, the employees initially agreed to a deduction of 6d. a loom from their wages to prevent the mill closing down, but when objections to this practice were raised by the Weavers Union Messrs Bibby 'decided to lay off many of the operatives and they dismissed all who lived in Kirkham'.[34]

In July 1941 Balderstone Mill closed down on the orders of the Government, to be used for storage by the US Air Force. On re-opening in about 1947 it was reported that the 'weaving shed was entirely filled with looms except for alleyways which had been considerably widened since the building was last used'; that in the engine room 'two 300 Horse power engines, John and Alla, were working at a tremendous speed'; and that the mill had been 'redecorated and better lighting installed'. The report added that 'the firm is well known for the manufacture of velvets and cords and corset cloth, which, however are still being made in a utility quality'.[35] By 1949 some 510 looms were in full production.[36]

By 1962 the number of weavers required to work the same number of looms had been halved from those needed a quarter to half a century earlier. When Thomas Threlfall retired in 1961 he was reported as saying that 'since I have been there the main change at Balderstone Mill has been in the looms – from four to eight – as well as better machinery'.[37] James Threlfall, his father, had been first employed at the mill in 1879, becoming manager in 1908, and between them father and son managed Balderstone Mill for all but fourteen of the sixty seven years that it was owned by the Bibby family.

The opportunities for days of such long service, however, were coming to an end and, 'crippled by cheap foreign imports and a thinning order book',[38] John Bibby & Sons closed Balderstone Mill on 26 January 1968, with the loss of over 100 weaving jobs. On 19 June in the same year the company was voluntarily wound up. In January 1969 the mill was sold to the Rossendale firm of J. H. Birtwistle who operated it until 1980, but on 20 December that year it was reported that 'the few remaining employees of Freckleton's textile mill forced to close down because of the recession left work for the last time yesterday'.[39]

This final closure brought to a close an era in the history of Freckleton that spanned not only Balderstone Mill but stretched back to the linen industry of the sixteenth century. Apart from the name stone of Balderstone Mill, fixed into the roadside wall near the junction of Lytham Road and Clitheroes Lane, there is now no visible evidence of an industry that once provided employment to many generations of local families.

CHAPTER 23

The Port of Freckleton

The Trading Port

Whilst there is no evidence to support previous claims that Freckleton was the 'Portus Setantiorum' of the Roman era, there can be little doubt that from at least the seventeenth century, and probably much earlier, the Pool along the Dow Brook had been used for the Irish Sea coastal trade and other commercial activities. Some evidence of the Irish Sea trade is perhaps provided by the marriage in 1732 of John Salthouse, a Freckleton mariner, to Jane Woodall, at Brigham, a village near the Cumberland port of Workington. Other evidence of early maritime activity is provided by Colonel Thomas Bellingham, who recorded in his diary on the 7 February 1689 that he 'came to Mr Chaddock's ship at the neb of Neas [Naze]. Met Mr Richmond there. Eat and drank and played [cards?] about an hour'.[1] And in 1720 the magistrates ordered a watch to be kept 'at the water side within the said township of Freckleton, by two persons, both day and night, for thirteen weeks, or more together. During part of which said time a ship called Jaxon's Sloop was under quarantine within the view of the said watch'.[2]

It was, however, the Douglas Navigation Act of 1720 that began the transformation of the Pool at Freckleton from a relatively quiet backwater into a small but busy port. The Act proposed making the River Douglas navigable and passable with boats from the River Ribble, into which it runs, to Miry Lane End at Wigan. It was built primarily to provide an alternative means of supplying Liverpool with coal from the Wigan coalfields, rather than by road which was costly and only possible in the summer months. According to the Act this would be 'very beneficial to trade, advantageous to the poor, and convenient for the carriage of coals, cannel, stone, slate and other goods and mechandize to and from the towns and parts adjacent, and will very much tend to the employing of watermen, and be a means to preserve the highway'.[3]

Construction work began in earnest in 1738 and in the following year the Earl of Derby conveyed to Robert Hall land for a wharf at Freckleton.[4] In 1742 the appointed commissioners declared the works certified by the Act were finished and in addition to the coal trade, described later in this chapter, there is evidence that very soon after its establishment the port was being used for a range of other commercial activities. In 1747 a broken bell from Kirkham Church was carted to Freckleton and from there shipped to Gloucester, and three years later when the bells were recast they were again shipped from Freckleton, on this occasion to Bristol.[5]

In 1760 the Exchequer appointed a commission to define the customs port of Preston, of which Freckleton wharf formed a part. The commissioners defined the port area as 'the key or wharf called ffreckleton key extending along the shore from north to south about twenty yards upon which a warehouse is now built known by the name of ffreckleton New Warehouse, from thence along the shore in a southerly direction towards Neas [Naze] Point a space of sixty yards in length, and from the north side of the said key or wharf in a line northerly along the shore towards Park Pool an hundred and forty yards in length bounded by the shore westwards and the River Ribble eastwards'.[6]

Part of William Yates' map of Lancashire published in 1786. It clearly shows the location of the warehouses built at Freckleton following the establishment of the port, also the ford across the Ribble sands from Hesketh Bank. (*Courtesy of Lancashire Record Office*)

When Whitaker visited the Naze sometime in the 1760s he wrote 'And here is even now a tolerably commodious harbour. The Ribble forms a large half moon facing south, and receiving a small backwater into it from the north. This is secured from the violence of the wind by the highlands which skirt it, is secured from the force of the tide by the projection of the Ness, and has a breath of a quarter of mile and a depth of fifteen feet upon the ebb. And here is even now the little port of Preston, a large warehouse being erected upon a mote in the channel and several vessels coming to it from London, Wales and Ireland'.[7]

By the middle of the eighteenth century groups of merchants in Kirkham, such as the Langton and Birley families, were already trading from Wardleys on the Wyre to the Baltic, importing flax for the production of sailcloth and ropes. However, this trade was only possible during the summer as the Baltic ports were frozen in winter and consequently the development of the port facilities at Freckleton, though difficult to access for the larger Baltic ships, provided a convenient alternative for smaller vessels bringing flax from Ireland. In addition Freckleton was used to bring in consignments from Liverpool, as in August 1782 when William Langton at the sailcloth warehouse, Dry Dock, Liverpool, was advised by his father, 'If you find the remains of the Petersburg 12 heads please you as to colour and quality would have you ship it by the first coast boat to Freckleton'.[8]

By the late eighteenth century it was not only the Kirkham merchants who were using the facilities at Freckleton but also local men, and evidence of their commercial activity is provided in an account book[9] of a vessel trading out of Freckleton during the years 1796 to 1820. The book has the word 'Active' on the spine, a term used to describe 'on the credit side of the balance sheet', and if this is so in this case then the book refers to a vessel that cannot be identified. However, the *Active* was also the name of a round-sterned sloop of 50 tons built at Freckleton in 1790 and it possible that the book actually relates to that vessel. In either event it is an invaluable source of information providing, as it does, an account of the sailings of one vessel over a twenty four year period. The sub-owners were named as John Goodshaw and Thomas Mayor with John Mayor described as a non-subscriber. George Richardson was named as the master. From 10 March 1796 to 27 March 1797 the trading profit made by the vessel amounted to £133 18s. 9d., of which three quarters went to Goodshaw and Mayor and one quarter to George Richardson.

In 1796 the vessel sailed mainly from the Wyre to Liverpool and Chester but from 1797 to 1807, particularly during the months April to December, it sailed principally from Freckleton to Liverpool, taking canvas, sacks, sacking, rope and yarn for companies that included Messrs Hornbys and Messrs Langton Birley & Co. of Kirkham, and John Mayor & Co. and Henry Sharples of Freckleton. On the return journey the cargo included items as diverse as flour, gin, glass, nails, oranges, potatoes, soap, sugar and even, on one occasion, a tarring machine.

In 1802, and subsequent years, the vessel was often operating around the small ports of Cumberland and south-west Scotland during the months of January through to April, carrying cargoes ranging from coals to oats and wheat. In April 1806 it was at Drogheda in Ireland with a cargo of coals before returning to the Liverpool 'run' for the remainder of the year. From 1808, and continuing throughout the following nine years, the vessel made regular journeys to several ports around Anglesey, transporting coal, and returning with limestone and other unspecified cargoes, but which presumably included slate, whilst at other times it appears to have been used for delivering coal brought from the Wigan coalfields.

Most of the these locally built vessels were owned by Freckleton men, with the Goodshaw and Mayor families predominating, and who, by investing their capital in this way, clearly intended to make their trading more lucrative by cutting out the middleman. Often the vessels were owned jointly between several people who held 'shares' in it, each vessel comprising 64 shares which were then divided between two or upto thirty two individuals. This method of ownership no doubt helped to spread any financial loss when disaster struck, as in April 1794 when the *Delight*, a round-sterned sloop built at Freckleton in 1782 and owned by George Richardson, mariner, James Goodshaw, husbandman and James Blundell, mariner, was sunk off the Welsh coast.

It was probably soon after the commissioners had defined the bounds of the port at Freckleton that a resident coastwaiter was first appointed, though it is not until 1781, when William Lucas was in post, that it is possible to identify anyone by name. A coastwaiter was a customs official who examined vessels and goods, duitable and free, in the coastwise trade, and which on the evidence of a notice issued in 1810 by the 'principal owners of the Coasting, Canal & Ribble Vessels'[10] included a wide range of items that included ale, canvas, cheese, glass, lead, mahogany, molasses, oats, pitch, soap and tobacco. By 1826, when Ralph Dewhirst was the coastwaiter, it was recorded that 'many vessels discharge

Freight of Merchandise

BY SEA, CANAL AND RIBBLE,

FROM

LIVERPOOL,

TO

LYTHAM, FRECKLETON AND PRESTON,

AGREED UPON THIS DAY

By the Principal Owners of the Coasting, Canal & Ribble Vessels:

	SEA. S.	SEA. D.	CANAL. S.	CANAL. D.
A.—Ashes, per Barrel,	1	9	2	0
Do. per Ton,	10	0	11	8
Ale, per Barrel,	2	0	2	4
Allum, per Ton,	10	0	11	8
Alabaster or Chalk, per Ton,	10	0	11	8
B.—Bark, per Ton,	23	0	25	0
Barley, per Winchester Bushell,		3		3½
Bottles, per Dozen,		6		8
Brandy, per Puncheon,	7	0	8	0
Do. per Piece,	7	6	8	6
Beans, per Bushel,		3		3½
Butter, per Ton,	10	0	11	8
C.—Canvas or Cloth, per Cwt.		7		8
Cases or Boxes, light Goods, per Foot,		2½		3
Cheese, per Ton,	10	0	11	8
Cotton Wool, per Ton,	23	0	25	0
D.—Deals, per solid foot,		2½		2½
Deal Balk, do		3		3
F.—Flax, per Ton	13	2	14	10
Flower, per Pack, twelve score,	1	1	1	2
Do. per Sack, fourteen score,	1	2	1	3
Fruit, per Ton,	10	0	11	8
Fullers Earth, per Ton,	10	0	11	8
Furniture, per foot,		2		3
Figs, per Tapnet,		3		4
G.—Glass, per side, not accountable for breakage,	4	0	4	3
Do. per Box, do.		8		9
H.—Hair, per Cwt.		10		11
Hemp, per Ton,	17	0	18	2
Do. per Cordilla,	25	0	26	0
Herrings, per Barrel, dried,	[illegible]	2	1	4
Do. salted,	1	6	1	8
Hides, Cow or Ox, &c. each,		6		7
Hops, per Pocket,	2	6	3	0
I.—Iron Liquor, per Pipe,	7	0	8	0
Do. per Puncheon,	6	0	7	0
Iron, in Bars or Pigs, per Ton	10	0	11	8
Do. Bundles, per Ton,	10	0	11	8
Junk, per Ton,	12	0	13	0
K.—Kelp, per Ton,	10	0	11	8
L.—Laths, per Bundle,		4		5
Lead, in Pigs, per Ton,	10	0	11	8
Lead, Red or White, per Cwt.		6		7
Lathwood, per Fatham, four feet	24	0	26	0

	SEA. S.	SEA. D.	CANAL. S.	CANAL. D.
Lathwood, per Fatham, three feet	18	0	20	0
Lemons, per Box,	1	0	1	2
Do. per Chest,	2	0	2	2
Logwood, per Ton,	10	0	11	8
M.—Mahogany, per foot,		4		4½
Malt, per Bushel,		3		3½
Molasses, per Hogshead	5	6	6	6
Madder, per do.	7	0	7	6
N.—Nuts, per Bag,	1	3	1	4
O.—Oak Billets, per foot,		3		3½
Oat Meal, per Load,	1	1	1	2
Oats, per Bushel, 45lb.		2½		2¾
Oil Cake, per Ton,	10	0	11	8
Oil, per Hogshead	5	6	6	0
Oil Vitriol, per Carboy,	2	6	3	0
Oil, per Jar,	4	6	5	0
P.—Pipe Clay, per Ton	10	0	11	8
Pitch or Tar, per Barrel,	2	0	2	3
Porter, per Butt,	7	0	7	6
Do. per Barrel,	2	0	2	3
R.—Raisins, per Basket,		3		3½
Do. in Bags, per Cwt.		6		7
Rice. per do.		6		7
Rum, per Puncheon,	6	6	7	6
Rosin, per Barrel,	2	0	2	3
S.—Seeds in Sacks,		6		7
Salt, per Bushel,		3		3½
Shumack, per Ton,	10	0	11	8
Soap, per Box,	1	0	1	2
Staves, per Ton,	12	0	13	0
Sugar, per Ton,	10	0	11	8
Do. in Loaves or pack'd per Cwt.		7		8
Soap, per Firkin,		6		7
Spirits, in small Casks, per Gallon		2		2½
T.—Tallow, per Cwt.		6		7
Tobacco, unmanufactured per do.		7		8
Do manufactured, per do.		8		9
Tin, per Box,		7		8
V.—Vinegar, per Hogshead	3	6	4	0
Do. per half do.	1	9	2	0
W.—Wheat, per Bushel, 70lb.		3½		4½
Wine, per Pipe,	7	6	8	6
Do. cased, per Pipe,	8	6	9	6
Wolds, per Mat,	3	0	3	6

The Owners of the Vessels employed in the above Trade GIVE NOTICE, that they will not be accountable for any Loss or Damage that may be sustained in consequence of the Act of God, Fire, the King's Enemies, any Riot or Commotion, nor from all or any the Dangers and Accidents of the Seas, Rivers, or Navigations of whatever Nature or Kind; nor will they be liable for any Deficiency in Weights or Measures, nor in the Gauge of Wine or Spirit, unless the same be dipped along-side the Vessels, in the Presence of the Masters, and proved to be improperly stowed.—The Owners of Goods are to bear the Expence and Risk of Porterage in Loading and Landing from the Vessels.

N. B. The Ton is to consist of 20 Hundred-weight of 112lbs Gross Weight. When there is not sufficiency of Water to bring the Vessels up to Preston Quay, such Goods as are entered for Preston will be discharged at Savic, and the Owner or Owners of the Vessels will pay the Toll at the Barr, and One-fourth of Cartage. Goods will in all cases of Litigation or Bankruptcy, be detained to cover Book debts.

——ooo——

March 27th, 1810. *(Addison, Printer, Preston)*

A contemporary document of 1810 showing the charges made on a remarkable range of goods and items shipped from Liverpool to Lytham, Freckleton and Preston. (*Courtesy of Lancashire Record Office – DDPr 138/9*) their cargoes here [i.e. the port], from Ireland and coastwise, and also take in coals brought in leighters [sic] from the Leeds and Liverpool Canal'.[11]

The decline of the port began in the 1830s with the building of the training walls of the River Ribble, which enabled vessels to proceed up the river to Preston without lighterage. The opening of Lytham dock in 1846, with its linked railway siding allowing connections for onward transportation to inland destinations, also contributed to a loss of trade as cargoes from Tarleton proceeded there instead of to Freckleton.

However, despite this apparent economic decline, the census returns for the period from 1841 to 1891 show that in addition to the shipbuilding industry, described later in this chapter, a number of men continued to find employment in maritime trades throughout the second half of the nineteenth century. The 1851 census recorded one master mariner, one master mariner (retired), nine mariners, seventeen mariners' wives (their husbands obviously being out on their boats on census day) and two sailors, whilst forty years later the 1891 census recorded one master mariner, twenty one mariners, two retired mariners and seven sailors.

There are several poignant reminders of the ever present dangers that such men constantly faced. In September 1861 the *Pryde*, owned by Peter Rigby, was totally lost in the Bristol Channel, and eleven years later the *Unity*, built at Freckleton in 1865, was also lost in the same area. Memorial inscriptions on gravestones in Holy Trinity churchyard include those to Captain Henry Richardson, his wife Elizabeth and their son Thomas who were lost at sea on 8 February 1860, and to Thomas Whittle aged 30, Thomas Riley aged 29 and William Sumner aged 28 who were all lost at sea in separate incidents between the years 1866 and 1868.

In the early 1890s Peter Hall, captain of the *Lancashire Lad*, and his brother Robert Hall, captain of the *Harvest Maid*, were earning their living from the sea by taking coal to Polperro/Charleston in Cornwall. On other occasions journeys were made to Ireland and even as far as Holland. The vessels returned from Cornwall with china clay to either Liverpool, for the chemical industry, or Lancaster, for the linoleum industry, and it was on one of these return journeys, in December 1891, that the *Harvest Maid* was lost with all hands during a violent gale off Bideford Bay in Devon.[12]

By 1927 it was reported that 'the village has lost its sailors and instead of scores of men earning their livelihood on the sea, the number now so employed can be counted on the fingers of one hand'.[13]

The Coal Trade

Even before the opening of the Douglas Navigation the ford across the Ribble at Freckleton may have been used for bringing coals into the Fylde, as suggested by an entry in the accounts of the steward for the Clifton family of Lytham, who on 25 July 1721 recorded 'paid my charges in going over Ribble about coals'.[14] If in fact this is what was taking place then the means used to transport the inevitably limited amounts of coal was presumably by packhorse. With the opening of the Navigation all this would have changed and in 1753 a parcel of land for a coal yard, with the right of navigating vessels along Freckleton Pool from the River Ribble, was let on an annual tenancy to James Hall and others at a rental of 18s. 0d. per annum.[15]

Coal from the Wigan coalfields was brought to Freckleton on vessels known as flats and the surviving account book, for the years 1764 to 1768, of a flat named *Success*[16] provides an insight of the workings of the trade. Between June and November 1765 the vessel came to Freckleton on seven occasions and delivered a total of 102 tons of coal, at 8s. 0d. per ton, to Richard Atkinson, a Freckleton innkeeper from 1766 to 1770. A further 182½ tons were delivered to him between March and December 1766, and 190½ tons during the same months in 1767. In addition coal was also delivered to other local men, including Thomas Cowburn of Freckleton and John Shepherd of Kirkham.

It is unlikely that the *Success* was the only flat delivering coal to Freckleton and by 1774 the trade was such that it was considered necessary to set up a subscription for repairing the roads within the township. Although the second page of the subscription document is missing it nevertheless provides fulsome evidence of how important the coal trade had become by the last quarter of the eighteenth century.

> Whereas the Roads within the Township of Freckleton Leading from the Coalyards there to the Township of Kirkham have been of late years very ruinous deep and in wet Seasons Impassable by reason of the Traffick through the same to fetch Coals to Kirkham Poulton and the Country adjacent whereby Numbers of Famalys have been deprived of a proper supply; And altho the Inhabitants of Freckleton have for many years past laid out and expended Considerable sums in Repair thereof as well as in performing Statute Labour as required by Law. Yet their utmost Endeavours are found insufficient to maintain and keep the said Road in proper Condition; nor is the same likely to be done with Effect; unless a substantial Cart Causey be Paved & Carryed through the same; And as it will require

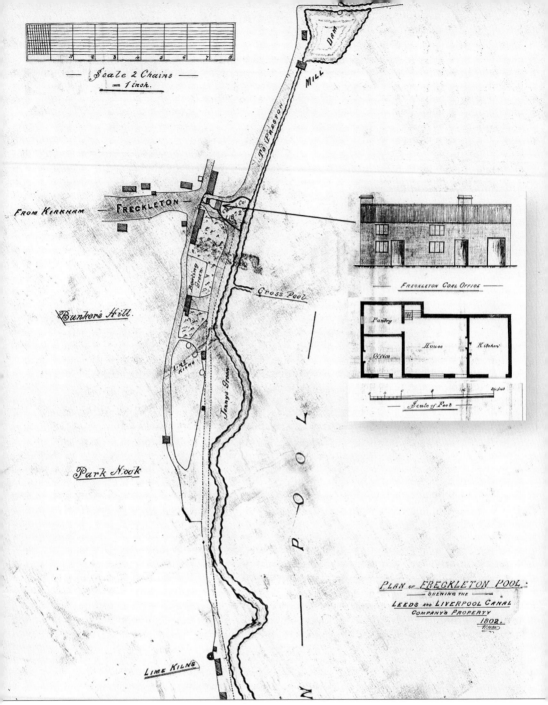

As a result of the Douglas Navigation Act of 1720 a wharf was established at Freckleton in 1738, and in 1753 land for a coal yard was let on an annual tenancy to James Hall and others. In 1783 the Leeds & Liverpool Canal Co. purchased the Douglas Navigation Company and by 1802 a Counting House had been built on the Coal Hill. (*Courtesy of British Waterways*).

the sum of Four to five Hundred Pounds to Compleat the same; A sum which the Inhabitants being mostly farmers, who clear their estates are not able nor Competable to raise; And to keep their Highways in Repair Whereby this Road may still remain in the same improper State. And as there appears no other means for makeing the Cart Pavement proposed speedily and Effectually without the Aid of the Publick. The Inhabitants of Freckleton find themselves under the Necessity to apply for Subscription to Enable them to do it. If in this they receive that Encouragement which it will be the Publick Interest to promote They propose as follows That in the space of four years from the 29th of September 1774 They will Pave the said Road with a substantial Causey; to be Ten Feet wide from the Coalyards to the Headless Cross which divides the Townships of Freckleton and Kirkham and Maintain the same ever after at their own Expence'.

The Necessity and usefulness of this work to the Publick is apparent as the Extravagant Toll imposed on Teams Passing over Ribble by Tarleton Turnpike has almost put a Total stop to the fetching Coal from ...[17]

In 1783 the Leeds and Liverpool Canal Company purchased the Douglas Navigation Company and by 1802 had built a counting house on the Coal Hill, presumably in order to collect dues from vessels using the navigation to deliver coal to Freckleton. In the following year, however, the Company was expressing concern at the scarcity of coal and accordingly increased the dues required. This decision only made matters worse and following protests which revealed 'that coal carried to Preston on the Lancaster Canal was being sold more cheaply than supplies taken via Tarleton and the Ribble, the newly opened tramroad from Walton Summit to Preston proving to be less of an inconvenience to traffic, despite transhipment, than the hazards of the estuary and road transport from Freckleton wharf' the Leeds and Liverpool agreed to a discount of up to 1s. 3d. per ton on coal sold at Freckleton.[18]

The account book for the *Active* reveals that during the years 1817 to 1819 coal was being bought at between 14s. 0d. and 16s. 6d. per ton, but despite being sold at between 18s. 0d. and 23s. 0d. per ton there were still complaints that trade at Freckleton had diminished due to competition from the Lancaster Canal. However, in 1823, following an investigation carried out at the request of the Leeds and Liverpool Canal Co., it was reported that trade in coal was actually increasing at Freckleton, mainly for shipment to Ireland with return cargoes of corn and cattle. In 1827 a scheme was published to unite the Lancaster and Leeds and Liverpool via the Douglas. The scheme proposed that lines of wooden booms be moored across the Ribble from the Douglas mouth to Freckleton to form a floating towpath. Two navigation channels were to be left in the middle and from Freckleton a new canal would rise 79ft 4in by ten locks to join the Lancaster Canal at Salwick.[19]

During this period at least three companies or individuals traded as coal merchants at Freckleton. The partnership of John Worthington, John Higham and William Higham appears to have traded around the years 1818–1820,[20] whilst in 1814 James Blundell was described as 'formerly a coal merchant'.[21] It was, however, Goodshaw Mayor that was clearly the principal company. As early as 1791 they brought a complaint against (William) Whalley concerning trespass on their land. The opening submission described them as a 'Company of Coal Merchants' who 'bring their coals in vessels of about 30 Tons Burthen, and land them upon the Strand or soil adjoining their own lands. Vessels of 60 tons may come up at spring Tides'.[22] Twenty years later a letter sent by the company to a Mr Barker of Low Wood, near Cartmel on 27 December 1810, provides further evidence of their extensive trade:[23]

Sir,

Yours of the 24 Inst we rec[eive]d yesterday and have to inform you that at present all our vessels are engaged or we sh[oul]d have sent you One on trial the Terms for Shipp[in]g the best coals from the pits where we have most Measure is 17/– Money or 17/6 three Months the Vessels has 5/- per ton freight Clear of every expence at Your end – they may be ship[pe]d at 6d. less from some of the Collierys but are not so Good in Quality nor near the Quantity if you choose to take a Trial in Summer please to let us know that we may prepare accordingly

we are Sir your
Ob[edien]t Serv[an]t
Goodshaw Mayor & Co.

Following the death of James Goodshaw in 1813 and John Mayor in 1815 the Goodshaw Mayor business was carried on, until his own death in 1821, by Thomas Mayor the elder, nephew of John Mayor, who had married Ann Goodshaw, daughter of James Goodshaw, in 1784. The business then passed to their son Robert Mayor who in 1839 bequeathed his 'counting house and weighing machine situate near the Coal yard in Freckleton' to his wife, his brother, and his two sons, Robert and Thomas.[24] In view of this bequest it would seem that by 1839 the lease of the counting house had been purchased by the Mayor family from the Leeds and Liverpool. In his own will, made just before his death in 1858, Robert (junior) also refers to a counting house and weighing machine near the coal yard which he held as tenant in common with his brother.[25]

A contemporary account of the nineteenth-century wharf is provided by the jottings made on the back of an envelope, postmarked 'Southport Jy 27 83', by an unknown employee of the Leeds and Liverpool Canal Co. who recorded that:

> Thos Turner has known Freckleton Wharf for 56 years – well.
>
> There was a small warehouse for storing Sacks & Tackle – being a Village mostly of Sack Weavers and was occupied by Robert Mayor and Two Sons after him – Mayor Sack Makers & Coal Merchants Broke [up] about the year 1850 – & since that the yard and small Warehouse stood empty for sometime. Then Peter Rigby took it till he died, then his Son Marsden Rigby had it till CW [?] saw it and let it for 5£ per ann. Marsden Rigby is now dead and the place is occupied by his widow and is used as Coal Merchant – Mayor had 3 or 4 Flats for Coal etc. etc.
>
> The Quay was [re]built by L & L about the year 1840. T. Turner worked at it when building and the Companys frontage extends from the Pool up to the main street in Freckleton [Preston Old Road]
>
> Trade at Present to Freckleton Wharf 1 Flat owned by Rigby – and usually 1 Load per Wk 35 Tons.[26]

The agreement dated 5 May 1845 by which Peter Rigby leased the land for a coal yard was entered in the township minute book[27] and records that nineteen perches of land were let at a yearly rent of 9s. 6d.; at the same time a further thirty two perches were let to his brother Thomas Rigby at a yearly rent of 16s. 0d. The business subsequently passed to the Hall family who were related through marriage to the Rigby family. In the nineteenth century the flats onto which the coal was loaded were punted across the river when the tide conditions were suitable, including night-time, with a man at each end of the flat, neither of whom could see the other due to the height of the coal. In the final days of the coal trade the flats were towed by a small steamer which was also loaded with coal. Each flat carried about twenty tons of coal which was either offloaded into sacks or sometimes onto carts.[28] Coal continued to be carried to Freckleton until the 1920s and the trade only ceased when Balderstone Mill began to have coal delivered direct from Kirkham railway station.

Shipbuilding

By an Act of Parliament, passed in 1786, all owners of British ships with a deck and a burden greater than 15 tons were required to register them with the customs at their home port. The information included details of the owners' names and addresses, master's name, place and date of where the vessel was built and technical specifications. Vessels registered at the customs port of Preston include those built at Freckleton and although the list is not complete there is a wealth of information about Freckleton ships, though unfortunately less about their builders.[29]

The earliest vessel recorded as being built at Freckleton was the *Delight* in 1782, which, as already mentioned, was lost at sea in 1794. In 1801 a second vessel of the same name was built for John Mayor, James Goodshaw and George Richardson. Between 1782 and 1801 at least six sloops and two flats were built, including the sloop *Unity* in 1785, when the owners again included John Mayor, James Goodshaw and James Blundell, together with William Hornby of Kirkham and local master mariner Richard Wright.

Other sloops included the *Active* and *Hero*, and when the *Hero* was sold for £120 in 1836, by members of the Mayor family to Robert Wright, it was described as having 'one Deck and one Mast, that her length from the fore part of the main Stern to the after part of the Stern Post aloft is fifty nine feet one inch her breadth at the broadest part taken above the Main Wales is fifteen feet ten inches her depth in the Hold is five feet seven inches that she is sloop rigged, with a standing Bowsprit, is round sterned carvel built, has no Galleries, and no Head'. Her burthen weight was recorded as sixty one 83/94th tons and the master was William Swann.[30]

Due to a missing shipping register for the period 1815 to 1840 the name(s) of the leading Freckleton shipbuilder(s) are unknown. However, the 1823 militia list for Freckleton includes the name of Thomas Wright, ship carpenter, who, almost certainly, was the Thomas Wright born to Robert and Betty Wright of Warton in 1784, and appears to have gone to Skerton, Lancaster, sometime prior to 1807, presumably to learn his trade as a shipwright. Thomas was married in 1807 at Lancaster, where his first children, Robert and Margaret, were baptised, but returned to Freckleton by 1817 where further children were born. On the 1841 census he was living in Lower Road next to his son Robert, both men being described as a ship carpenter.

The first vessel that can be positively identified as being built by Thomas Wright was the schooner named *Ann* in 1842. By 1851 Thomas had died and the shipbuilding business had been taken over by his son Robert who, in 1851, was recorded as employing two men and eleven boys increasing by 1861 to ten men and four boys. The last vessel to be built by Robert Wright was an 83 ton schooner completed in 1870 named the *Spencer* and in which he initially retained 56 of the 64 shares, with James Spencer, ropemaker, holding the other eight. In 1873 Robert Wright sold 24 of these shares to John Kirby, master mariner, which, no doubt, helped to finance his retirement as by the 1871 census return he was described as a retired ship builder

The same census also shows that shipbuilding had been taken over by Peter Rawstrone, who was described as a master ship builder employing four men and three boys. In 1881 Peter Rawstrone and Henry Allanson were both described as shipbuilders and it would seem that at some time in the preceeding decade the two men, who were cousins, had established a joint company. During the years 1872 to 1885 some of the largest vessels built at Freckleton were launched from the yard including the schooners *Isabella, Jane, Perseverance, J. C. Swindlehurst* and the *Welcome.*

Of all these vessels it is perhaps the *Welcome,* an 88 foot, three-masted, round-sterned schooner designed for the coasting trade, that is now the most fondly remembered. An unsigned handwritten document, that appears to be an summary of the events leading up to the launch, reveals a considerable pride in the fact that most of the men employed building the vessel were members of the Rechabite temperance movement in Freckleton:

> The Shipbuilding firm of Messrs Rawstrone and Allanson of Freckleton has a wide reputation for having teetotal workmen. The firm employs 13 men including masters and out of this number no less than 11 are members of the Freckleton [Rechabite] Hall tent.
>
> On the [blank] inst there was launched from the yard a three masted schooner of 200 tons burthen the Keel of which was laid on the 8 Dec 1883 and during the whole time of the building of this vessel not a drop of intoxicating drink has been seen upon the premises; the vessel is named 'Welcome' and is classed A1 at Lloyds for 12 years this testifying to the efficient workmanship of the men under the supervision of their Rechabite masters.
>
> The Welcome will be commanded by Capt J Banks who is also a member of the above named tent, her managing owner is Mr J Ascroft he too a member of the [blank] Tent, Tarleton in the North Meols District.
>
> The Welcome is now fully equipped and ready for sea and is bound from Preston to London, and we wish her 'God speed' earnestly hoping she may ever remain a silent exemplar of Rechabitism, advocating through her captain in every port she enters the principles of total abstinence.[31]

Shipyard Freckleton

Records of boats built at Freckleton are available from 1782. During part of the twentieth century the yard acquired the prestigious work of overhauling and repairing lifeboats for the RNLI.

The launch took place at 11.30 a.m. on Saturday the 13 June 1885 'amidst the hurrahs' of the large crowd that had gathered to watch the event. The vessel was 'christened' by a Mrs Firth of Dukinfield and after the launch 'dinner was partaken of at the Ship Inn, where about 45 guests sat down'. At the same time it was reported that 'work at the yard continues to be brisk, despite the bad times'.[32]

Due to an absence of any known documentary sources little is known of the commercial activities at the yard during the early years of the twentieth century. Ownership of the boatyard passed into the hands of George Allanson, the son of Henry, and then to his own son, also called Henry, and for many years the company overhauled and repaired lifeboats for the RNLI. This was prestiguous work as the RNLI were, and are, very strict about the quality of workmanship and would have no hesitation in dropping a yard if it consistently failed to reach the standard required. The fact that they were a RNLI yard also attracted other work as people knew they must be good to keep the contract. During World War II lifeboats came to Allansons for overhaul from as far afield as Kirkcudbright in Scotland and Pwllheli in Wales. At the beginning of 1945 the French Lifeboat *Jean Charcot*, an escapee from Finistere and used by the RNLI during the war, was overhauled at the yard before being taken to Newlyn by members of the Lytham Lifeboat crew and handed back to a French crew.

By 1970 the yard had passed into the ownership of Jim Wearing who continued the work previously carried out by the Allanson family. Early in the morning of Thursday 11 June 1970 the 200 × 60 foot building at the boatyard was completely destroyed by fire. The fire brigade sent appliances from all local stations, but they could only prevent the fire from spreading to adjoining property. By good fortune there were no lifeboats in the yard at the time, although fourteen light craft were lost in the fire.[33]

Although the fire ended the era of lifeboat servicing, other work at the yard continued, and the present owners, the Booth family, whose company trades as Freckleton Boatyard, have since 1988 carried out maintenance and fitting out work, as well as building the occasional new boat. The most recent vessel to be built and launched from Freckleton was a 35 foot steel yacht called the *Northern Rose* on 29 August 2000.

CHAPTER 24

Inns

Licensing and Control

Inns and innkeepers have been subject to legislation since the days of the Anglo-Saxons. From 1495 the law required every alehouse keeper to apply for a recognizance supported by two sureties; and a statute of 1753 required the clerk of the peace to keep a register of the recognizances filed. A recognizance was granted yearly and required that the innkeeper 'shall keep and maintain good order and rule and shall suffer no Disorder nor unlawful games to be used in his/her said house nor in any Outhouse Garden or backside thereunto belonging during the said term then this recognizance shall not be void'.

By the early nineteenth century any person who had not been licensed for the preceding year was also required to 'produce a certificate under the hands of the Minister and major part of the Churchwardens and overseers, or else three reputable and substantial householders of the place where he inhabiteth, setting forth that he is of good fame and sober life and conversation'. Evidence that the church took an interest in the drinking habits of its parishioners is provided by a entry in the Kirkham parish vestry book for 1813 that 'ordered that the Churchwardens be directed to take care that no public houses be kept open after the hour of 9 on Sunday Evenings'.[1] Whether the wardens confined their interest just to Kirkham or extended it to the other townships in the parish is not known.

On 6 October 1821 the Freckleton township committee also considered it necessary to exercise some control over Sunday drinking and paid 4s. 6d. for 'Notices printing for Publicans'. Three days later they met again to appoint Henry Fisher and Thomas Riley as special constables who were then paid 2s. 11d. for 'Expences Serving Publicans' on Friday 12 October. Thereafter for the next six months these special constables appear to have commenced a regular Sunday inspection of all licensed premises in the township, and on 10 January 1822 received a quarterly payment of £2 12s. 0d. for 'visiting Publick Houses on the Sabbath Day', and on 8 April they received a further £1 6s. 0d. for identical work.[2]

Inns as Public Institutions

Apart from the Quaker meeting house there was no other building suitable for public meetings until the opening of Trinity School in 1839, and consequently the local inns provided an important alternative as a common meeting place in the social economy of the township. The annual township meeting was held in one of the inns and in the nineteenth-century township disbursements books there are annual entries for 'Yearly Towns Meeting', at which an amount ranging from 10s. 6d. to 15s. 0d., presumably for 'refreshments', was allowed. It is probable that one of the inns was also the meeting place of the friendly society which was in existence by the early 19th century.

Seventeenth- and Eighteenth-century Inns and Innkeepers

Although there is no indication as to the location of their inns the first recorded innkeepers in Freckleton were Richard Browne and James Tomlinson, both of whom were granted licences for the years 1635 to 1637. There is no further information until 1661 when the recognizance entry for Freckleton states 'none' and it is not until 1671–72 that the next known innkeeper, John Crompton, was granted a licence. During the first third of the eighteenth century recognizances are only available for the year 1722 when Richard Southworth and another Richard Brown (who as we will see later in this chapter was almost certainly innkeeper of the inn later known as the Bush Inn) were named. However, in his will dated 1727 Robert Housmond described himself as 'an Innkeeper and Taylor'.[3] He left his messuage to his son Edward and the 'little house' to his wife, but unfortunately the will does not provide any clues as to the location of these properties, nor is there any inventory associated with the will which might have told us more about how Robert combined his two trades.

From 1740–41, until his death in 1753, Thomas Bamber was an innkeeper, followed by John Pearson, who retained his licence until 1766. Although it is not possible to pinpoint the location of 'Pearsons' it was most probably the Ship Inn as there are several references to it during the rebuilding of the clow in 1764, including: 'To spent at Pearsons one night when the flood was stopped of the Marsh 2s. 9d.' and 'Jno Roads [Rhodes] Debit to Jno Pearson Nine Days meat at 6d. per [day] 4s. 6d. and Ale 2s. 6d.'[4] From the mid-eighteenth century there is an almost complete record of all innkeepers in Freckleton and in 1766 three are named for the first time. However it is not until 1777 that it is possible to positively identify the inns that they kept.

Ship Inn

Although probably already an ancient inn the earliest known deeds for the property now known as the Ship Inn date only from 1 May 1777, when John Swann of Kirkham (woollen draper), James Goodshaw of Freckleton (husbandman) and William Harrison of Freckleton (yeoman) conveyed the property to John Mayor of Freckleton (yeoman) and mariner James Blundell of Liverpool (as trustee).[5] James Hargreaves was named as the tenant of the house and garden. The deeds do not make any mention of the name of the property but it was probably about

The deeds of the Ship Inn date from 1777. From the late eighteenth century until the mid-nineteenth century it was known as Bunkers Hill, after the battle fought in 1775 between the British and the American colonists. The early name has been preserved in the name of Bunker Street.

Ship Inn, Freckleton.

this time that it became known as 'Bunkers Hill' after the battle fought in 1775 between the British and the American colonists.

It was certainly known by that name in 1812 as an agreement for re-erecting the 'clow' (clough) refers to 'the Clough which lately stood in the Pool or Arm of the River Ribble opposite the Public House called Bunkers Hill'.⁶ A plan of Freckleton Pool prepared for the Leeds and Liverpool Canal Company in 1802 clearly shows the inn, together with its adjacent bowling green, which existed to at least 1830, to the east of the building. In about 1810 Robert Clifton became the innkeeper but it is not until shortly before his departure in 1824 that the inn is first referred to as the Ship.

Following the Mayor family bankruptcy in 1830 the property was sold in 1833 to Joseph Ditchfield of Lytham. On his death in 1838 he instructed that his trustees apply the rents and profits of his 'public house situate in Freckleton – commonly called or known by the name of Bunkers Hill' to the use of his wife and children. The property remained in the ownership of his heirs until it was sold in 1857 to Henry Robert Marcus, of Liverpool, agent. From about 1838 to 1853 the tenant had been James Harrison who combined his role of innkeeper with that of sailmaker, but at the time of the sale in 1857 the property was unoccupied.

On the census of 1861 the occupier was Thomas Seed, a mechanic in the cotton mill. The building, however, was named as Bunkers Hill and described as a beerhouse and not an inn. Thomas Seed was still the occupier in 1869 when the property was sold to Thomas Grime, a Preston innkeeper, and this appears to have been the last occasion when it was referred to by the name Bunkers Hill. In 1877 Thomas Grime sold to Thomas Moss, who in turn sold to Catterall and Swarbricks Brewery in 1895. Five years earlier a return of public houses and beerhouses reported that there were 'three beds for travellers, that 80 could be fed any refreshments and that there was stabling for five horses'.⁷

In 1904 Catterall and Swarbricks sold to Thomas Snalam of Freckleton, and in 1920 Edward Entwisle of Bolton, as executor of Susannah Snalam, conveyed the property to himself. In 1923 it was sold to Samuel Entwisle, who in 1934 sold it to Samuel Johnstone Entwisle, in whose ownership it remained until 1962 when it was purchased by J. G. Swales & Co. It is now (2000) owned by the Scottish & Newcastle Group.

Coach and Horses Inn

As we saw in chapter 19 the Coach and Horses almost certainly owes its origins to the trade created by traffic using the marsh road in the early nineteenth century. The inn would seem to have been built by the Hornby family because in 1830 the heirs of Thomas Hornby were recorded as the owners of a 'new Public House & Outbuildings'.[8] It first opened in 1824–25 when Robert Clifton, who the previous year had been innkeeper at the Ship Inn, was described as innkeeper of the Coach and Horses.[9] Robert Clifton combined his role as innkeeper with various other commercial activities and when he died in 1834 he left several closes of land, including three closes in Clitheroes Lane which he had inherited from the Coulborn family, and where he had had a house built (now 19 Bush Lane). The tenancy of the Coach and Horses passed to his widow Jane, and was run by herself and her son-in-law Henry Watson for the next twenty years.

Jane Clifton died in 1854 and the following year the Coach and Horses, described as 'All that Inn or Public House in Freckleton – with the Cottages, Yards, Stables, Outbuildings and Croft thereto – now in the occupation of Mr Henry Watson and others' was sold to Anne Hornby (née Seed) of Lytham for £937 10s. 0d.[10] The new landlady was her sister Ellen Rigby, the widow of Marsden Rigby, who as we will see,

The Coach and Horses was almost certainly built and opened by the Hornby family in 1824–25 to serve the trade created by the remade road across the marsh. The first landlord was Robert Clifton who had previously been landlord at Bunkers Hill.

had combined the roles of beerseller and farmer when he had been the occupier of Lamaleach Farm. Ellen Rigby remained at the Coach and Horses until about 1866 when James Seed took over. By 1881 the tenant was William Threlfall who in turn was followed by George Helm. At some date prior to her death in 1889 ownership passed from Anne Hornby to her nephew John Robert Knowles, a Lytham butcher. On his own death in 1898 ownership then passed to his sister Anne Jane Jackson who died in 1925.

During the period of horse drawn traffic the Coach and Horses served as a staging inn, where horses could be exchanged on vehicles coming from Preston to Blackpool, and vice-versa on the return journey. Land behind the inn and up to Croft Butts was used for grazing, and the rings to which horses could be tied were still to be seen on the outside walls of the inn until the 1930s. In 1890, however, despite its central location, it could provide only one bed, though 60 travellers could be fed with any refreshments.[11] From about 1904 until 1922 James Parker, previously at the Plough Inn, was landlord. In 1926 the inn was purchased by Swales Brewery and soon afterwards Jack Fielding became landlord. He was succeeded by his son-in law William Carter Hankinson, who became the first of the three generations of the same family that still continues to trade at the Coach and Horsess.

Plough Hotel

The opening of a beerhouse, which the 1838 tithe map shows to have been approximately on the site of the present day Plough Hotel, was an outcome of the 1830 Beer House Act which enabled any householder whose name was on the rate book to sell beer. The township survey of 1830[12] records the owners of a 'Public House at Thomas Bambers' as the heirs of John Grimbaldeston. These heirs were in fact James Cross and John King, James Cross being the nephew of Thomas and John Grimbaldeston, whose parents had lived at Hall Cross. The original building, known subsequently as the Plough Inn, continued in the ownership of this family until it was sold by William Higham King in 1871 to Robert Richardson.

Innkeepers during the 1850s and 1860s were Henry Whiteside, Christopher Bamber and Thomas Adamson. By 1881 Thomas Parker was innkeeper and he was succeeded first by his widow Ellen and then by his son James Parker. In 1890 the *Plough Inn* could provide beds for two travellers, any refreshments for up to forty persons and stabling for

The first Plough Inn was opened in 1830 and was an outcome of the Beer Act which enabled any householder whose name was on the rate book to sell beer. In this *c.*1926 photograph the then landlord John Threlfall (left) and Jack Parkinson are standing at the entrance of the building that was demolished following the construction of Preston New Road.

two horses.[13] Robert Richardson died in 1900 and ownership of the inn passed to Jane, his widow, who remained the owner until her own death in 1913. The inn was then sold at a public auction to John Threlfall, who had been the landlord from about 1907, for £650. Following the constuction of Preston New Road the old Plough Inn was demolished and the present building, now known as the Plough Hotel, was opened in about 1930. It is now (2000) owned by the Scottish & Newcastle Group.

Bush Inn

In 1635 the distance between Ormskirk and Kirkham was recorded as being only eleven miles, and as Preston was said to be twelve miles from Ormskirk and Kirkham six miles from Preston it suggests that the common highway was the passage across the Ribble sands. On Yates' map of Lancashire, published in 1786, the Ribble is noted as being 'Fordable at Low Water' from Hesketh Bank to a point near to a

building called Guide House at Freckleton – not to be confused with
Guides House at Warton which is also marked on the map. The track
leading to the ford was also shown on maps produced in 1816 and 1829,
and anecdotal evidence suggests that a crossing point from Hesketh Bank
to Freckleton was in use until the cutting of the new river channel in
the middle of the nineteenth century. In 1891 it was recorded that 'roads
in connection with it [the ford] still exist, on the one hand to Freckleton
and Kirkham, and on the other to Tarleton'.[14]

In the days when such a crossing was in regular use an inn situated
at or near to the Naze would be the obvious meeting place for those
who perhaps required a guide to take them across the river. Although
Yates' map does not provide a precise location of Guide(s) House the
Ordnance Survey map of 1842 clearly shows a dwelling of that name
situated on the site of the now demolished Bush Inn (a bush was used
by the Romans to denote accommodation and its use in England is
supposed to have been adopted from them and is considered to be
among the earliest of English inn signs). However, the inn at Freckleton
does not appear to have acquired this name until about 1860 and its
adoption seems to be a late reintroduction of the old tradition.

It is not known when an inn first opened but it appears to have
been established by 1723, as in that year the baronial court of Penwortham
instructed Richard Browne 'Alekeeper of Freckleton' to lay 'a Sufficient

Almost certainly of ancient origin the Bush [Pool] Inn probably served as an arrival and
departure point for travellers using one of the fords across the River Ribble. A southward
route out of the township is mentioned in a thirteenth-century charter. The inn ceased
trading in 1910 and became a farmhouse before being demolished in 1974.

Hollow Cart plat as hath been accustomed in the Poole Houses Lane'.[15] (As we have already seen present day Bush Lane was still known as Pool Lane in the nineteenth century.) The fact that four other men were also ordered, at the same court, to cut their hedges and ditch their ditches along Pool Houses Lane supports the assumption that the lane was then a regular route leading to a crossing point over the River Ribble.

Richard Browne was probably only the tenant of the alehouse and although the court did not name the owner it is possible that it was a member of the Hall family who owned land in that part of the township from the seventeenth to the nineteenth century. In 1675 Richard Hall 'of the poole house belonging unto Freckleton' was described as having 'tented the water mill at Preston marsh for Elizabeth Wearden'.[16] Further evidence of the existence of an inn on this site is provided by the will of Robert Hall, who in 1829 gave instructions as to the disposal of 'all that my messuage (now occupied as a Public House and called Pool house) with the Outbuildings – now in the occupation of Robert Breckell as tenant'.[17] Robert Breckell is first mentioned as having been granted a licence in 1812 and he retained it until his death in 1832.

In 1834 *Pigots Directory* named Elizabeth Breckell as an innkeeper at an inn where 'letters' could be received. The inn was presumably Pool House but she must have left soon after as by 1841 William Grimbaldeston was the innkeeper. In 1851 Pool Lane appears to have been known as Guides Lane (again, not to be confused with Guides House at Warton), and by this time John Harrison had taken over from William Grimbaldeston. The inn remained in the ownership of the trustees of the Hall family until the 1860s when a Mr Baron became the owner.

The census return of 1861 names Matthew Cross as innkeeper of the Bush Inn in Guides House Lane. In 1871 and 1881 he is described as both innkeeper and farmer (of 12¾ acres), a dual role perhaps necessary due to the inn no longer being on a well-used route. Its greater reliability on the 'excursion' trade seems to be confirmed by the statement that 'at weekends waggonettes in large numbers rumbled down to the Bush for ale, porter, pies and peas and it became a popular rendezvous both for Prestonians and even as far away as Blackpool'.[18] In 1890 the inn could provide two beds for travellers, any refreshments for up to twenty persons and stabling for two horses.[19] At some unknown date Matthew Cross purchased the inn and following his death in 1887 was succeeded as owner by his son Thomas. When Thomas died in 1908 ownership passed to his widow Jane who continued to trade until 1910, whereafter the building was occupied as a farmhouse. The farmhouse was ultimately purchased by British Aerospace who demolished it in 1974.

'Mariners Arms'

Situated on the 'bottoms' road adjacent to the premises of the Freckleton Boatyard is the property known latterly as Poolside Farm but which, in the late eighteenth and early nineteenth centuries, is said to have been the 'Mariners Arms'. Unfortunately there is no known documentation which refers specifically to an inn of that name and the only indication that the building was used for such purposes comes from the statement that 'it received its licence in 1790 and relinquished it in 1843'.[20]

However, assuming that the present building, particularly in view of its location, was indeed previously an inn then it is possible that, together with the Ship Inn/Bunkers Hill and the Bush Inn, it was one of the three inns that were licensed in 1766. In 1822 one of the then three licensed inns was known as the Masons Arms and perhaps this was the 'Mariners Arms' which the newly licensed innkeeper, Robert Alston, had decided to rename, though in practice the original name continued through tradition.

The 1830 township survey gives no indication of any inn called the 'Mariners Arms'. This, together with the fact that by 1833 Robert Alston was the innkeeper at Bunkers Hill, suggests that the 'Mariners Arms' had ceased trading by that date. In 1838 the property was owned by the Rev. James Fox, a master at Kirkham Grammar School, and the occupier was Peter Houghton. In 1841 Peter Houghton was still the occupier but there is nothing in the census return of that year to suggest that he was an innkeeper.

Cyclists Arms

This inn which stood opposite Holy Trinity Church can be first identified as a beerhouse from the 1851 census, when the occupant, John Clifton, was described as a beerseller and farmer. The 1853 township valuation shows the owner to be Jane Clifton, mother of John, who at the time she purchased the property was still tenant of the Coach and Horses. Prior to her death in 1854 Jane Clifton appears to have been in dispute with the Hornby family, the then owners of the Coach and Horses, though the reasons for the dispute are unclear. According to one story the beerhouse was for many years known as the 'Lower' Coach and

Horses, whilst the word 'Original' was added by the new owners to the existing Coach and Horses. Confirmation of this disagreement can be found in the 1868 township valuation when both properties are entered under the name Coach and Horses.[21]

Due once more to the absence of documentation its subsequent history is rather vague but at sometime between 1868 and 1881 the executors of Jane Clifton sold to Peter Wareing and it was probably soon afterwards that the building first acquired the name of *Cyclists Arms*. In 1922 the then owners, Burtonwood Brewery, sold the property to the landlord William Helm. The building was destroyed in the air disaster of 1944.

Stanley Arms

As already mentioned the present Stanley House stands on or near the site of the dwelling house which in 1783 John Foster bequeathed to his niece Dorothy Threlfall, the wife of William Threlfall. In 1823 the property – it is unclear whether it was the actual dwelling house or land attached to it – was sold to John Baker who built a new house on the site. Confirmation of this transaction is contained in the minutes of a township meeting held in 1850 when William Threlfall senior was recorded as saying that 'the property formerly belonged his father – [and] afterwards John Baker bought the property [and] built a house upon it'.[22] As we have seen John Baker did not live long to enjoy his new home and the property passed into the ownership of Cicely Wright of Kirkham. In 1838 Thomas Wright, shipbuilder, was the occupier but by 1841 it had become a beerhouse with Nancy Kirby as the beerseller. By 1853 Nancy Kirby had married Henry Young who in 1858 was described as a beer retailer and vessel owner, but it was Nancy herself who appears to have run the beerhouse until sometime in the 1870s. The Wright family were still the owners in 1868 but shortly afterwards it passed into the ownership of Dr William Shaw of Kirkham. By 1910 the owners were Walmsley & Co, of Preston and from about 1913 until 1922, when the Stanley Arms closed, Betsy Brindle was the landlady.

'Lamaleach Inn'

Situated almost on the Freckleton/Warton boundary the dwelling now known as Lamaleach Farm was built about 1840. On the 1851 census the occupant was named as Marsden Rigby senior (the son of Robert Marsden Rigby and Elizabeth Grayson), who was described as 'beerseller farms 14 acres', although it was probably Ellen, his wife, who was the actual landlady. Marsden Rigby died in 1855 and as we have seen it was presumably then that Ellen left Lamaleach to become landlady at the Coach and Horses. By 1861 John Etherington was combining beer retailing with farming at Lamaleach, but by 1868 he had left and John Townsend had taken over.

John Hargreaves, the owner since at least 1853, died sometime prior to 1868, as in that year his executors were entered on the township valuation as the owners of the property. In 1868 the building was still described as a beerhouse but by 1871, possibly following its sale to new owners, it appears to have been used solely as a farmhouse and its brief existence as a beerhouse had ceased.

Part IX

The Modern Township

CHAPTER 25

Victorian Freckleton

The Early Victorian Township

By 1841 the population had risen to 995, with the majority of those of working age finding employment at the linen factory owned by the Mayor family, as handloom weavers, at the port as either mariners or in shipbuilding, or on the local farms. In addition to those employed in industrial activities and allied trades there was also a barber, butcher, confectioner, six grocers, three shoemakers and three tailors; whilst the (Kirkham Road) Methodist Chapel, Holy Trinity Chapel and Trinity (National) School served the spiritual and educational needs of the community. Law and order was the responsibility of the village police-man, who lived in Higher Road,[1] and who had been appointed to Freckleton following the adoption by the county in 1839 of the Rural Constabulary Act. By 1851 a post office had opened in Lower Road with James Hargreaves as postmaster.

Until the middle of the nineteenth century the main street of the township was the present Preston Old Road and the historical significance of this part of the township is still preserved today by the use of the term 'down town'. On the 1841 census present day Kirkham Road and most of Preston Old Road as far Bunker Street was recorded as Higher Road, whilst Lower Road included present day Lower Lane and also that part of Preston Old Road from Bunker Street to the marsh gate.

On the Ordnance Survey map of 1840 the road leading to Warton was called Lamaleach Road, but on the 1841 census properties that stood around the Green and continued into the present School Lane were recorded as being in Chapel Street (so named after the chapel of Holy Trinity). Spring Gardens was known as Bedlam and Bunker Street was referred to as Bunkers Street, with the properties to the south of Bunkers

Hill (the Ship Inn) still retaining their ancient names of Dungeon Row and Park Nook. Clitheroes Lane, presumably so named after the family of that name who resided in the township in the late seventeenth century, and Strike Lane were known just as Clitheroes and Strike.

The tithe survey of 1838 recorded no less than seventy eight landowners in Freckleton, and although Hugh Hornby of Ribby owned the largest individual acreage he did not reside in the township. Several of the larger properties – Church House, Grove House, Mount House, Rigby House and the house that later became the first parsonage – were still owned and lived in by the members of the Mayor family. The owner of Raker House was Walton Bulcock, a grandson of Robert Freckleton. Members of the Goodshaw family resided at Ivy Cottage and Holly House, whilst Naze House was still occupied by Jane de la Pryme, a member of a Blackburn merchant family resident in Freckleton since the beginning of the century. The handloom weavers and factory workers were concentrated in Higher Road and in Bunkers Street, where families associated with maritime trades also lived.

Bunker Street. Named after the inn called Bunkers Hill (now the Ship) it was called Bunkers Street on the nineteenth-century census returns until 1891, when the 's' was dropped and it became known as Bunker Street.

Township Administration

For most of the Victorian period township affairs were administered by the long established practice of holding an annual town meeting at which the ratepayers elected or selected a township committee. The township minute book shows that from 1848 until 1894 the township (committee) annually appointed two overseers of the poor, two collectors of property and income tax, and one surveyor of the highways, until 1864 when that office also became the responsibility of two men.[2]

Some of the decisions taken at these meetings suggests that a small number of ratepayers were determined to keep expense to a minimum unless it was to their advantage, as in 1863 when at a township meeting to discuss the Local Government Act 1858 the motion that the Act 'shall not be adopted in this Township' was carried without dissent. In 1880 a proposal by the Kirkham Gas Company to supply gas to Freckleton was met with the unanimous decision 'that the Township of Freckleton rejects the application of the Kirkham Gas Company' followed, as we will see shortly, by the almost unbelieveable decision in 1883 that there was no need to sewer the township.

The commitee did, however, have to allocate an amount each year for the maintenance of the highways. Of particular contention for many years was Naze Lane and in March 1852 Mr Crossfield (of Naze Mount) and Mr Myres (of Naze House) managed to have a resolution passed (it was rescinded three months later) that required the township to pay for its repair. Twenty five years later John Crossfield was still attempting to have the lane maintained at the expense of the township and it was not until legal advice was obtained that it was decided that 'the Ratepayers have no powers to order the Surveyors to repair Naze Lane'.

The Local Government Act of 1894, however, brought much needed reform to an outdated system, and in elections for the first Freckleton parish council no less than eighteen candidates stood for the nine seats allocated to the township. Richard Mason of Lower House Farm topped the poll with 147 votes, and Richard Cookson was chosen as chairman of the council – a post he retained until 1904.

Health and Sanitation

Early concern about the spread of disease can be detected in an order made at a township meeting in 1756 when it was agreed 'to cause the Earth [nightsoil] to be removed from the side of Joseph Lancaster's garding [garden] as used or take what befalls the owner of the land'.³ It was, however, not until almost a century later that the 1848 Public Health Act first gave power to local authorities to appoint a medical officer of health. Some idea of the sanitary conditions then prevailing in the district can be obtained from the report made in 1851 by Dr William Gradwell, who was appointed by the General Board of Health to inspect conditions in Kirkham.⁴ In Kirkham, for example, he reported that 'at the bottom of Freckleton Street, opposite the police station' and where 'the stench was abominable' there was 'a semi fluid nightsoil coming down a covered passage between two houses, and then along the street'.

In his report Dr Gradwell also noted that 'scarlet fever prevailed epidemically about seven years ago, and of a very malignant character. – It was all round about as well as in the town [of Kirkham] – I had upwards of 300 cases – We had a few cases of cholera, about a dozen in 1849 – The diarrhoea cases were very numerous – Measles has not been very prevalent, but the cases have been severe, and many children

Central Terrace. During the early to mid-Victorian years cottages on the present site were occupied by sacking weavers and at one period the area was known as 'Hungry Hill'. According to the datestone Central Terrace (right) was rebuilt in 1882 and was perhaps one of the earliest attempts at improving living conditions in the village. Facing Central Terrace is the entry to the former ropeyard of Henry James Hall. (*Courtesy of* Lancashire Evening Post)

after appearing to get over measles well, have died of pneumonia'. Although the report makes no specific reference to Freckleton the fact that, in spite of an increase in population from 701 in 1811 to 995 in 1841, the number of houses had increased by only forty to 186, no doubt meant that in parts of the village conditions were probably little better than those in Kirkham. Indeed infant mortality remained high throughout the second half of the nineteenth century and an analysis of the burials recorded in Holy Trinity burial register from 1860 to 1900 reveals that 200, or 35%, of the 555 burials were of infants aged up to 6 years.

By the middle of the nineteenth century it was becoming recognised that the spread of diseases such as cholera and diarrhoea were caused by an infected water supply and poor drainage. In 1845 a township pump had been installed and in 1848 the township committee received 6*d.* from Henry Whiteside 'for the ground rent of the Pump placed upon the Smithy Green, he having a sum of money in his hands which he had collected from different parties who subscribed towards the Pump'.[5]

During the 1850s and 1860s there is not a single mention in the township minute book of the need for proper sewering of the township and it was only at the instigation of the Rural Sanitary Authority in 1873 that consideration began to be given to the matter. By the mid-1870s it would seem that part of the township already had some form of sewerage system, as in 1875 the attention of the parochial committee was drawn to the nuisance caused by the outlet of the sewer opposite Holy Trinity Church. Such a nuisance cannot have been reassuring for those still using the township pump on the Green, which in December 1876 was noted to be in a defective state.

In September 1879 Rev. W. Scott complained of 'the flow of sewage through his garden'[6] and at the same time his neighbour, Charles Mayor of Rigby House, also complained of an unspecified, though no doubt related, problem. Sometime early in 1883 Charles Mayor instructed his solicitor to complain 'of the want of sewage [disposal] in Freckleton' and it was possibly this that prompted the Sanitary Authority to write to the overseer of Freckleton suggesting the appointment of a parochial committee 'for the purpose of considering what additional sewerage is necessary'.[7] The suggestion was discussed at a township meeting in April 1883 when it was proposed by William Cookson, seconded and carried that no committee be appointed 'as in the opinion of this meeting it is not necessary to sewer the township'.[8]

By 1888, however, possibly due to pressure from the Rural Sanitary Authority, a more realistic attitude was taken and those present at the township meeting that year were of the opinion that the proposed sewer along Warton Lane (Lytham Road) 'was not sufficient' and 'that it should be extended so as to sewer as much of the village as possible'. At the same meeting it was decided that the money collected by Mr E. Bonney from persons on the Green 'be used in keeping the Towns pump in repair'.[9]

At a meeting of a parochial committee held in June 1889 it was agreed that 'A sewerage scheme was becoming an absolute necessity and required attention'.[10] When in December the same year a scheme was adopted a newspaper report described the village as having:

> developed considerably, and in one section of it [Lytham Road] a large number of houses have been erected by Mr Sowerbutts, to accommodate the increased population which has been attracted by the extensions effected in his mill.
>
> Again, the new coast line to Blackpool will pass through Freckleton, and in prospect of this houses have been erected, whilst many others will undoubtedly be built.
>
> The refuse from the new erections has hitherto passed into tanks, and thence into the waterways at the road sides, where its presence has been anything but productive to a continuation of the healthy condition of the district. The other portion of the village has already a system of sewerage in use, but to receive the sanction of the Local Government Board it was necessary to deal with the whole township.[11]

In order to pay for the system to be installed £3,000 was borrowed by the Rural Sanitary Authority from the Prudential Assurance Company at 3½%, repayable by 30 equal yearly instalments. However, in view of the fact that in June 1892 the Sanitary Authority ordered that 'a call be made on the Overseers of Freckleton for £163 2s. 4d. being the first instalment of Loan and Interest to the Prudential Assurance Co. Ltd', it would seem that the actual costs fell on the ratepayers of Freckleton. In 1890 Fylde Waterworks laid a water main from Kirkham to Freckleton and by 1893 the sewerage system was complete. This only partially resolved the problem, however, and as we will see in the next chapter even in the 1920s calls were still being made for better sanitation.

Workhouse to Welfare

In 1834 amendments to the Act governing the administration of the Poor Law placed responsibility for the poor in the hands of Poor Law Unions, controlled by elected boards of guardians. Each guardian was elected locally, though the franchise was restricted to ratepayers and landowners, and was responsible for the day to day management of parochial poor relief. The Act minimised the provision of outdoor relief and made confinement in the workhouse the central element of the new system, whilst at the same time actively discouraging all but the most desperate from seeking assistance. In 1837 the Fylde Union was established, and in 1844 a Union Workhouse was built in Station Road, Kirkham. This in turn was replaced by a new workhouse at Wesham in 1907.

The earliest record of the appointment of a guardian for Freckleton is in 1848 when Robert Mayor was appointed. He served until at least 1851 when he was succeeded by John Watson. The two men who gave the longest service in Freckleton were Thomas Green, guardian from 1864 to 1875, and William Segar Hodgson from 1876 to 1891. Unlike the period 1803 to 1834 there is little first hand information about the conditions of, and relief given to, the poor during the years 1844 to 1894, apart from the paying of doles, usually 1s. 0d., to approximately thirty recipients each 23 December.[12]

Life for many, however, must have continued to be a struggle for survival, as exemplified by James Blackhurst, a sacking weaver born in Freckleton in 1795 who received intermittent relief throughout his life and died in Kirkham Workhouse in 1871. As we saw previously it was necessary, during the 1862–63 cotton famine, to request outside assistance in order to maintain the large number of residents requiring relief. Remarkably at no annual township meeting held in those two years was there any mention of the state of the poor, nor did either the guardian or overseer of the poor appear to have played any part in the providing of relief, though in the absence of perhaps now lost documentary evidence to the contrary this may be unfair criticism.

Friendly Societies

As we saw in chapter 7 one means whereby workers could ensure they received some form of assistance during periods of unemployment, due to sickness or other difficulties, was to make contributions to a friendly society. It is probable that a friendly society existed in the township during the middle years of the nineteenth century and certainly by the 1870s this important social function was being fulfilled by two societies – the Rechabites and the Mechanics.

A tent (society) of the Independent Order of Rechabites was established in 1873–74, and in 1875 George Wylie Rigby, 'the energetic secretary', was recorded as saying that 'the tent was opened two years ago with 13 members, and that they now numbered 29 persons'. At the same time it was also reported that 'they have also a juvenile tent, and hope to enlist the female portion of the village into a female tent. We understand they have not yet been called upon for any sick pay since the tent was opened'.[13] The Rechabites were also a temperance movement and in 1884 it was reported that 'they have not been altogether unsuccessful, for it is stated that drunkeness is gradually on the decline'.[14] In his 1884 report the secretary stated that there were 49 honorary members and 200 paying members. Six members had received sick allowance of £19 18s. 4d. and the Order had a balance of £146 10s. 6½d., of which £134 11s. 0d. had been invested in the Kirkham Savings Bank. The worth per member was £2 19s. 9½d.

It is not known in which year the Freckleton branch of the Independent Order of Mechanics was established but by 1883 they had £443 invested in the Kirkham Savings Bank. In 1884 they numbered 126 and it was reported that during the year the amount of money expended on sick members had been £96 10s. 6d., outlay on the funeral fund had been £37 15s. 0d.[15] and expenditure on the tribute fund came to £2 9s. 3¾d. Unlike the Rechabites the Mechanics were not associated with the temperance movement and met on a Saturday at the Coach and Horses Inn. During the last two decades of the nineteenth century and the early twentieth century their secretary was John Hargreaves.

Both the Rechabites and the Mechanics continued to fulfill a necessary role into the twentieth century, but with the advent of social reforms such as the National Insurance Bill of 1911 the state itself gradually began to take over the work previously done by such societies.

Club Day

The origins of Club Day almost certainly began with the establishment of the friendly societies in the early nineteenth century. Traditional club days appear to have been held on the first or second Monday in August, and although it is not known when the first club day processions took place it was reported in 1911 that Mr William Pilkington of Preston had attended the annual festivities for fifty years.[16] From 1875 an annual Rechabite procession also took place on a Saturday in September in order to publicise the benefits of membership and temperance. The earliest mention of a forthcoming club day fair is contained in two proposals passed at the township meeting held in May 1879:

The origins of Club Day almost certainly began with the establishment of Friendly
Societies in the nineteenth century and by the 1880s the churches also participated in the
annual parades. In this pre-1915 photograph the Holy Trinity procession is lined up by
the village green on which can be seen the travelling fair.

> that the village or smithy Green be taken into care of the Parish and that
> a rent be paid by the occupiers of it such as Showmen and Photographers
> tents Shooting galleries etc.;
>   that the amount or rent to be paid by the aforesaid strolling occupants
> of the Green be one shilling per night. The cash to go to the Highway
> Rate.[17]

In 1884 it was reported that 'the village green was especially gay.
Around it were the usual catchpenny contrivances – a photographic
establishment, try-your-strength machine, a few Aunt Sallies, sundry
stalls, and a swing-boats – while on the green itself bands were playing
the greater portion of the day. Altogether, the amount of interest taken
in Freckleton club day seems to increase annually, and the village, in
respect of club days, most assuredly holds its own with, if it does not
even outvie its neighbour Kirkham'.[18] On Monday 3 August 1885 when
the Order of Mechanics walked with Holy Trinity Church in the morning
and the Primitive Methodist Church and Wesleyan Methodist Church

walked in the afternoon, the occasion was described as being when 'the inhabitants of Freckleton determined the best use of the opportunity of enjoying themselves by participating in the sports and pastimes attending the celebrations of so auspicious an event'.[19] The Rechabites, however, did not participate, presumably preferring as in former years to have their own separate procession at a later date.

During the late Victorian period Balderstone Mill ceased work on the previous Saturday, and in addition to the club day events of the following Monday festivities also took place on the Tuesday. In 1886 it was reported that the day after club day between 200 and 300 people went by train from Kirkham to Liverpool, whilst others went to Blackpool and Southport. Others took a sail on the paddle steamer *Winnie*, built at Freckleton that year, starting from Naze Point shortly after 8 a.m. and calling at Lytham, Southport and Blackpool before returning home just after 7 p.m.[20] In 1896 the newly established parish council 'let the fair rights for the sum of £4 10s. 0d. to Peter Rawstrone and his brother-in-law William Iddon'[21] who then 'let off coconut shies, swing-boats and a roundabout'.[22]

Pastimes and Sports

One of the few surviving first hand accounts of the secular social activities that took place during the early years of Queen Victoria's reign relates to the annual Gooseberry Show, 'where berries of extraordinary size and succulence were exhibited, and prizes such as tea-kettles and tea services were distributed'.[23] On 3 August 1848 Adam Wright recorded in a letter to his great-neice, 'in the morning I went to Freckleton to see [Edward] Houseman's gooseberries as Friday is the Show Day. I am sorry to say that many of his best have cracked and burst from the wetness of the weather, so that unless other people's have done the same, he will not have so good a chance of a kettle, he has still some fine ones'.[24]

For most people, however, the various church functions were the focal point for their social activities and the Christmas and New Year tea parties continued to be an annual event for all the churches throughout the Victorian period. In addition there was a wide range of other events, as revealed by the following selection of entries from the Trinity School log book:

> 20 Nov. 1876   School work ended at 3.30 p.m. to prepare for a lecture
> on Phrenology.

25 June 1887	Jubilee Tea Party and treat to scholars – past and present – under 18 years of age, with Old people over 60 years of age.
10 Sept. 1888	Mr T H Myres called to leave notices of Primrose League meeting and Lecture on Lighthouses.
5 Nov. 1892	Concert by Wesleyans.
12 Nov. 1892	Tea & Concert by Co-operative Society.
12 Oct. 1898	Missionary meeting and magic lantern exhibition [held] last night.
21 Nov. 1898	A dance was held in the Schoolroom on Saturday night.

The still evident musical tradition first began in the nineteenth century, and in 1886 the Freckleton Brass Band was formed. In 1955 two surviving members of the original band, Robert Rawstrone aged 89 and James Hawthornthwaite aged 87, recalled that they and their friends 'used to meet in a cottage in Kirkham road'[25] and that it was at one of these social gatherings that someone suggested forming a band. Having managed to raise £50 to buy a set of secondhand instruments, which according to tradition 'were taken around the village on a hand cart to see if

The earliest known photograph of Freckleton Brass Band taken at the beginning of the twentieth century.

From the mid-sixteenth century until the twentieth century the surname Coulburn
(and its several variants, Coulborne, Cowburn and Colebrand) was one of the
commonest village surnames. In this photograph taken in the 1890s, John and Ann
Coulburn, together with three of their sons Robert (turning handle), Lawrence and
William, are engaged in some unidentified process involving potatoes. In 1898 John
Coulburn was described as a rope and twine maker at Park Nook Farm.

anyone was interested in having a go',[26] 'they started to practise hard
in a room above an inn in Bunker Street'.[27]

Within two years of its formation an entry in the school log book
for 28 May 1888 records: 'school premises used by Freckleton Brass Band
on Saturday night last'. The earliest known outside public performance
of the band was at the laying of the memorial stone of the new Primitive
Methodist Chapel in August 1891. On 10 December 1892 there was a
'Band concert in the Schoolroom' and on 14 February 1896 'the School
[was] closed all day to allow the Freckleton Brass Band the use of the
rooms for a Sale of Work to be opened at 7 p.m.' In September 1900
the band headed the procession at the opening of the Holy Family
Church.

Known sporting activities were confined to football and cricket. In
December 1884 Mr Bramwell recorded in the school log book that 'the
boys of the village are intensely fond of the game of football and no
attempt is made by the police authorities to stop it in the main road
near the School and Church. The Schoolmaster has forbidden the kicking

SMITHY, FRECKLETON.   E. BEATTIE·Delt 1892.

This pen and ink drawing by Beattie was made in 1892 and whilst the smithy was the focus of his attention the drawing also depicts the Cyclists Arms and the 'old' Plough Inn. Also shown is the pump on the village green which was a regular topic of discussion and concern at Victorian township meetings.

of anything about the School Yard but very rough play goes on in the road near the Church'.

Due to an obvious lack of recreational facilities within the village the marsh seems to have been the favoured alternative venue for team sports. In June 1885 a special meeting of the marsh gate owners was called to consider 'if any steps should be taken to prevent parties playing Foot Ball on the Marsh', and the following February the owners resolved that a deputation be appointed 'to wait upon the football and cricket players with powers to make some arrangements either to let them some gates if convenient and that Dr Shaw be empowered with the marsh managers to make some terms with them'.[28] The outcome of the meeting is unknown but it is possible that it resulted in the establishment of the first Freckleton football team, an assumption partially supported by an undated photograph, probably taken sometime in the 1880s, of a

Freckleton football team captained by John Hacking who was born in 1864. The progress of this club is not known but by 1898 the present club had been formed under the name of Freckleton United Football Club.[29]

The Late Victorian Township

By 1900, even though some properties had been rebuilt, the layout of the village was essentially that of sixty years earlier. First time properties had been built on the east side of the Green during the 1860s, whilst the beginnings of the development of Lytham Road followed the purchase of Balderstone Mill by William Sowerbutts and the subsequent building of dwellings for some of his employees. Population growth during the Victorian period had been somewhat erratic as the township experienced the changes brought about by the demise of some trades, the vagaries of the cotton industry, and changes in agriculture practices. From the high of 995 in 1841 the population had dropped to 879 in 1861, thereafter rising rapidly until it reached 1308 in 1891.

Although a slight decrease took place during the next decade, by 1898 village retailers and tradesmen included six grocers, two of whom were also cab proprietors, one fruiterer and one greengrocer, two butchers, a fried fish dealer, three lamp and oil dealers, a draper and a milliner, four boot and shoe makers, a painter, a plumber, a hairdresser, four (general) shopkeepers and the Co-op Store. The township, however, was to remain effectively isolated until the development of road transport that took place after World War I.

CHAPTER 26

Twentieth-century Freckleton

Township Administration

As we saw in the last chapter Freckleton Parish Council was established in 1894 and from then until 1974 the township was administered as part of the Fylde Rural District Council. Since 1974 it has come within the jurisdiction of the Fylde Borough Council. After the first parish council election in 1894 no poll was necessary until 1904, when councillors were elected by a show of hands by those attending the annual meeting. In 1907 a full election took place followed by another in 1910 when twenty two men stood for the nine seats; a similar situation prevailed in 1922, whilst in 1925 more votes were recorded than in any previous election.

In 1939 the County of Lancaster (Township of Freckleton) Order laid down that parish councillors 'shall be elected by nomination, and when

Village Green – Presentation of coronation mugs in 1911. In former times the location of many village events, in 1924 part of the Green became the site of the War Memorial and this, together with the completion of the new road in 1926, removed forever an ancient village landmark.

Village Green – *c.* 1920. Within twenty years of the Beattie drawing the smithy had been purchased by the District Bank who subsequently erected a new building on the site. However, as the war Memorial has not yet been built this photograph must have been taken before 1924.

the number of nominees exceeds the number of vacancies, by a poll'. In 1958 the number of councillors was increased to twelve and in 1964 the township was divided into East ward and West ward, with six councillors representing each ward. Councillors such as Walter Rawsthorne (1913–53) and Richard Spencer MBE (1946–95) served continuously from the time of their first election without ever being defeated. Several others have given twenty or thirty years' service and, together with those who served for less, have all made their contribution to the steady progress of the township. Since 1958 an increasing number of women have served on the parish council and in 1995 Marlene Dowling became the first person from Freckleton to be appointed a Deputy Lieutenant for the County of Lancaster.

Local Affairs

Some of the responsibilities of the parish council, such as the poultry allotments, have already been mentioned, whilst the role played by the council in establishing recreational facilities will be described later in this chapter. In the years leading up to World War I the council dealt with such local matters as road and bridge maintenance, the collection of rubbish, and burst sewer pipes. The problem of 'night soil' also required attention and in 1911 Coun. T. Slater suggested 'that some kind of disinfectant ought to be got and stored away for the use of any inhabitant when emptying ashpits',[1] whilst in 1922 Robert Wilson, on behalf of the ex-servicemen's association, called 'for better sanitation' and 'that ash pits be abolished and water closets put in'.[2]

In 1919 the parish council resolved to make presentations to two Freckleton men in recognition of their services and bravery during the World War I. Sergeant James Halsall had been awarded the Military Medal on 16 August 1917, and one month later, on 17 September 1917, Private Harry Hall was also awarded the Military Medal whilst serving as a stretcher bearer in the Loyal North Lancashire Regiment. Sixteen Freckleton men were killed on active service during World War I and

Barkers Cottages, Preston Old Road. Built in 1906 to replace older dwellings on the same site the name derives from the Barker family who acquired, through marriage, many of the Mayor family properties.

Stanley Terrace, Kirkham Road. The houses on the left of the picture, up to the junction with School Lane, were demolished in *c.*1925 to make way for the new road. At the time the middle left corner shop was occupied by the Fylde Industrial Co-op Stores.

their names are inscribed on the village war memorial that was unveiled in 1924.

The difficulties posed by a lack of any accessible public transport meant that for the first quarter of the twentieth century the township was effectively isolated. In 1901 plans were drawn up by the Blackpool, Lytham & St Annes Tramways Co. to extend the tramway from Lytham through Warton and on to Freckleton, where it was to run onto a new light railway to connect with the Preston system at Ashton. Permission for the extension was refused, but had it been granted the tramway would have entered the village just to the south of Lamaleach Farm, continuing to run parallel with Lytham Road before cutting across Clitheroes Lane by Refuge Farm. It would have then have passed behind Holy Trinity Church curving slightly as it crossed Preston Old Road, by Grove House, before crossing the present school playing fields. Finally, after crossing Lower Lane, and passing just north of Brades Farm, it would have followed a straight line to the toll house.[3]

Even after World War I 'the only means of public transport was a one-horsed covered waggonette which ran, or more often walked to Preston on four days a week',[4] and in fact the village had to wait until the early 1920s for its first bus service, operated by Laws, to commence. This service was followed soon after by John Bull buses.[5] The completion of Preston New Road in 1926 was therefore arguably the most important event of the last century as it provided, for the first time, easy access to neighbouring towns, and by 1927 there was 'an excellent bus service to Preston, Lytham and Kirkham'.[6] However, such was the apparent increase in traffic that 'owing to the dangerous cross roads in the centre of the village' it was the opinion of the parish council in February 1927 that 'there ought to be some one on regular point duty'.[7] In the same year the council also made an unsuccessful request to the Ribble Bus Company for a bus shelter.

The War Memorial was unveiled in 1924 and recorded the names of the sixteen Freckleton men who died in WWI. The names of those who died in subsequent conflicts have also been inscribed. (*Courtesy of* Lancashire Evening Post)

New Road to Preston. An undated photograph but presumably *c.*1926. The site of the Co-op stores has been reduced to rubble and a vehicle is entering the village on the new road. The butcher's shop on the opposite corner of School Lane was owned by James Bonney. The business later passed to the Snape family and is now the oldest in Freckleton having been established in 1864. (*Courtesy of* Lancashire Evening Post)

In 1928 the Lytham St Annes Electricity Department began laying a service cable to consumers and on 18 June 1929 the mayor of Lytham St Annes switched on the supply of electricity to Freckleton. The parish council also had an agreement with Lytham St Annes Corporation that the Lytham St Annes fire brigade would attend any fire in the village. However in 1932 this arrangement was not renewed as the parish council considered the terms unacceptable, and it would appear that thereafter it was the engine from Wesham that attended any serious incident.

Following the outbreak of war in 1939 the village was very soon surrounded by military camps and a large tented RAF camp was established on land near to Hall Cross between Kirkham Road and Lower Lane. On the night of Sunday 15 September 1940 a lone German aircraft dropped sixteen bombs in the Warton and Freckleton area causing some damage to property, but not casualties. It resulted in the destruction of the blacksmith's shop, situated next to Kirkham Road Methodist church, occupied by Mr & Mrs Fred Rayton and his family. Because of wartime reporting restrictions the location of the bombing raid was reported as having taken place 'in a rural area near a North-west coastal town'. The damage to the smithy was described in a subsequent propoganda broadcast, made by 'Lord' Haw Haw, as the destruction of an iron foundry! In 1941 Freckleton set the whole country an example when the 'Dig for Victory' campaign began and in May that year the campaign was inaugurated in the village with a visit from the Duke of Norfolk.

In the previous year the government began to build the aerodrome at Warton and in 1942 it was handed over to the United States Army Air Force (USAAF) and used as an aircraft assembly plant. Known as Base Air Depot 2 (BAD2), over 10,000 American servicemen were stationed in the area, including at Freckleton, on land around and at the rear of Lamaleach Farm (Site 10), along Naze Lane, now the Naze Lane Industrial Estate (Site 11), and adjacent to the Recreation Ground, along Croft Butts Lane and next to Further Ends Farm (Site 12).

The 1944 Air Disaster

The disaster occurred at approximately 10.45 a.m. on Wednesday, 23 August 1944, when an American Liberator aircraft was hit by lightning and fell onto the infants department of Trinity School, setting it on fire. This was followed by further violent explosions and after the crash 'firemen had difficulty in preventing the flames enveloping the senior school from which children had fled in terror'.[8] It also destroyed the café facing the school, owned by Alan and Rachel Whittle, known as the Sad Sack, and two other properties. There are many graphic accounts of the subseqent rescue attempts and although, to quote the words of the then deputy coroner, 'it would be invidious to single out anyone for what they did in their attempts at rescue in this appalling tragedy', there are certain individual or collective acts that should not go unrecorded in what was the worst ever disaster in the history of Freckleton.

Section Leader Hunt, of the National Fire Service, in giving an account of how difficulties had to be overcome at the outset of the disaster, told how, after rushing to the scene from Kirkham, that he found 'both sides of the road were ablaze and the main water supply was blocked with debris'. Three men were put on rescue work but as this was practically impossible without water, he got 50 Americans to carry the trailer pump over the debris in the road to the mill lodge. He added 'I found some more Americans and organised a rescue party to clear the debris off the children. By then another pump had arrived from St Annes, so we were able to concentrate one hose on the school, and another on the other side of the road'.[9] A further tribute was paid to the American military by Police Superintendent Hinds, of whom he said 'there is no praise too high. They did an admirable job, working in great danger when the fire was at its height, in rescue work and removing bodies'.[10]

Writing in his capacity as deputy chief warden Mr W. S. Durant referred to the fact that '50% of the local personnel attached to Freckleton's Warden Post, were on the scene and in action almost immediately and rendered valuable assistance in every possible way'. Warden W Banks, 'who saw the incident occur from his place of employment, the Post Office, informed the Police Station at Kirkham at the same time as it was actually happening'. Warden Miss C. Allsup 'was on the scene immediately and guided personnel of the American Air Force who were there from the front of the School whence approach was impossible on the account of the intensity of the fire to the back of the school where some attempt at rescue might be possible'. Warden Miss M. Wharton 'was undoubtedly outstanding for her work with regard to maintaining morale and for her untiring efforts in visiting the various houses. At her request I accompanied her to the American Crash

Memorial – Holy Trinity churchyard. The memorial to the victims of the 1944 air disaster was unveiled on 24 May 1947. The cost of nearly £1100 was mostly subscribed by the families of the bereaved and their friends.

Hospital for the purpose of obtaining definite knowledge about the casualties there and in an endeavour to stop or substantiate rumours there were in the area'.[11]

The highest praise was reserved for the headmaster Mr F. A. Billington who 'himself was a member of the Wardens Service in Freckleton and, although his own child was in another part of the School, by his action in an effort to rescue the children and the members of his Staff in the Infants department, he maintained the highest traditions of the Service. There is abundant testimony of the gallant rescue work he performed and no doubt that his action was the means of saving several lives. He sustained considerable injury (by burning) to his hands whilst engaged in this work. Reference too must be made to the great amount of work carried out by him throughout the rest of that day in the interest of the children and their parents'.[12]

The funeral service took place on Saturday 26 August when thirty six children, together with their teacher Miss Jennie Hall, were buried together in one large communal grave. The six adults and one child who had been in the Sad Sack café were placed in an adjoining grave. The Bishop of Blackburn preached the sermon and amongst those who assisted in the service was the vicar, the Rev. J. W. Broadbent; the two local Methodist ministers, the Rev. R Armstrong and the Rev. A. Bell; and Chaplain H. Knies of the USAAF. The American Army authorities undertook to bear the whole of the expenses. Further internments took place in the following week and the final death toll of sixty-one comprised thirty eight schoolchildren, two teachers, seven British civilians, four RAF personnel and ten USAAF airmen, including the three crew members of the Liberator.

At the inquest for the victims a verdict of 'misadventure in all cases' was recorded, whilst the investigation board of the USAAF concluded that 'the cause of this accident is unknown'. There are memorials to the victims in Holy Trinity churchyard, unveiled on 24 May 1947, and at the headquarters of the United States 8th Air Force Division, Savannah, Georgia. Annual wreath laying ceremonies take place at each memorial every 23 August by British and American members of the BAD2 association.

Following the disaster three appeals were launched. The American appeal for a children's memorial playground in due course provided the playground and memorial park that is now maintained by the parish council. The fund set up by the Church of England contributed towards the building of the New Memorial School. The fund set up by the parish council is now administered by trustees.

Club Day

Traditional club days were held up to the outbreak of World War I. In 1919 it was decided to hold peace celebrations and throughout most of that summer discussions took place as to the events to be held and how they should be funded. The date for the celebrations was fixed for Monday 4 August but unfortunately on the actual day the planned procession was washed out due to continuous rain. However, on the 12 August the parish council confirmed that four days later sports would take place for children in the afternoon and for adults in the evening and that there was also to be maypole and morris dancing.

In the 1920s club day processions resumed but without the involvement of the friendly societies and in effect became, and continue to be, processions of witness organised by the churches. Although the annual Monday event remained the most important date in the village calendar the actual day of the event was not to the liking of the owners of Balderstone Mill. At a special meeting of the parish council held in April 1922 it was said that 'At present the holidays cause great annoyance

Club Day, *c.* 1920. When club days recommenced after the First World War only the churches took part, and in this photograph Emma Webster is leading the Sunday school scholars of the Primitive Methodist Church.

to the owners and managers at the Mill when Freckleton holidays come on one week and Preston holidays on another'.[13] After some discussion it was proposed and agreed that the holidays in August be on the same dates as Preston. In response the mill management agreed that the employees could have any full Saturday for a club day provided they gave up the Saturday before Whit week or the Saturday before August holidays, to which the employees agreed that Whit Saturday be given up as a holiday. When club day recommenced after World War II the date was fixed on the third Saturday in June.

From 1922 until 1962 the club day sports were organised by the parish council but since 1962 this responsibility has been undertaken by the Club Day Sports Committee. Following the unveiling of the War Memorial in 1924 the annual fair moved from its traditional site on the Village Green and has since been held at different locations, including the field which is now the site of the village car park, the Memorial playing field and finally Bush Lane playing fields. Although no longer club days in the older sense the present club days provide not only a yearly opportunity for all residents to share in an enjoyable day but also remain a tangible link with the first friendly society that sought to protect its members almost two hundred years ago.

Freckleton Brass Band

As we saw in the last chapter the band was formed in 1886 but the absence of any late nineteenth- or early twentieth-century minute books means that very little is known about band activities until the 1930s. The band, however, had clearly established itself as a strong competitor and in 1910, when the bandmaster was Peter Rawstrone, won second prize in a contest held at Crystal Palace, London. On return from London the band was met at Kirkham railway station 'and walked from there to Freckleton playing en route, accompanied by some 200 villagers'.[14] On several occasions during the early 1930s the band paid for the professional services of William Halliwell, who had conducted the band at Crystal Palace in 1910, and also Harold Moss. As a result of their tuition, combined with the continuing leadership of Peter Rawstrone as conductor, the band were 1st prize winners at contests held at Oldham and Leyland in 1931. Then as now the band was also annually engaged in local club days and other events such as concerts at the Public Hall, Preston. Revenue for the band was raised by holding Sunday concerts in the village, tea parties, whist drives and collections.

The disruptions to village life caused by World War II also had its effect on the band and following a meeting in August 1948, attended by just 13 members and one non member, it was resolved 'that the band terminates its activities and that the Secretary informs the Parish Council of this decision and to ask for guidance on the matter of instruments and uniforms'.[15] At a parish council meeting the following month it was decided to call for a public meeting to try to promote interest in the band, as it was felt that 'Freckleton without a Brass Band would be a calamity'.[16] Within a month a new committee, under the chairmanship of Thomas Banks, was established and they decided to appoint Alec Prosser to take charge of the band for one month at a weekly fee of 7s. 6d. It was also agreed that each band member pay 6d. weekly. Alec Prosser was to remain with the band until 1962 and during his fourteen years as musical director many competition successes were achieved, including the North-West Area Championship in 1952. The band also represented the north-western area in the All Britain brass band finals in London in 1954.

Before World War II the band consisted mainly of members of the Freckleton families of Butcher, Rawstrone, Threlfall and Whittle. James Threlfall, who died in 1938, was said to have been a founder member and in 1957 his two sons, Tom and Jack, each received recognition of their fifty years service to the band. In its early days band rehearsals were held in an upper room of the Ship Inn but at a later date moved to the now demolished stables at the rear of the Coach and Horses Inn. At present (2000) the band have their own band room situated at the entrance to the Memorial playing fields. In 1983 Paul Dalton was appointed resident conductor, becoming principal conductor in 1995. Under him the band has achieved considerable success and has worked its way from the fourth section to the championship section of the national finals and in 1997–98 were National First Section Champions.

Social Activities

It was not only Freckleton Brass Band that maintained the strong musical tradition established in the nineteenth century. In 1906 the Kirkham Road Methodist Chapel Choir began to compete at music festivals and in 1921 a ladies choir was also formed. Both these choirs were conducted by Peter Rawstrone, the conductor of Freckleton Brass Band, whose father, also called Peter, was leader of the Kirkham Road Methodist Chapel Choir from 1855 to 1895.

In June 1940 Richard Spencer organised the first Freckleton Competitive Musical Festival at Kirkham Road Methodist Church. The initial event attracted 41 competitors but when held again in December the following year this number increased to 150. The Festival continued throughout World War II and by the 1950s was a well established event that has continued to grow in popularity. It is now one of the leading music festivals in the North West, with about 1,500 people from England, Scotland, Wales and the Isle of Man attending each year.

National and international musicians who have started their musical career by performing at the festival include Amanda Roocroft, John Tomlinson and Constance Shacklock, and other outstanding musicans who have appeared include Jacqueline Delmond and Owen Brannigan. The festival finale is traditionally a performance of Handel's *Messiah*. Since 1997 the festival has held a master class each year for school choirs and to date seven schools have participated, including pupils from Freckleton Church of England School. Since its inception there have been only three organising secretaries: Richard Spencer 1940 to 1978; Bernard Whittle 1978 to 1987; and Jean Lancaster since 1987.[17]

Richard Spencer was also secretary to the committee that helped organise the first Freckleton Chysanthemum Society Show held in 1929 at Kirkham Road Methodist Church, the proceeds being for the church. From 1932 proceeds were used to endow beds at Preston Royal Infirmary and Lytham Hospital and also to help maintain the Freckleton, Warton and Bryning, and Wrea Green District Nursing Association. From 1935 to 1938 the show included an annual floral fete, brass band concert, and queens pageant, as well as a flower and produce show. In 1936 the show was opened by Lord Derby, accompanied by several other titled guests, and attracted more than 1000 entries in addition to various pageants and band competitions. There was also a trade exhibition housed in a marquee on the recreation ground.

Throughout the late 1930s the show continued to attract a large number of entries and in 1936 six thousand people were reported to have paid admission to the event. Even in 1940, despite the difficulties caused by the outbreak of war, a show was held at which Richard Spencer and the Chrysanthemum Society committee were congratulated for raising funds for the Red Cross and other local charities. The society continued to hold an annual flower show until 1945.

One of the longest-established village organisations is the Freckleton branch of the National Federation of the Women's Institute. The branch was established in 1922 and on 20 April that year the parish council

The Hodgson Institute was demolished in 1975 and replaced by the present Memorial Hall in 1977. The building also serves as a venue for meetings of the parish council.

The Sports and Social Club was built on the site of the old factory and opened in 1967.

agreed to them using the Hodgson Institute at 1*s*. 0*d*. a meeting. Among the founder members were Mrs Beck, Mrs Eastham, Mrs Margaret Joule, Miss Alice Mason, Mrs J. Rawstrone and Mrs Elizabeth Throp. The branch now (2000) meets at the Memorial Hall.

The 1st Freckleton Scout Group was formed in October 1936, with Peter Hall as scoutmaster and George Kirby as assistant scoutmaster. It was an open group, met at Kirkham Road Methodist Church, and continued to operate until September 1942. The 2nd Freckleton Scout Group was formed by Harry Morris in September 1952 and their present headquarters, at the entrance to the Memorial playing fields, was opened in 1966. The Freckleton Girl Guide Company was formed in the mid-1930s with Miss Roberts, a teacher at Trinity School, where the group met, as captain. Her lieutenant was Eileen Sumner of Naze Mount. It is not known when the group ceased to operate but in April 1951 a further company, styled 1st Freckleton, was established with Mrs D. French as captain, and in September 1983 the 2nd Freckleton Guide Company was formed. Their present headquarters is adjacent to that of the Scout Group.

The Memorial Hall, opened in September 1977 and occupying the site of the Hodgson Institute, continues to provide a venue for village events and to serve as the meeting place of the parish council. The Sports & Social Club, situated in Preston Old Road on the site previously used as a linen factory, tanyard and egg packing station, was opened in October 1967 and this too provides a focus for social gatherings and is the venue for the village snooker and darts teams.

Sport and Recreation

As we saw in the last chapter Dr Shaw, on behalf of the marsh owners, held discussions in 1886 with representatives of the football and cricket players, about letting part of the marsh for organised events. An arrangement of some sort must have been reached as even in the 1930s matches were still being played on land just inside the entrance to the marsh in Preston Old Road. The marsh, however, was far from ideal for other sports and in April 1914 the secretary of the Hodgson Institute wrote to the parish council requesting the use of land in Bush Lane known as Little Ends field, which lay adjacent to Long Ends field, for use as a bowling green. No doubt due to the outbreak of World War I no further action was taken but in October 1919 the parish council received a petition from about ninety ratepayers asking that Long Ends Field be laid out for recreation and a bowling green. The field was being used by James Parker, then landlord of the Coach & Horses, for grazing his cattle, but in May 1922, when his tenancy expired, the council agreed that the field 'be thrown open for recreation and that the pit be fenced at once with chestnut paling'.[18]

When in July 1927 two plots of land, at a site behind Holy Trinity church measuring four acres and two acres, became available a majority of the council were of the opinion that it ought to be bought for the village. As the land was being offered for sale later in the same week the council clerk had an urgent meeting with officials of the county council and was told that if the site could be bought for £600 to £700 there should not be any difficulty in getting the sanction of the Ministry of Health to a loan to extend over a period of thirty years.[19]

The purchase was successfully completed and on 21 July 1928 the bowling green was officially opened, and in 1929 both the football and cricket clubs were granted use of parts of the land as pitches. Tennis courts were also laid out, thereby meeting the request of the tennis club, which as early as 1921 had asked for a portion of Long Ends field. The recreation ground served as the principal sports area until it was redesigned by the Americans as the Memorial playing fields. This, however, meant that whilst the bowling club retained its green both the football and cricket clubs lost their pitches, and in the years immediately following World War II the football club used the RAF pitches in Lower

FRECKLETON F.C.
West Lancs. League & Cup Winners 79–80

P. Eddleston G. Ashworth G. Richardson M. Turner A. Clydesdale R. Wright

K. Bamber P. Mullen J. Molloy P. McCann M. Threlfall S. Paine

Freckleton Football Club, 1980. The present club had been formed by 1898 and was a member of the Fylde Amateur League for many years. In 1961–2 the club joined the West Lancashire League and were first division champions in three successive seasons from 1979–80 to 1981–82.

Lane opposite Higher House and a pitch in a field loaned by Jack Sudell of Lower House Farm.

In 1953 the matter of the 'chaotic' state of Long Ends field was debated by the council who, as they drew no monetary value from it, decided to invite representatives from the football and cricket clubs to discuss the future of the field. In August 1954 a tender of £1,883 was accepted for work in developing Long Ends field as a playing field, and at the council meeting held in July 1955 it was resolved 'that the football and cricket clubs be jointly responsible for the maintenance of the New Playing Field at an [agreed] annual rental'.[20]

As we have seen the present football club can trace its origins to the late nineteenth century and to its joining the Fylde League in 1898. In the season 1908–09 the club won the Bannister Cup, a feat repeated in 1910–11 and 1911–12 when the captain was William Salthouse. Following their third cup success the club joined the West Lancashire League, remaining there for the next two seasons until the league was disbanded. It would appear that after World War 1 the club returned to the Fylde League where it remained until the 1961–62 season. During those fifty-two years the second division championship was won in 1956–57 and the first division championship in 1960–61, together with Bannister Cup triumphs in the late 1950s and early 1960s. The club rejoined the reformed West Lancashire League in 1961–62 and were first division champions in three successive seasons from 1979–80 to 1981–82. There have also been four cup successes, the last being the Jobling Cup won in 1999–2000.[21]

A cricket club was in existence by 1910 but it is not clear when it was formed nor is anything known about its subsequent history. The present cricket club was formed in 1930 and among the first members were Tom Birch, John Broadbent, Bill Coulton, George Lonsdale, Tom Parker, Marsden Rigby and Taylor Woods. After World War II, when the club lost its ground on the former recreation ground, the club was kept together by Stan Muncaster, Tom Parker, Marsden Rigby and Dick Rossall playing friendly matches away from home. In 1961 the club joined the Fylde League when they finished as runners-up and in the following year were accepted into the Palace Shield, winning the Barcroft Cup, 3rd division, in 1962, 1966 and 1967. In 1969 the league formation changed and the club were placed in the second division where they have twice been champions in 1977 and 1999, and currently (2000) play in the top division.[22]

The inaugural meeting of the bowling club took place in November

1927 with John Kirby as first chairman and William Banks as secretary. By the time of the official opening of the bowling green in 1928 fund raising events and donations had also enabled a club pavilion to be erected and this building served the club until it was replaced in 1985. Until 1932, when the club entered a team in the 2nd division of the Fylde League, friendly matches were played against other local teams. In 1946 the club entered a team in the Lytham St. Annes League, winning the league championship in 1950. In 1967 a team was entered in division nine of the Preston and District League, progressing to the premier division within nine years. In 1983 two teams were entered in the Fylde League where the senior team gained promotion in successive seasons to reach division one, and in 1990 a ladies team was formed.

In 1975 the club won the Lytham St Annes League and repeated the feat in the renamed Lytham St Annes Mens League in 1980, 1981, 1982, 1985 and 1986. In addition to club successes there have also been individual achievements, including those of Billy Sudell which extended from his winning of the league merit award in 1939 to his appearance in the quarter finals of the Waterloo Cup thirty one years later. Perhaps, though, the outstanding individual achievement was that of Billy Houghton in winning the Waterloo Cup in 1974. At present (2000) the club has teams in the Lytham St Annes Mens Bowling League, the Lytham St Annes Womens Municipal League, the Lytham St Annes Mens Veteran League, the Lytham St Annes Senior Ladies League, the Fylde Amateur League and the Preston & District League.[23]

In 1975 both the Bowling Club and the Cricket Club were among the beneficiares of the will of Robert Rawstorne, with the residue of his estate being left to the village 'for such recreational and religious purposes in the village as is thought fit'. One outcome of this generous gift was the opening in 1981 of the Rawstorne Centre on Bush Lane playing fields which provides social facilities and changing rooms for the football and cricket teams. Outside the centre is an all weather surface used for netball and tennis.

The Modern Village

With the ending of World War II, in which eight Freckleton men died on active service, the large number of USAAF personnel, who since 1942 had occupied the three military sites in the village, began to leave for home. Before they did, however, a ceremony held on 20 August 1945 saw over 2,000 people attend the formal handing over of the Memorial

Avalon Drive. Built in the late 1950s properties in Avalon Drive were part of the major development of the area east of Preston Old Road.

playing fields. Constucted by personnel of BAD2 the unveiling of the memorial was made by Colonel Tom Scott and bears a bronze plaque in memory of those who died in the disaster of 1944. By 1946 the RAF occupied the former USAAF sites and were to remain as part of the village scene until the early 1960s.

The 1926 'new' road was the first major alteration to the road system within the township since the 1780s, but within thirty years both Naze Lane and Bush (Pool) Lane were also bisected to allow for a runway extension at English Electric (now British Aerospace). In order to provide access to land and property in the south of the township the parish council signed an agreement with Lancashire County Council in 1956 regarding the purchase of a portion of Wades Croft which enabled a roadway (Naze Lane) to be built around the airfield extension. By this date it was already becoming apparent that a by-pass around the village would also be necessary, though it was not until June 1991 that work finally commenced to the north of the village centre.

Since 1946 the population of the township has grown from approximately 2,500 to almost 7000 in 2000, and consequently the last fifty years has seen an ever increasing number of modern dwellings, notably the development of the areas around Avalon Drive and at Lamaleach. This, in turn, has led to an expansion of services including, for example, the opening of a purpose-built library in 1980. Other changes such as new schools, the opening of the Sports and Social Club and

In 1796 the site, which then fronted onto School Lane, comprised two cottages, a barn, a shippon, and a stable and was occupied by Cuthbert Kirkham. By 1850 the two cottages had been converted into four cottages and a weaving shop. Following the completion of the new road in 1926 the then property was re-oriented to face onto Preston New Road. It is now the site of the Caravela restaurant. This everchanging scene is an example of the economic and social changes that have occurred throughout the history of the township.

the building of the Memorial Hall have already been described. Following the closure of Balderstone Mill in 1980 British Aerospace at Warton and British Nuclear Fuels at Salwick have been the principal employers.

The village continues to evolve and as old buildings are demolished, and other features vanish, they are replaced by new ones, thereby continuing the pattern of change that has been the story of the ancient township of Freckleton since the first settlers arrived some four and a half thousand years ago.

Appendices

APPENDIX A

Charter Relating to Land Granted in Freckleton to the Benedictine Priory of Lytham (mid-thirteenth century)

Grant in free-alms, by Richard son of Roger, lord of Freckleton, brother of the house of St Cuthbert of Lytham, with the consent of his heirs, to God, blessed Cuthbert of Durham and the Durham Monks at Lytham, of the land between that of Richard son of Robert de Mora and that of William son of Hawisia, confirming in free-alms to them the butt on which the pound fold stands granted by Swain son of Osbert of Freckleton.

1 acre in Whittingham granted by Roger of Freckleton his father,
1 acre 1 perch in the vill of Freckleton granted by Swain of Freckleton,
1 toft in the vill of Freckleton which was Uthred son of Matilda's, and 2 adjacent lands held by Uthred, with 4 selions with the messuage by the Pool of Warton held by Richard Breton granted by Matilda daughter of Robert son of Raynward,
3 selions in a field of Freckleton above Uttlonewra granted by Richard son of Walthef of Freckleton,
1 perch of land in the vill of Freckleton granted by the same Richard son of Walthef,
2 and a half perches in the fields of Freckleton granted by the said Richard son of Walthef,
half an acre in a field of Freckleton by the land of St John held by Swain de Mora at the Housesteads granted by the same Richard son of Walthef,
1 selion in a field of Freckleton above short Faldwrigis and half land in the same field above Tustehorn›furlong granted by the same Richard son of Walthef all the croft in front of Richard of Pemberton's house with the ditch to the north, and half land granted by the same Richard son of Walthef,
1 selion in the vill of Freckleton in the field called Strik by the oftsaid Richard son of Walthef,
half acre in a field of Freckleton above Longerodes stretching from the way called Phustor to the moor granted by Adam son of Osbert of Freckleton,

5 perches with 1 toft in the fields of Freckleton by the houses of the pool granted by Adam son of Osbert of Freckleton and Swain his brother, and 1 toft with buildings adjacent land in the vill of Freckleton on the moor held of St Cuthbert by Richard de Mora.

APPENDIX B

Resident Curates and Vicars of Holy Trinity Parish Church

Resident Curate:	Rev. G. H. Waterfall	1860–1861
Resident Curate:	Rev. W. Scott	1861–1874
Vicar:	Rev. W. Scott	1874–1892
Vicar:	Rev. E. J. Hack	1892–1917
Vicar:	Rev. F. P. Mansfield	1918–1920
Vicar:	Rev. W. Preston	1921–1922
Vicar:	Rev. R. Hayward	1922–1929
Vicar:	Rev. J. W. Broadbent	1930–1950
Vicar:	Rev. H. C. Pope	1950–1959
Vicar:	Rev. N. S. Saul	1959–1966
Vicar:	Rev. D. L. Sears	1966–1974
Vicar:	Rev. J. R. Armfelt	1975–1979
Vicar:	Rev. T. Unsworth	1979–1983
Vicar:	Rev. J. W. S. Wilson	1984–1987
Vicar:	Rev. S. F. Brian	1988–1997
Vicar:	Rev. M. Gisbourne	1998–

Resident Parish Priests of Holy Family Roman Catholic Church

Parish Priest	Rev. J. Roche	1907–1922
Parish Priest	Rev. F. Carr	1922–1927
Parish Priest	Rev. T. Kenny	1927–1929
Parish Priest	Rev. F. Hayward	1929–1935
Parish Priest	Rev. E. McGough	1935–1937
Parish Priest	Rev. P. O'Sullivan	1937–1938
Parish Priest	Rev. J. Rawlinson	1938
Parish Priest	Rev. B. Hornby	1939
Parish Priest	Rev. J. Rawlinson	1940–1951
Parish Priest	Rev. F. Whiteside	1951–1971
Parish Priest	Rev. T. Carey	1971–1974
Parish Priest	Rev. B. Roney	1974–1977

Parish Priest	Rev. Canon A. Boyle	1977–1987
Parish Priest	Rev. J. Collins	1987–1990
Parish Priest	Rev. J. Gibson	1990–

Resident Ministers of Freckleton Methodist Church

Resident Minister Rev. S. Finch   1959
Resident Minister Rev. S. Routh
Resident Minister Rev. J. Peacock
Resident Minister Rev. G. Bruce   Resident ministers
Resident Minister Rev. V. Cowell   1960 to 1982
Resident Minister Rev. . Lockwood
Resident Minister Rev. J. Moorehouse
No Minister resident from 1982 to 1986
Resident Minister Rev. D. Hamfleet
Resident Minister Rev. D. Tidswell   Resident ministers
Resident Minister Rev. R. Bradshaw   1986–
Resident Minister Rev. J. Baldry

APPENDIX C

Constitution of Freckleton Marshgate Owners.
Dated 10 May 1670

We the major part of the Inhabitants of Freckleton whose names are hereunto subscribed do (upon due consideration) make these ensuing orders and constitutions for the right Governing of our stinted Marsh & Lands within Freckleton aforesaid all our Acts & deeds, this 10th day of May 1670, And to be & remain of force & virtue until allowed by full consent of the said Inhabitants.

first. it is ordered & agreed upon by the foresaid inhabitants That six beast gates & no more shall be the stint for every oxgang of Land within the said Township The several sorts of Goods there to be put on viz:-

one Gelding or Mare for two beast gates, four sheep for a beast gate, & four Geese for a beast gate, every Lanb shall go for a made sheep after the 24th day of June, but every Gosling at the first putting down (because of their great annoyance to the said Marsh) shall go for an old goose & not under.

2. It is ordered by the said Inhabitants That the Marsh men which are to be elected yearly by the said Inhabitants shall have the power hereby to demand, receive & take for every Mare or Gelding 4*d.*, every beast 2*d.*, every sheep 2*d.*, and every goose a penny before the goods shall be put down to the said Marsh, also the said Marsh men shall receive what trepasses may happen be, with the profits of the Land, and with the said several sums of money, they the said Marsh men are forthwith to Hire one or more Herdsmen or Shepherds to look carefully unto all and every the said goods until Michaelmas day (29 September), or the 25th day of March at which time the said Marsh men shall have hereby power to set what Marsh gates they think needfull only to the necessary repairs of the stone platt, the dungeon, & outland hill with the head room there & shall make their true accounts unto Inhabitants their neighbours every 25th day of March yearly.

3. The said Inhabitants do hereby order that if any the said goods do commit any wilful trespass upon the said Marsh or Lands from the time of putting on until Michaelmas day (above the space of six hours & that only in the hot season when they shall by reason of some head room casually left open gadd or run down) shall for the trepass of every mare or gelding pay a forfeit forthwith to the Marsh men for the towns

use 4d, for every beast 2d, every sheep 2d, & every goose 1d, before they redeem their said goods so trepassing out of the Towns fold.

4. it is ordered That the marshmen shall not permit or suffer any foreigner or stranger for any beast gate they shall take upon the said Marsh, to put down either sheep or geese for their gate or gates so taken; as well of the inhabitants as strangers goods, these orders to continue for this year only.

Marshmen	Rich. Harrison	G. Sharples
for this	John Sharples	Rich Harrison himselfe &
present year		Ralph ffreckleton
shown		Mathew Kirkhame
		Willm Buckk (Marke of)
		Edw Rigby by Do Browne
		Henry Mereley
		Rich Badger
		Thomas Waede
		Richard Browne
		John Marser
		Christopher ...
		Lawrence Coulbourne
		Jo. Sharples senr (Marke of)
		Law Webster (Marke of)
		Thomas Hankinson
		James Colborn
		... Taylor

APPENDIX D

Bill of Complaint brought in 1746 by 22 Proprietors of Land in Freckleton against Thomas Grimbaldeston. Information Supplied by Mr Shawe, Solicitor, to Edward Starkie, Barrister

The township of Freckleton belongs to several charterers and Freeholders there And there is no chief Lord of the said Township or other person who claims to be Lord of the Manor or the royalty of the said Township or to the soil of the wastes commons or Marsh grounds on or belonging to the said township, but such commons wastes & Marsh grounds jointly belong to the said several charterers and Freeholders.

Belonging to the said Township there is a considerable quantity of Marsh Land adjoining to the River Ribble within the Flux and Reflux of the Sea; and this marsh ground is stinted and divided into a considerable number of Beast Gates and which are appropriated to the ancient enclosed Lands in the said Township; so that each Estate in the township turns yearly to the said Marsh grounds such a number of Cattle as hath been anciently agreed upon, or which they lately purchased from other Estates, and no more, and they keep yearly accounts to whom the Beast Gates belong, and yearly appoint amongst themselves officers they call Marsh Tenters whose business is to see that no person turns more cattle to the Marsh than he has a Right to do by Ancient custom or purchase.

Adjoining to Freckleton Marsh is Newton Marsh and there the charterers by Ancient custom or Agreement amongst themselves carry away the soil from their Marsh into their Ancient Inclosed grounds and the same custom prevails in some neighbouring Townships who have also Marsh belonging to them: But in Freckleton this custom has never prevailed save in one instance or two and then leave was asked at a Towns Meeting of the inhabitants, and granted upon payment of some small consideration in satisfaction of the trepass.

The soil carried from the Marsh grounds is very rich Till and greatly improves the Land whereon it is laid, though at the same time it considerably impoverishes the said Marsh grounds ...

A P P E N D I X   E

Articles for the Regulations of the Proposed Road Over Freckleton Newton & Clifton Marshes

Article 1
That the affairs and concerns of the said road shall be conducted and managed by a Committee of Six Persons to be annually chosen as follows viz:

Two by John Clifton in right of his property on Clifton Marsh. Two by a majority of the Owners of Gates on Freckleton Marsh and Two by a Majority of the owners of Gates on Newton Marsh and in case of the Death of any of the Committee (or refusal to act) others to be chosen as aforesaide.

Article 2
That the great object of the Committee shall be to provide a Fund for the repairs of the said road and that Money shall be raised by subscription and borrowed on the security of the Tolls to make the Road over Newton Marsh and build a House for the Toll Keeper whose Salary shall be paid out of the Tolls and who shall attend to and take care of the Cattle to be put upon Newton Marsh without any expense to the owners of the Gates.

Article 3
That a plan shall be made as to the direction and width of the road over the three Marshes and an estimate got as to the Expenses over each Marsh separately.

Article 4
That the Road over Freckleton Marsh being already made the same shall be delivered up in such good and substantial repair at the time the Road over the other two Marshes shall be opened as a Majority of the Committee shall approve.

Article 5
That the Road over Clifton Marsh shall be made under the discretion of the said John Clifton and his Agents going from Lea Toll Gate upon the present paved Road to or near Clifton Marsh Gate and then turning southward to the corner of the enclosed Land and from thence Westward to Newton Marsh and the same shall be completed to the satisfaction of the committee or a majority thereof on or before the ... day ... provided the sum of £ ... shall be first raised for that purpose.

Article 6	That the Road over Newton Marsh shall be made out of the subscription money and shall be under the direction and completed to the satisfaction or a majority thereof on or before the ... day of ...
Article 7	That the Toll house and Toll Gate shall be erected and placed at ... and shall be the property of all the three Marsh Owners.
Article 8	That heavy Carriages (viz) of ... cwt shall not go or pass upon the Road unless the same have broad wheels (viz) ... inches at the least upon the Sole or bottom of the Tellies of the Wheels under the penalty of ... and that Certificates of the Actual Weight of the Carriages shall be given by the Owners or drivers to the Toll Gate Keeper if required who shall deliver the same to the Committee who may if they think necessary require proof to be made to their satisfaction otherwise the penalty shall be paid and on refusal shall be prevented passing another time.
Article 9	That after the Road across the three marshes shall be completed and opened the whole of the same Road shall be kept in repair and be under the direction of the Committee or a Majority of them out of the Fund and tolls which shall be raised.

Article 10   That the Toll shall be taken as follows (viz)

A cart or carriage laden with Hay, Straw, Dung, Manure, Wheat, Oats, Barley or Beans drawn by

4 Horses shall pay	6*d.*
3 " " "	4*d.*
2 " " "	2*d.*
1 Horse " "	1*d.*

Ditto laden with Timber and Merchandise of all sorts and all other things and Materials drawn by

4 Horses shall pay	8*d.*
3 " " "	6*d.*
2 " " "	3*d.*
1 Horse " "	1½*d.*

Article 11	That no Wagon or Cart shall be suffered to pass the Toll gate drawn by more than 4 Horses.
Article 12	That every Horse passing first from Freckleton to Newton Marsh to pay 0½*d.*

"	"			from Freckleton to Clifton to pay	1*d.*
"	"			from Clifton to Newton to pay	0½*d.*
"	"			from Clifton over Freckleton to pay	1*d.*
"	"			from Newton over Freckleton to pay	0½*d.*
"	"			from Newton over Clifton to pay	0½*d.*

A Chaise and other Carriage and a pair of Horses
to pay   6*d.*

| " | " | " | " | " | with 4 horses to pay | 9*d.* |
| " | " | " | " | " | with 6 horses to pay | 1*s.* 0*d.* |

Any Carriage Caravan & having only 1 Horse   2*d.*

Notes and References

Historical societies, record offices etc.

CS	Chetham Society
LPRS	Lancashire Parish Register Society
LRO	Lancashire Record Office
LSF	Library of the Society of Friends, London
PRO	Public Record Office
RSLC	Record Society of Lancashire and Cheshire
THSLC	Transactions of the Historic Society of Lancashire and Cheshire
TLCAS	Transactions of the Lancashire & Cheshire Antiquarian Society

Chapter 1: Origins of the Township

1. Jackson, J. Wilfrid., 'Prehistoric Archaeology of Lancashire', in *TLCAS*, vol. 50 (1934), p. 74.
2. Whitaker, Rev. T. D., *History of Manchester* (J. Murray, London, 1773), vol. 1, p. 269 [hereafter Whitaker, *History of Manchester*].
3. Singleton, F. J., *Kirkham, a Short History* (Kirkham and District Local History Society, 1980), p. 8.
4. Howard-Davis, C. and Buxton, K., *Roman Forts in the Fylde* (Centre for North-West Regional Studies, Lancaster University, 2000), p. 77.
5. Higham, Dr M. C., Course Notes – 'Place Names and the Early History of the North West', Lancaster University, 1998.

Chapter 2: Medieval Freckleton

1. Cunliffe Shaw, R., 'The Townfields of Lancashire', in *THSLC*, vol. 114 (1963), p. 30.
2. Farrer, W., *Lancashire Pipe Rolls* (Henry Young & Sons, Liverpool, 1902), pp. 323–5 [hereafter Farrer, *Lancashire Pipe Rolls*].
3. Farrer, *Lancashire Pipe Rolls*, p. 410.
4. *A New English Dictionary on Historical Principles* (Clarendon Press, Oxford, 1908).
5. Farrer, *Lancashire Pipe Rolls*, p. 410.
6. Farrer, W., 'Lancashire Inquests Extents and Feudal Aids', in *RSLC*, vol. 48 (1903), p. 152.
7. Farrer, W., 'The Chartulary of Cockersand Abbey', in *CS*, NS, vol. 38 (1898), p. 199.
8. Farrer, W.,'The Chartulary of Cockersand Abbey', in *CS*, NS, vol. 38 (1898), p. 198.
9. Farrer, W.,'The Chartulary of Cockersand Abbey', in *CS*, NS, vol. 64 (1909), p. 1114.
10. I am indebted to Dr A. Piper of the University of Durham for allowing me to use his transcipts of the Lytham Priory Charters.
11. *The Victoria County History of Lancashire* (1906) [hereafter *VCH*], vol. vii, p. 170.
12. *VCH*, vol. vii. p. 169.
13. LRO, Calendar of Sharples family, No. 97. Transcribed by R Walker [hereafter LRO, Calendar of Sharples family, No. –].

14. Farrer, W., 'Lancashire Inquests Extents and Feudal Aids', in *RSLC*, vol. 54 (1907), p. 109.
15. Farrer, W., 'Lancashire Inquests Extents and Feudal Aids', in *RSLC*, vol. 54 (1907), p. 195.
16. Tupling, G. H., 'South Lancashire in the Reign of Edward II', in *CS*, third series, vol. 1 (1949), p. 68.
17. LRO, Calendar of Sharples family, No. 47.
18. Rylands, J. Paul., *The Exchequer Lay Subsidy Roll* (Wyman & Sons, 1896), p. 64.
19. Ziegler. P., *The Black Death* (RU Edition 1969), p. 184.
20. Walker, R., 'Freckleton Water Mill' in *THSLC*, vol. 94 (1943), p. 100.
21. LRO, Calendar of Sharples family, No. 98.

Chapter 3: The Tudor Township

1. *VCH*, vol. vii, p. 169.
2. Cunliffe Shaw, R., *Clifton Papers* (The Guardian Press, 1935), p. 20.
3. LRO, Calendar of Sharples family No. 120.
4. Sharpe France, R., 'The Registers of Estates of Lancashire Papists 1717–1788', in *RSLC*, vol. 108 (1960), p. 64.
5. Fishwick, H., 'History of Kirkham' in *CS*, OS, vol. 92 (1874), p. 93.
6. Coward, B., 'Lords Stanley and the Earls of Derby 1385–1672', in *CS*, third series, vol. xxx (1983), p. 35.

Chapter 4: The Sharples Family

1. LRO, Calendar of Sharples family – from which the information in this chapter is taken unless indicated otherwise.
2. LRO, DDH Loose Items.
3. LRO, DDF 207.
4. LRO, DDCL 1025.
5. Beaumont, W., 'A Discourse of the Warr in Lancashire', in *CS*, OS, vol. 62 (1864), p. 62.
6. LRO, WRW(A) 1661.
7. LRO, WRW(A) 1691.
8. LRO, WRW(A) 1691.

Chapter 5: The Stuart Township

1. Harrison, M. J., *Early History of the Harrisons* (for private circulation, 1922).
2. LRO, Calendar of Sharples family, No. 35.
3. Deeds courtesy of Mr P. Hall.
4. Deeds courtesy of Mr and Mrs D. Gregg.
5. *VCH*, vol. vii, p. 170.
6. Cunliffe Shaw, R., 'The Parish Registers of Kirkham', in *LPRS*, vol. 99, p. ii.
7. Lytham Priory Charters courtesy of Dr Piper.
8. LRO, P147/14.
9. LRO, MF1/28.
10. Cunliffe Shaw, R., 'The Parish Registers of Kirkham', in *LPRS*, vol. 99, p. xii.
11. Cunliffe Shaw, R., 'The Parish Registers of Kirkham', in *LPRS*, vol. 99, p. viii.
12. LRO, QSB 1/9/17.
13. Beaumont, W., 'A Discourse of the Warr in Lancashire', in *CS*, OS, vol. 62 (1864), pp. 56–7.
14. Ibid., p. 57.
15. LRO, QSP 435/29.
16. Laslett, P., *The World We Have Lost* (3rd edn, Methuen, 1983), p. 43 [hereafter Laslett, *The World We Have Lost*].
17. Ibid., p. 44.
18. Hey, D. G., *An English Rural Community: Myddle under the Tudors and Stuarts* (Leicester University Press, 1974) p. 56.

Chapter 6: The Georgian Township

1. LRO, DDX 1482/4.
2. LRO, DDX 1482/5.
3. LRO, DDX 194/54.
4. Spencer, R., *Remembrances of Freckleton* (publisher not named, 1990), p. 3 [hereafter Spencer, *Remembrances of Freckleton*].
5. LRO, DDX 1482/7.
6. LRO, QSP 1322/12.
7. LRO, DDF 306.
8. LRO, QAR 7/1/16.
9. Township highway account book, 1802–17. This and all subsequent entries courtesy of Mr D. Kirby.
10. LRO, DDX 1482/12.
11. LRO, DDX 1482/17.
12. Information courtesy of Mr and Mrs R. Banks.
13. LRO, LXA 6.
14. Lancashire Directory, 1828.

Chapter 7: The Poor

1. Cunliffe Shaw, R., *Records of the Thirty Men of the Parish of Kirkham* (Helen G. Shaw, 1930), p. 37 [hereafter Cunliffe Shaw, *Records of the Thirty Men*].
2. Ibid., p. 44.
3. LRO, QSP 122/20.
4. LRO, WRW(A) 1681.
5. LRO, QSP 749/5.
6. LRO, QSP 971/5.
7. LRO, QSP 1094/14.
8. LRO, QSP 1150/4.
9. LRO, DDD 365.
10. LRO, DDD 369.
11. LRO, PR 2067.
12. LRO, WRW(A) 1693.
13. Fishwick, H., 'The History of the Parish of Kirkham', in *CS*, OS, vol. 92 (1874), p. 164.
14. LRO, WRW(A) 1709.
15. LRO, WRW(A) 1730.
16. LRO, WRW(A) 1765.
17. LRO, DDX 1482/2.
18. LRO, DDX 1482/4.
19. LRO, FRP 14/14.
20. LRO, FRP 18/17/37.
21. British Parliamentary Papers.
22. Township disbursement books, 1803–12. This and all subsequent entries courtesy of Mr D. Kirby.
23. Township disbursement books, 1817–26. This and all subsequent entries courtesy of Mr D. Kirby.
24. LRO, PR 2969/1/1.
25. *Baines's Lancashire* (1824–25), vol. 2. p. 644 [hereafter *Baines's Lancashire*].
26. LRO, LXA 6.
27. Marshall, J. D., 'The Lancashire Rural Labourer in the Early Nineteenth Century', in *LCAS*, vol. 71 (1963), p. 108.

Chapter 8: The Church of England

1. LRO, DDX 35/1.
2. Cunliffe Shaw, *Records of the Thirty Men*, p. 13.

3. LRO, P147/14.
4. LRO, QSJ 8/3/no. 36.
5. LRO, PR 2067.
6. LRO, PR 2067.
7. LRO, WRW(A) 1780.
8. Cunliffe Shaw, R., *Kirkham in Amounderness* (R. Seed & Sons, Preston, 1949), p. 195 [hereafter Cunliffe Shaw, *Kirkham in Amounderness*].
9. LRO PR 2969/1/1.
10. Baines, E., *The History of the County Palatine & Duchy of Lancaster* (Fisher Son & Co., London, 1836), vol. 4, p. 396.
11. Charity Commissioners Inquiry 1902/3 (quotes Newton Charity Minute Book 1837).
12. Cunliffe Shaw, R., *The Records of a Lancashire Family* (The Guardian Press, Preston, 1940), p. 242.
13. Cunliffe Shaw, *Kirkham in Amounderness*, p. 204.
14. LRO, DP 376/4.
15. Hewitson, A., *Our Country Churches and Chapels* (Simpkin Marshall & Co., 1872), p. 279 [hereafter Hewitson, *Our Country Churches and Chapels*].
16. LRO, DP 421.
17. LRO, PR 3216/2.
18. *Lytham Times*, 20 February 1892.
19. LRO, PR 3216/2.

Chapter 9: Congregational Church
1. Nightingale, B., *Lancashire Congregational Union* (John Heywood, Manchester, 1890), p. 95.
2. LRO, QDV 9/21.
3. LRO, QDV 4/66.
4. LRO, QDV 4/74.

Chapter 10: Wesleyan Methodist Church (Kirkham Road)
1. Taylor J., *Apostles of Fylde Methodism* (T. Woolmer, London, 1885), p. 131 [hereafter Taylor, *Apostles of Fylde Methodism*].
2. Ibid., p. 53.
3. *Preston Guardian*, 21 May 1910.
4. Spencer, R., *Freckleton, Kirkham Road Methodist Church Jubilee Souvenir Brochure* (1960). p. 3.
5. Pilkington, W., *Preston and District Methodism* (W. Pilkington, 1890), p. 126 [hereafter Pilkington, *Preston and District Methodism*].
6. *Jubilee Souvenir Brochure*, p. 3.
7. Pilkington, *Preston and District Methodism*, p. 126.
8. Church deed courtesy of church officials.
9. Church deed courtesy of church officials.
10. *Methodist Magazine*, 1838. p. 397. I am indebted to Mr N. Cunliffe for this information.
11. LRO, MPr 50 Acc 5573 Box 3.
12. LRO, MPr 50 Acc 5573 Box 3.
13. Cunliffe Shaw, *The Records of a Lancashire Family*, p. 246.
14. *Preston Guardian*. 21 May 1910.
15. LRO, QDV 4/61.
16. Township disbursement book, 1817–18.
17. LRO, MGa Acc 5829 Box 3.
18. Chapel Account Book 1819–48 courtesy of Mr D. Kirby.
19. LRO, QDV/9/21.
20. LRO, MPr 50 Acc 5573 Box 3.
21. Ibid., p. 33.
22. Pilkington, *Preston and District Methodism*, p. 33.
23. Church deeds courtesy of church officials.

24. Church accounts courtesy of church officials.
25. Pilkington, *Preston and District Methodism*, p. 33.
26. Hewitson, *Our Country Churches and Chapels*, p. 284.
27. Pilkington, *Preston and District Methodism*, p. 34.
28. Note found in Chapel Class Register Book 1833–48, courtesy of church officials. (Now deposited at LRO, reference LRO, MPr 50 Acc 8653.)
29. Hewitson, *Our Country Churches and Chapels*, p. 285.
30. Trustees Minute Book, 1883–1900, courtesy of the church officials. (Now deposited at the LRO, reference LRO, MPr 50 Acc 8653.)
31. Trustees Minute Book, 1883–1900.
32. Ibid.
33. Ibid.

Chapter 11: Primitive Methodist Church (Preston Old Road)

1. Preston Old Road Methodist Church, *Centenary Programme, 1861–1961*. Author not named.
2. Preston Old Road Methodist Church, *Centenary Programme*.
3. Ibid.
4. Ibid.
5. LRO, MPr 2/2/1.
6. Ibid.
7. Ibid.
8. Hewitson, *Our Country Churches and Chapels*. p. 286.
9. LRO, MPr 2/2/1.
10. *Lytham Times*, 29 August 1891.
11. Church minute book, 1923–66. This and all subsequent entries courtesy of Mr M. Lancaster.
12. Church minute book, 1923–66.

Chapter 12: Plymouth Brethren

1. LRO, PR 3216/2.
2. I am indebted to Mr and Mrs T. Butcher and Mrs J. Joule for most of the information contained in this part of the chapter.

Chapter 13: The Quakers

1. Porteus, T. C., 'Roger Haydock of Coppull', in *LCAS*, vol. 52 (1937), p. 13.
2. Besse, Joseph, *Sufferings of Early Quakers* (facsimile published by Sessions Book Trust, 2000), Chapter 22, p. 321.
3. LRO, QSP 705/11.
4. LSF, Meetings for Sufferings Vol. 9, July–October 1694.
5. LRO, FRL 1965.
6. LRO, QSP 1003/3.
7. LRO, FRP 1/7.
8. LRO, WRW(A) 1720.
9. LRO, QSP 737/17.
10. LRO, FRP 1/7.
11. LRO, WRW(A) 1696.
12. LRO, WRW(A) 1716.
13. LRO, FRP 13/2.
14. LRO, DDF 264.
15. LRO, WRW(A) 1724.
16. 'History of the Quakers in Freckleton' (typescript; title page missing; author and date unknown; copy in Fleetwood Library).
17. LRO, FRP 13/1.
18. LRO, FRP 4/1.
19. LRO, FRP 15/1/14.

20. Abbatt, D., *Quaker Annals of Preston and the Fylde, 1653–1900* (Headley Brothers, 1930), p. 112 [hereafter Abbatt, *Quaker Annals of Preston and The Fylde, 1653–1900*]
21. Ibid, p. 112.
22. Hewitson, *Our Country Churches and Chapels*, p. 283.
23. LRO, FRP 13/1.
24. LRO, QSP 2573/12.
25. Butler, D.M., *The Quaker Meetings Houses of Britain*. (Friends Historical Society 1999), Vol 1 page 306.
26. LRO, FRP 18/4/1
27. Hewitson, *Our Country Churches and Chapels*, p. 284
28. *Preston Guardian*, 30th July 1904

Chapter 14: Roman Catholic Church

1. *Catholic Record Society*, vol. 6 (1909), p. 182.
2. Ibid. Vol 15 (1915), p.222.
3. LRO, WRW(A) 1685.
4. LRO, DDTs/Box 3/2.
5. LRO, RCKi/15.6.
6. LRO, RCKi/15.6.
7. Spencer, R., *Reminiscences of Freckleton* (publisher not named, 1975), p. 2 [hereafter Spencer, *Reminiscences of Freckleton*].
8. *Preston Guardian*, 6 October 1900.
9. Ibid.
10. Singleton, F. J., *Mowbreck Hall and The Willows* (Willows R. C. Church, 1983), p. 47.

Chapter 15: Education, 1551–1839

1. Cunliffe Shaw, *Kirkham in Amounderness*, p. 466.
2. Ibid., p. 469.
3. Ibid., p. 540.
4. Ibid., p. 540. Also LRO, DDD 260.
5. LRO, WRW(A) 1724.
6. LRO, FRP 13/1.
7. LRO, FRP 13/1.
8. LRO, FRP 13/1.
9. Township disbursement book, 1803/4.
10. Methodist Church Class Register Book, 1833–48.
11. Preston Guardian, 30 July 1904.

Chapter 16: Trinity School/New Memorial School

1. LRO, Freck SP.
2. LRO, DDCL 1195/25.
3. LRO, DDCL 1199/3
4. Cunliffe Shaw, *Records of a Lancashire Family*, p. 257.
5. *Preston Pilot*, 2 January 1864.
6. *Lytham St Annes Express*, January 1941.
7. PRO, ED 49/3714
8. LRO, DP 376/4.
9. I am indebted to Mr G. Worthy, the Headmaster of Freckleton Church of England School for allowing me the free use of the School Log Books for the years 1876 to 1981, without which it would have been impossible to write the remainder of this chapter or to have obtained information that appears in other chapters of this book.
10. PRO, ED 49/371419.
11. Newton Charity Minute Book. This and all subsequent entries courtesy of the Secretary – Mr J. Tomlinson.

Chapter 17: Strike Lane School
1. School Log Book courtesy of the Headmaster – Mr L. Pimlott.

Chapter 18: Marsh Gates and Marsh Owners
1. LRO, The Marshlands of Newton with Scales and Freckleton (R. Walker, handwritten 1942) [hereafter LRO, The Marshlands of Newton with Scales and Freckleton].
2. Ibid.
3. Ibid.
4. Ibid.
5. LRO, DDS 2/1.
6. LRO, WRW(A) 1692.
7. LRO, DDS 2/6.
8. LRO, DDS 2/8.
9. LRO, DDS 2/3.
10. LRO, DDS 2/10.
11. LRO, DDD 153.
12. Walker, R., 'Freckleton Water Mill' in *THSLC*, vol. 94 (1943), p. 98.
13. LRO, DDS 2/1.
14. LRO, DDS 2/4A.
15. LRO, The Marshlands of Newton with Scales and Freckleton.
16. Ibid.
17. LRO, DDS 2/17.
18. LRO, PR 5010/12.
19. Dakres., J., *The Last Tide* (Carnegie Press, 1986), p. 51.
20. LRO, DDD 153.
21. Marsh Gate Owners Minute Book, 1841–1922. This and all subsequent entries courtesy of the Secretary, Mr R. Banks. (Now deposited at Lancashire Record Office – LRO, DDX 2200.)

Chapter 19: The Marsh Road
1. LRO, DDCL 580A.
2. LRO, DDS 2/2.
3. LRO, DDCL 581A.
4. Marsh Gate Owners Minute Book, 1841–1922.
5. 'New Road over Freckleton Marsh' Account Book. This and all subsequent entries courtesy of Mr D. Kirby.
6. Ibid.
7. LRO, DDK 835/5.
8. LRO, DDX 1794.
9. Marsh Gate Owners Minute Book, 1841–1922.
10. LRO, DDK 835/5.
11. LRO, DDX 1794.
12. LRO, DDX 1794.
13. Rogers, P., *A Short History of Freckleton* (published privately, 1947), p. 12.
14. LRO, DDS 2/23.
15. LRO, DDD 175.
16. LRO, DDX 1794.

Chapter 20: Water Mill and Wind Mills
1. *VCH*, vol. vii, p. 167.
2. LRO, DDHO 1293.
3. Fishwick, H., 'History of Kirkham', in *CS*, OS, vol. 92, p. 9.
4. *VCH*, vol. vii, p. 169.
5. Ibid.

6. LRO, Calendar of Sharples family, no. 63.
7. LRO, Calendar of Sharples family, no. 114.
8. Walker, R., 'Freckleton Water Mill', in *THSLC*, vol. 94 (1943), pp. 104–7.
9. Ibid., pp. 100–1.
10. LRO, Calendar of Sharples family, p. 9.
11. LRO, WRW(A) 1688.
12. Walker, R., 'Freckleton Water Mill', in *THSLC*, vol. 94 (1943), pp. 102–7.
13. Walker, R., 'Freckleton Water Mill', in *THSLC*, vol. 94 (1943), p. 108.
14. LRO, QSP 435/2.
15. LRO, DDF 242.
16. LRO, DDF 252.
17. LRO, DDTS/ Box4/14.
18. LRO, WRW(A) 1830.
19. Walker, R., 'Freckleton Water Mill', in *THSLC*, vol. 94 (1943), p. 107.
20. LRO, DP 376/6.
21. Marsh Gate Owners Minute Book, 1841–1922.
22. Ibid.
23. Newton Charity Minute Book.

Chapter 21: Agriculture

1. Cunliffe Shaw, *Kirkham in Amounderness*, p. 226.
2. Ibid., p. 224.
3. Ibid., p. 236.
4. LRO, DDH Loose Items.
5. Cunliffe Shaw, *Kirkham in Amounderness*, p. 711.
6. Ibid., p. 276.
7. Moffat Louis. W., *England on the Eve of the Industrial Revolution* (Frank Cass & Co. Ltd, 1963), p. 73.
8. Tait, J., 'Lancashire Quarter Sessions Records', in *CS*, NS, vol. 77 (1917), p. 115.
9. LRO, WRW (A) 1683.
10. LRO, DDX 189/2.
11. Deeds courtesy of Mr G. Rhodes.
12. LRO, Calendar of Sharples family. Historical summary.
13. LRO, DDNW 8/1–6.
14. LRO, DDCL 521A.
15. LRO, Calendar of Sharples family, No. 131.
16. Holt John., *General View of the Agriculture of the County Of Lancaster* (Augustus M. Kelley, New York, 1969; reprint of 1795 edn), p. 51 [hereafter Holt, *General View of the Agriculture of the County of Lancaster*].
17. Ibid., p. 128.
18. LRO, DDX 1794.
19. *Preston Pilot*, 9 January 1864.
20. Hewitson A., *History of Preston* (S. R. Publishers Ltd, 1969; reprint of 1883 edn), p. 216.
21. Messrs Wignall, Butcher & Banks, *Report on the Allotments and Poultry Industry of Freckleton* (Freckleton & District Liberal Association, typescript, 1927). p. 4 [hereafter Wignall, Butcher & Banks. *Report on the Allotments and Poultry Industry*].
22. Information courtesy of Mrs E. Mason.
23. Information courtesy of Mr and Mrs R. Banks.
24. Wignall, Butcher & Banks, *Report on the Allotments and Poultry Industry*, p. 9.
25. LRO, PR 5010/3.
26. Information about Lower House Farm post 1966 courtesy of Mr C. Fare.

Chapter 22: Linen and Cotton

1. Cunliffe Shaw, *Kirkham in Amounderness*, p. 711.
2. PRO, PL6/1 F82.44167.

3. LRO, WRW(A) 1680.
4. LRO, WRW(A) 1658.
5. LRO, DDPr 94/4.
6. LRO, DDS 2/21.
7. Deeds courtesy of Mr and Mrs J. Langley.
8. LRO, DDS2/21.
9. Roberts, E. (ed.), *A History of Linen in the North West* (Centre for North-West Regional Studies, Lancaster University 1998), p. 49.
10. *Baines's Lancashire*, (1824/25), vol. 2, p. 627.
11. Lancashire Directory, 1828.
12. Information courtesy of Mr P. Hall and Mr M. Lancaster.
13. Barrett's Directory, 1898.
14. LRO, WRW(A) 1839.
15. LRO, DP 376/1.
16. LRO, DP 376/1.
17. LRO, DP 376/1.
18. LRO, DDX 1482/20.
19. LRO, DP 376/5.
20. LRO, DP 376/4.
21. LRO, DP 376/5.
22. LRO, DP 376/5.
23. LRO, DP 376/5.
24. LRO, DP 376/9.
25. Deeds courtesy of Mr and Mrs H. Fisher.
26. Trinity School Log Book.
27. Information courtesy of Mr G. Hall.
28. *Lancashire Evening Post*, date unknown, *c.* 1980.
29. Information courtesy of Mrs J. Foster.
30. Information courtesy of Mrs E. Mason.
31. Information courtesy of Mr S. Till.
32. *Lancashire Evening Post*, date unknown, *c.* 1980.
33. LRO, PR5010/3.
34. *Lancashire Evening Post*, date unknown *c.* 1980.
35. Un-named and undated newspaper article, *c.* 1947; scrapbook of Mrs A. Hartley now in Freckleton Library
36. *Lytham St Annes Express*, 7 December 1962.
37. Ibid., 5 January 1961.
38. *West Lancashire Evening Gazette*, 26 January 1968.
39. Ibid., 20 December 1980.

Chapter 23: The Port of Freckleton

1. Hewitson, A., *Diary of Col. Bellingham* (Geo. Toulmin & Sons, Preston, 1908), p. 49.
2. LRO, QSP 1194/21.
3. Barron J. A., *A History of the Ribble Navigation* (Guardian Press, 1938), p. 444 [hereafter Barron, *A History of the Ribble Navigation*].
4. Document courtesy of British Waterways.
5. Cunliffe Shaw, *Kirkham in Amounderness*, p. 169.
6. Barron, *A History of the Ribble Navigation*, p. 452.
7. Whitaker, *History of Manchester*, vol. 1. pp. 180–1.
8. Singleton, F. J., 'The Flax Merchants of Kirkham' in *THSLC*, vol. 126. p. 90.
9. Information courtesy of Mr D. Kirby.
10. LRO, DDPr 138/19.
11. Barron, *A History of the Ribble Navigation*, p. 454.
12. Information courtesy of Mr G. and Mr P. Hall.
13. Wignall, Butcher & Banks, *Report on the Allotments and Poultry Industry*, p. 2.

14. LRO, DDCL/400.
15. Document courtesy of British Waterways.
16. LRO, PR 2851/5/5.
17. LRO, DDX 1482/8.
18. Ms Statistical History of the Leeds and Liverpool Canal Co by Law Clerk *c.*1898 (BTHR) quoted by Hadfield and Biddle, *Canals of NW England* (David & Charles, 1970), vol. 1, pp. 162–3. The British Transport Historical records are deposited at the PRO, London under reference ZLIB. The above quoted Ms has not been inspected.
19. LRO, DDHE 69/2.
20. Deeds of Ravald House Farm courtesy of Mr G. Rhodes.
21. Deed of Kirkham Road Methodist Chapel 1814 courtesy of church officials.
22. LRO, DDD 143.
23. Document courtesy of Mr T. Doughty.
24. LRO, WRW(A) 1839.
25. LRO, WLA 1.
26. Document courtesy of British Waterways.
27. Township minute book, 1844–95. This and all subsequent entries courtesy of Mr D. Kirby.
28. Information courtesy of Mr P. Hall.
29. LRO, SS8/1–5.
30. Bill of Sale courtesy of Mr G. Parker.
31. Found in Wesleyan Methodist Class Register Book, 1833–48.
32. Unidentified newspaper report courtesy of Mr R. Banks.
33. Information on RNLI lifeboat servicing courtesy of Mr D. Forshaw.

Chapter 24: Inns

1. LRO, PR 2067 (Kirkham Vestry Book 1813).
2. Township disbursement book, 1821/22.
3. LRO, DDX 33/96.
4. LRO, Marshlands of Newton with Scales and Freckleton.
5. Information courtesy of Greenalls Brewery.
6. LRO, DDS 2/17.
7. LRO, QAD 5/1.
8. LRO, DDS 2/21.
9. *Baines's Lancashire* (1824–25) vol 2, p. 627.
10. LRO, DDX 1482/19.
11. LRO, QAD 5/1.
12. LRO, DDS 2/21.
13. LRO, QAD 5/1.
14. Harrison, W., 'Pre-Turnpike Highways in Lancashire and Cheshire', in *TLCAS*, vol. 9 (1891), p. 130.
15. LRO, DDF 225.
16. LRO, WRW(A) 1675.
17. LRO, WRW(A) 1829.
18. Spencer, *Reminiscences of Freckleton*, p. 18.
19. LRO, QAD 5/1.
20. Spencer, *Reminiscences of Freckleton*, p. 18.
21. Ibid., p. 19.
22. Township minute book, 1844–95.

Chapter 25: Victorian Freckleton

1. Deeds courtesy of Mr F. Hunter. (Property now numbered 67 Kirkham Road.)
2. Township minute book, 1844–95.
3. LRO, DDS 2/9.
4. Board of Health Report, 1851.
5. Township minute book, 1844–95.

6. LRO, SAF 1/1 (Rural Sanitary Authority minutes).
7. LRO, SAF 1/1.
8. Township minute book, 1844–95.
9. Ibid. August/September 1885.
10. Ibid. August/September 1886.
11. LRO, DP 376/6.
12. Township minute book, 1844–95.
13. LRO, DP 376/4.
14. LRO, DP 376/8.
15. Unidentified Preston newspaper report, August 1885. From scrapbook in possession of Mr D. Kirby.
16. *Lytham Times*, 11 August 1911.
17. Township minute book, 1844–95.
18. Unidentified Preston newspaper report, August 1884. From scrapbook in possession of Mr D. Kirby.
19. Ibid. August 1885.
20. Ibid. August 1886.
21. Spencer, *Remembrances of Freckleton*, p. 16.
22. Ibid., p. 10.
23. Cunliffe Shaw, *Kirkham in Amounderness*, p. 736.
24. Cunliffe Shaw, *Records of a Lancashire Family*, p. 257.
25. Unidentified newspaper report courtesy of Mr M. Rossall (probably *Lancashire Evening Post*, October 1954).
26. Freckleton Brass Band Centenary Concert. Commemorative programme (1998).
27. Unidentified newspaper report courtesy of Mr M. Rossall (probably *Lancashire Evening Post*, October 1954) ...
28. Marsh Gate Owners Minute Book, 1841–1922.
29. *Lancashire Evening Post*, 23 December 1961.

Chapter 26: The Twentieth Century

1. LRO, PR 5010/1.
2. LRO, PR 5010/2.
3. Plans courtesy of Mr J. Tomlinson.
4. Wignall, Butcher & Banks, *Report on the Allotments and Poultry Industry*, p. 5.
5. Information courtesy of Mr G. Hall.
6. Wignall, Butcher & Banks, *Report on the Allotments and Poultry Industry*, p. 5.
7. LRO, PR 5010/3.
8. *News Chronicle*, 24 August 1944.
9. *West Lancashire Evening Gazette*, 24 August 1944.
10. Ibid.
11. Documents in possession of author.
12. Documents in possession of author.
13. LRO, PR 5010/2.
14. Spencer, *Remembrances of Freckleton*, p. 14.
15. Freckleton Band Minute Book 1948–52, courtesy of Mr M. Rossall.
16. LRO, PR 5010/5.
17. Information courtesy of Mrs J. Lancaster.
18. LRO, PR 5010/2.
19. LRO, PR 5010/2.
20. LRO, PR 5010/5.
21. Information courtesy of Mr R. Hardy.
22. Information courtesy of Councillor L. Rigby.
23. Information courtesy of Mr M. Dean from his privately published *A Brief History of Freckleton Bowling Club*.

Surname Index

Place-name Index

A

Avalon Drive 12, 257

B

Balderstone Mill 102, 179, 185, 191, 193–6, 234, 238, 248, 258
the Bank 69, 166
Bannister Flatt 109
Bedlam (Spring Gardens) 178, 225
'Bonney's' Field 195
Bottoms Farm 171
Brades Farm 96, 243
Bramwell Close 123
Brethoughmoor 9
Brickfield (Long Raker) 185
Brook Lane 46
Bunkers Hill (Ship Inn) 137, 214–15, 221, 226
Bunker(s) Street 184, 187, 190, 225–6
Burying Yards 99
Bush Inn 213, 218–21
Bush Lane (Pool Lane) 46, 95, 220, 249, 253, 256–7
Butlers House (Higher House) 13

C

the Cage 43
Chapel Street 225
Church House 226
Clitheroes Lane 140, 196, 226, 242
Coach & Horses 83, 147, 183, 215–17, 221–3, 253
Coal Hill 47, 190
the Croft 109
Croft Butts Lane (Croftebutts) 12, 46, 183, 245
Coulborns Yard 99
Cyclists Arms 221–2

D

Derwent Close 87
Dibbs Farm 52
Dow
  Brook 137, 142, 143, 158, 160, 164, 197
  River 137
Dungeon (Row) 132, 226

E

(Old) Earth 164
(Further Old) Earth 164

F

(New) Factory 179, 185
(Old) Factory 85, 90, 179
Foldside Farm 12, 99, 168
Freckleton Cottage 181
'Freckleton Hall' 104
Freckleton Pool 137, 146
Further Ends Farm 183, 245

G

Gaulters Tenement 167
Grange Farm 171
the Great Croft 99–100
the Green (Smithy Green) 225, 229–30, 233, 238
Green Lane 121, 183–4
Grimbaldestons House 22, 164, 167–8, 171
Grove House 226, 242
Guide House 219
Guides House Lane 220
Gwelfolong 98

H

Halfpenny Hall 145
Hall Cross 29–30, 69–70, 104, 168, 181, 244
Hall Cross House 22, 164, 167–8, 171
the Hannings 135
Headless Cross 70
Headless Cross Bridge 45–6

Higher House 13, 22, 27, 29, 32, 167–8, 171, 255
Higher Road (Kirkham Road) 46, 181, 225–6
Hillock Lane 22, 46, 61–2, 168
Hodgson Institute 103
Holly House 76, 226

I

Ivy Cottage 226

J

James Smith 51

K

Kettleswick (Kettleswra) 12
Killn Bridge 143
Kirkham Road 14, 46, 88, 178, 225, 244

L

Lamaleach Bridge, 45–6
Lamaleach Farm 222, 242, 245
Lamaleach Inn 222–3
Lamaleach Lane/Road 46, 225
Little Ends Field 253
Long Ends Field 253–5
Longerodes (Longroots) 12
Long Raker 185
Lorimers 178, 180
Lower Coach & Horses 221
Lower House (Farm) 13, 24, 27, 29, 57, 71, 101, 105–6, 120, 133–5, 143, 153–4, 156–7, 159–60, 165, 168, 170–2, 176, 227, 255
Lower Lane/Road 12, 58, 88, 208, 225, 243–4, 255
Lytham Road 87, 94, 196, 230, 238, 242
Lyulph's Croft 10

M

'Mariners Arms' 221
Marsh View Farm 79
Masons Arms 221

List of Subscribers

A dash (—) in this following list indicates where a subscriber requested anonymity.

1 Irene Alice Gallagher, Freckleton
2 Connie Lee Porter, Freckleton
3 Roger and Wynne Parkinson, Freckleton
4 R. H. Latham, Freckleton
5 Mrs Mary Worthington, Freckleton
6 Miss Christine Hodge, Freckleton
7 Mrs Jane O'Sullivan, Freckleton
8 Mr and Mrs P. R. Dalton, Freckleton
9 Michael James Dean, Freckleton
10 Bernard and Marie Harrison, Pinner
11 Mr M. R. Parkinson, Freckleton
12 Mrs Sue Coward, Freckleton
13 Gordon and Pat Porter, Freckleton
14 Barbara Wilson, Freckleton
15 Timothy J. Palmer B.E.M., Freckleton
16 Colin L. Porter, Freckleton
17 Jacqueline A. Donaldson, Freckleton
18 Keith J. Porter, Freckleton
19 Geoffrey W. Anyon, Freckleton
20 Robert and Margaret Taylor, Lytham St Annes
21 Jennie Isabel Cookson, Freckleton
22 Linda Hansell, Freckleton
23 Mrs M. Dutton, Freckleton
24 Mrs Joan Richardson, Freckleton
25 Revd Michael Gisbourne, Freckleton
26 William Worthington, Penwortham
27 Linda Parkinson, Freckleton
28 —
29 Norman and Carole Lowe, Freckleton
30 Mrs Dorothy Day, Freckleton
31 Sylvia Mary Sanger, Freckleton
32 John and Margaret M. Hall, Freckleton
33 Brian E. Wright, Freckleton
34 Mr and Mrs G. Hesketh, Freckleton
35 Geoffrey Stork, Freckleton
36 —
37 J. A. and D. Sawyer, Freckleton
38 Mrs Marjorie Joan Hastwell, Freckleton
39 Mr D. E. Salthouse, Freckleton
40 Mrs M. Griffiths, Lytham St Annes
41 Harry Rawstrone, Freckleton
42 Barry John Wade, Freckleton
43 Mrs Janet Edwards, Freckleton
44 T. A. Birch, Freckleton
45 Rev. Judith Baldry, Freckleton
46 Mr Donald Smith, Freckleton
47 Mr John Wright, Freckleton
48 Alan Smith, Freckleton
49 Niel and Ann Stone, Freckleton
50 Eric Bickerstaffe, Freckleton
51 Mrs M. Crocker, Freckleton
52 Mrs Margaret Burns, Freckleton
53 Mrs May Kirby, Freckleton
54 Brian and Susan Hurley, Freckleton
55 Mr L. Hatton, Lytham St Annes
56 Alan and Pat Roberts, Freckleton
57 Joan and Stuart Capper, Southport
58 Mrs A. Sharp, Freckleton
59 Sue Humphreys, Freckleton
60 Mrs Erika Fidler, Freckleton
61 N. Spann, Freckleton
62 Ruth Burns (née Waite), Freckleton
63 Mr and Mrs F. Richardson, Freckleton
64 Ian Calderbank, Freckleton
65 David and Ros Bunting, Freckleton
66 Valerie and Vince Beech, Freckleton
67 Tony, Dorothy, Adam and Ruth Haynes, Freckleton
68 John Errington, Freckleton
69 Mr Patrick Howard, Freckleton
70 Mrs M. Scholz, Freckleton
71 Mrs S. Scholz, Freckleton
72 S. and J. Tudor-Jones, Freckleton
73 Maureen and Andrew Green, Freckleton
74 Mrs I. E. O'Leary, Freckleton
75 —
76 Frank Howard, Freckleton
77 Mr and Mrs R. Jebbitt, Freckleton
78 David Eastham, Freckleton
79 Rebecca Louise Eastham, Freckleton
80 Mark Robert Eastham, Freckleton
81 Andrew David Eastham, Freckleton
82 Mr Nicholas and Mrs Diane Glover, Freckleton
83 —
84 R. C. J. Sharples, Freckleton

85 Mr Hugh and Mrs Elsie Dollin, Freckleton
86 G. K. Taylor, Freckleton
87 Mrs Marie Britt, Freckleton
88 Gordon and Patricia Knight, Freckleton
89 Geoff Ogden, Freckleton
90 Ian Talbot, Freckleton
91 Robert B. Littlefair, Freckleton
92 Caroline Nicholson, Freckleton
93 Sylvester Till, Freckleton
94 Dorothy M. Mifsud (née Hall), Freckleton
95 Thomas Frank Dickinson, Freckleton
96 Alan Houlgraves, Freckleton
97 Mr Wilfred Blair, Freckleton
98 Mr and Mrs A. E. Stuffins, Freckleton
99 Mrs Shirley Delany, Freckleton
100 Mr Andrew Battersby, Freckleton
101 Kathleen Banks, Freckleton
102 Andrew Banks, Freckleton
103 Sarah Banks, Freckleton
104 Jack Woods, Freckleton
105 Robert Cooper, Freckleton
106 Barbara Ham, Freckleton
107 Michael, Susan, Thomas and Ben Rigg, Freckleton
108 H. Rayton, Freckleton
109 Mrs Margery Parkinson, Freckleton
110 (Mrs) Barbara Hall, Freckleton
111 Joan Martin, Freckleton
112 Mrs J. Draper, Freckleton
113 David and Sheila Halewood, Freckleton
114 Mr John Handley, Freckleton
115 Maureen Nixon, Freckleton
116 Mrs M. M. Dowling J. P. D. L., Freckleton
117 Alwyn and Colin Ashworth, Freckleton
118 Peter and Bernie Pedley, Freckleton
119 R. T. Taylor, Freckleton
120 Mr and Mrs Colin Robb, Freckleton
121 Mrs K. L. Cowburn, Freckleton
122 Mrs Margaret Dickinson, Freckleton
123 —
124 Mrs Janet Jackson, Freckleton
125 Denise Drinkall, Freckleton
126 Mike and Leni, Freckleton
127 Geoff Billington, Warton
128 Cllr. Mrs J. R. Maguire, Freckleton
129 Joy Rose, Freckleton
130 Mr J. Iddon, Freckleton
131 Ken Horner, Freckleton
132 Colin Birkill, Freckleton
133 Miss J. M. Lea, Lytham
134 Alan and Jean Watkinson, Freckleton
135 J. E. Hunter, Freckleton

136 Miss Jennifer Kay Oxton, Freckleton
137 Richard Peake, Freckleton
138 John Steven Cayzer, Freckleton
139 Robert Whiteside, Mirfield
140 Peter and Julie Armitage, Freckleton
141 Mr A. Barratt, Freckleton
142 Dave Hogg, Freckleton
143 Mr and Mrs D. R. Parkinson, Freckleton
144 William Whiteside, Warton
145 Garry Mitchell, Freckleton
146 Phil and Christine Gates, Freckleton
147 Denise and Mick King, Freckleton
148 Bill Blore - Freckleton Cycles
149 George Mason, Freckleton
150 G. and A. L. Hall, Freckleton
151 Adam R. Todd, Freckleton
152 Mrs Alvys J. Entwistle, Freckleton
153 Barbara Peake, Freckleton
154 Keith and Christine Buxton, Blackpool
155 Marjorie Chesworth, Freckleton
156 —
157 Paul and Debbie Coyle, Freckleton
158 Mr B. J. Whittle, Freckleton
159 Mrs P. Shields, Surrey, Canada
160 Jon Swift, Freckleton
161 —
162 Nellie Mason, Freckleton
163 Margaret Jaibaji, Laguna Niguel, USA
164 Mrs M. Williams, Eccleston
165 Mrs B. Cartmell, Freckleton
166 Linda Ball, Freckleton
167 Stella Bowman, Bolton
168 Peter Ford, Freckleton
169 Margaret Ann Rhodes, Freckleton
170 Michael and Sandra Collins, Freckleton
171 Myles Newton, Freckleton
172 Dr P. M. Bagley, Freckleton
173 Penny and Mike Pattinson, Grimsargh
174 Brian Rutter, Freckleton
175 Joan Bannister, Freckleton
176 B., R. and D. Haynes, Freckleton
177 David Winstanley, Freckleton
178 Pat Griffiths, Penwortham
179 —
180 Mr Richard Rayton, Freckleton
181 Mrs Maureen Hall, Freckleton
182 Mr J. Oddie, Freckleton
183 Mr Frank Gilman, Fulwood
184 Mr and Mrs T. Neilson, Freckleton
185 Mr and Mrs G. Parker, Freckleton
186 Mr G. N. Parker, Freckleton
187 Mr J. W. Parker, Freckleton
188 Mr and Mrs R. Brennan, Freckleton
189 D. Brian and Brenda Shaw, Freckleton
190 —

191 Thomas Butcher, Ashton-on-Ribble
192 Stewart Riley, Freckleton
193 Diane Coyne, Freckleton
194 Anthony J. Foster, Freckleton
195 Vera Cartmell, Freckleton
196 Mr Eric Hodgson, Fulwood
197 Mr and Mrs R. Holdsworth, Freckleton
198 A. N. Butler, Freckleton
199 Elizabeth Eastham, Freckleton
200 The Howell Family, Freckleton
201 Mary and Mark Rossall, Freckleton
202 Sarah and Warren Parkinson, Freckleton
203 John and Jo, Rossall, Northwich
204 Mrs Doris Lowe, Texas, USA
205 Christine Storey, Poulton-le-Fylde
206 Christine Wilson, Freckleton
207 Mrs Grace Edmondson, Freckleton
208 David Joule, Freckleton
209 Mr and Mrs D. R. Hardy, Freckleton
210 Mr and Mrs R. B. Hardy, Freckleton
211 Geoffrey and Reneé Finch, Freckleton
212 Tim Akeroyd, Freckleton
213 Colin Robb, Freckleton
214 Terry Lunt and Family, Freckleton
215 David and Pearl Elliston, Lytham St
     Annes
216 Mr and Mrs N. D. Critchley, Freckleton
217 Roger B. Hardy, Wrea Green
218 Marlene Wright, Freckleton
219 David R. Smith, Freckleton
220 Mr and Mrs Lindsay-Thinn, Freckleton
221 —
222 James R. Snape, Freckleton
223 —
224 Bernard and Sheilah Fishwick, Freckleton
225 Rosa Corey (née Kay), USA
226 Philip Kay, Lytham St Annes
227 Albert Kay, Australia
228 Mr Damian King, Freckleton
229 Noel Robert Emms, Freckleton
230 Jackie and Brian Singleton, Freckleton
231 David and Julie Hook, Freckleton
232 —
233 Mrs Frankie Hughes, St Anne's-on-Sea
234 Mr and Mrs P. Grady, Freckleton
235 Katie Taylor, Freckleton
236 Mrs H. Rawcliffe, Lytham
237 Jennie Keyes, Freckleton
238 Andrew Keyes, Goosnargh
239 Paul Keyes, Salwick
240 Roger Keyes, Limanton, France
241 Jennifer Billingham (née Keyes), Hyden,
     Western Australia
242 Daniel Keyes, Perth, Western Australia
243 B. B. Loughnane, Freckleton

244 R. M. Rigby, Warton
245 Mr K. Allanson, Chester
246 Mrs Sue Schofield, Freckleton
247 John Williamson, Freckleton
248 Philip J. Lewin, Elswick
249 Edwin and Alison Howarth, St Annes
250 Mrs J. Payne, Freckleton
251 Mrs E. Marquis, Lytham
252 Mr G. M. Payne, Blackpool
253 Bob and Beryl Barnes, Freckleton
254 Mrs William S. Threlfall, Freckleton
255 Roy Kiddle, Freckleton
256 Louise and Karl Gray, Frodsham
257 Linda, John and Samuel Frankland,
     Leyland
258 Susan and Ian Hudson, Whitehaven
259 David Fare, Lower House Farm,
     Freckleton
260 Mr Richard C. Cookson, Wrea Green
261 Richard Greenwood Iddon, Freckleton
262 —
263 Mr John Whiteside, Poulton-le-Fylde
264 Michael Threlfall, Freckleton
265 Mrs Doreen Ash, Freckleton
266 Mr Michael John Pearson, Freckleton
267 Mr J. and Mrs C. Garlick, Freckleton
268 Harold Hassall, Ross-Shire (Resident
     1939-1960)
269 Mrs Jessie MacFarlane, Freckleton
270 Harry Robinson, Freckleton
271 Mrs Mary Preston, Freckleton
272 William Singleton, Freckleton
273 Kenneth Singleton, Freckleton
274 M. and C. A. Monk, Freckleton
275 Mrs Vicky Fisher, Freckleton
276 Tracey Hopes, Fulwood (formerly of
     Freckleton)
277 Drena M. Crone, Warton
278 —
279 Douglas Seed, Fulwood
280 P. and M. Cronshaw, Freckleton
281 Mrs Cecilia Maxwell-Bradley, Freckleton
282 Peter James Bamber, Kirkham
283 Mr F. Whiley, Lytham St Annes
284 Norman and Beryl Cunliffe, Blackpool
285 —
286 Christine Halsall, Freckleton
287 Samuel J. Donaldson, Freckleton
288 Ken and Barbara Snibson, Freckleton
289 Derek and Christina Neale, Freckleton
290 Mrs Belle Gregson, Freckleton
291 Mrs Marsie Winder (née Harrison),
     Fulwood
292 Mr Llewellyn King, Freckleton
293 Matthew S. Donaldson, Freckleton

294 David Richard Whalley, Freckleton
295 Carole Christopher, Freckleton
296 Mr and Mrs M. De Nobrega of the
 Caravela Restaurant, Freckleton
297 Catherine Hughes, Freckleton
298 Miss K. Snape, Freckleton
299 —
300 Brian Rhodes, Longridge
301 Kath Harper and John Halsall, Freckleton
302 Mrs Lorraine Wareing, Freckleton
303 Mr Benjamin Hoggarth Walker,
 Freckleton
304 Mr J. J. Butcher, Freckleton
305 Mrs J. A. Butcher, Freckleton
306 Steven R. Baxendale, Freckleton
307 Roger De Nobrega, Freckleton
308 Barrie Fidler, Freckleton
309 Russell Helm, Bacup
310 Mrs Joyce Malin, Freckleton
311 Mr and Mrs J. A. Forster, Lea
312 Sheila Hanson, Freckleton
313 Mr and Mrs G. A. Boyd, British
 Columbia, Canada
314 Richard and Linda Rayton, Freckleton
315 Bob and Christine Pearson, Freckleton
316 Mr and Mrs R. C. Andrew, Freckleton
317 Edith Rhodes, Freckleton
318 Christine Anne Hancock, Bury
319 Eric Coates, Bolton le Sands
320 Rosemary Barnes, Pewsey
321 Mrs Vera Baldwin, Freckleton
322 Mr G. Eric Ray, St Anne's-on-Sea
323 Alfred Redfern, Lytham St Annes
324 John and Mary Wilson, Freckleton
325 Mr J. M. Turner, St Anne's-on-Sea
326 The Rev. and Mrs Stuart Westley,
 Blackpool
327 John Bainbridge, Freckleton
328 Ian and Jenny Pearson, Freckleton
329 Mr and Mrs R. Braithwaite, Freckleton
330 Mrs Vivien Topping, Lytham St Annes
331 Catherine Gray, Freckleton
332 Mr and Mrs Tom and Sylvia McGregor,
 Freckleton
333 Mrs Jane Foster, Freckleton
334 Mr Peter Foster, Croston
335 Mrs Robert Abram, Blackpool
336 Mrs Margaret Mullen (née Iddon),
 Freckleton
337 Jacqueline Regan, Freckleton
338 Lena and Jim Cookson, Freckleton
339 Louise Taylor (Miss), Freckleton
340 —
341 Teresa Hogarth, Freckleton
342 Jim and Margaret Rhodes, Preston

343 Bob Disley, Freckleton
344 Mrs P. Hogarth, Freckleton
345 Diane Newton, Freckleton
346 Andrew Townsend, Freckleton
347 Elizabeth S. Townsend, Freckleton
348 Peter Townsend, Freckleton
349 T. Fare, Freckleton
350 Maureen Janet Singleton, Thornton
 Cleveleys
351 G. Alan Edwards, Freckleton
352 Gregg Butler, Freckleton
353 Mrs J. Bergus, Freckleton
354 Andrew D. Slater, Freckleton
355 Mr and Mrs Edge, Freckleton
356 David and Heidi Hall, Kirkham
357 Sue and David Wade, Freckleton
358 Sally and Simon Crookes, Freckleton
359 —
360 Cllr Mr and Mrs Peter Rawstrone,
 Freckleton
361 Susan J. Wardell, Freckleton
362 Mr and Mrs Richard Wilson, Wray
 Green
363 Mr and Mrs Clarke-Roberts, St
 Anne's-on-Sea
364 Mr and Mrs A. Hinchliffe, Lytham St
 Annes
365 Jennifer Cartmell, Freckleton
366 Helen Patrica Gillett, Freckleton
367 Paul Richard Cartmell, Freckleton
368 Diane Cartmell, Freckleton
369 Mrs Gladys M. Sumner, Freckleton
370 Matt Durrant, Freckleton
371 Keith and Victoria McKay, Freckleton
372 Mr P. S. Hardman, Poulton-le-Fylde
373 Mr and Mrs S. Braithwaite, Freckleton
374 Mrs Christine E. Woodcock, Freckleton
375 Dr Gerald Sumner, Freckleton
376 Louise Freckelton, Cambridge
377 Mr Derek B. Hughes, Fleetwood
378 —
379 —
380 Catherine Wheldon, Freckleton
381 —
382 Mrs A. Coates, Warton
383 Dr A. Crosby, Preston
384 Mr and Mrs R. Banks, Freckleton
385 Dr M. Duggan, Haskayne
386 Mr and Mrs J. B. Frankland, Leyland
387 Freckleton Church of England Primary
 School
388 Mr and Mrs P. Hall, Freckleton
389 Holy Family RC Primary School, Warton
390 Mr and Mrs B. Hudson, Freckleton
391 Mr and Mrs K. Lawson, Goosnargh

392 Mrs M. McDonald, Freckleton
393 Mr and Mrs H. Robinson, Freckleton
394 Mrs E. Shakeshaft, Lytham
395 Strike Lane County Primary School,
　　　Freckleton
396 Mr R. Watson, Pilling
397 Tom Garlick, Freckleton
398 The Revd Norman S. Saul, Bamber
　　　Bridge
399 Melanie Greenall, Freckleton
400 Carole Kent, Freckleton
401 Mark Bolton-King and Jenny
　　　Bolton-King, Freckleton
402 Stanley Brown, Lytham
403 —
404 —
405 —
406 Barbara Garratt (née Procter), Freckleton
407 Mrs Irene Holt, Freckleton
408 Malcolm Jones, Freckleton
409 —
410 Steven Worden, Freckleton
411 Evelyn B. Munro (Ms), Freckleton
412 Mrs Jean Adam, Freckleton
413 Peter Williams, Freckleton
414 Mrs E. Cluley, St Anne's-on-Sea
415 William C. Smith, Freckleton
416 J. F. C. Crabbe, Freckleton
417 —
418 Mrs M. Hinks, Wesham
419 Malcolm and Anne Kay, Freckleton
420 Christopher Kay, Freckleton
421 T. G. and H. S. Berry (Berigood),
　　　Freckleton
422 Norman Benson, St Anne's-on-Sea
423 George W. Kirby, Penwortham
424 Mr George Hodgson, Wesham
425 John W. Butcher, Kirkham
426 Edward and Theresa Coles, Freckleton
427 Mrs Josephine Taylor, Warton
428 Melvin Rhodes, Freckleton
429 Mr H. D. and Mrs H. M. Barker, Lytham
430 Mrs Rita Taylor, Freckleton
431 Mr Terry Hough, Freckleton
432 G. and J. B. Awde, Freckleton
433 —
434 Jonathan and Martina Goodin, Freckleton
435 Mr Alan Burton, Freckleton
436 Mrs Jean Ann Burdon, Freckleton
437 Jim and Sandra Martin, Freckleton
438 Sally Kearney, Freckleton
439 John Mason, Freckleton
440 Mrs J. Godfrey, Morecambe
441 Mrs F. D. E. Baker, Lytham
442 Mr and Mrs Dennis Forsyth, Freckleton

443 Heather Notman, Freckleton
444 Rita Dunn, Freckleton
445 Patricia Bright, Freckleton
446 Samantha Bright, Freckleton
447 Mr R. H. Payne, Blackpool
448 Mrs Marion Crane, Lytham St Annes
449 R. C. Lightfoot, Carlisle
450 Mrs G. Rawson, London
451 Mrs P. Hope, Middlesex
452 James Patrick Valentine, Freckleton
453 Stuart and Jo-Anne Parkinson, Freckleton
454 Phyllis Welsh, Freckleton
455 Matthew P. Warhurst, Lytham St Annes
456 Michael and Denise Woods, Freckleton
457 Mrs June Hastwell, Newton
458 Mrs Joan Rebecca Taylor (née Cookson),
　　　Wrea Green
459 Mr M. J. Stewartson, Wesham
460 Mrs Betty V. Hudson, Freckleton
461 Irene E. Gannon, Lewes
462 Christine M. Burr, Solihull
463 Harry Hall, Freckleton
464 Jennifer M. Thompson, Greenhalgh
465 Jenny Brown, Wokingham
466 Mr S. J. Talbot, Freckleton
467 —
468 D. and P. Harper, Freckleton
469 Denis and Sheila Vickers, Freckleton
470 Brian and Wendy Carr, Freckleton
471 Valerie A. Whittle, Warton
472 Jane and Graham Findlay, Kilmacolm
473 John Hannan, Kirkham
474 B. J. Rafferty, Ribbleton
475 Graham and Vivienne Sudell, Lytham
476 Mrs Janet Boyd (née Snape), Blackpool
477 Mr R. Whitaker, Lytham St Annes
478 Dick Rossall, Freckleton
479 Mrs Vivien Lawler, Cottam
480 Beryl and Dennis Boardman, Freckleton
481 Mrs E. Willis, Freckleton
482 Jane E. Hamby, Preston
483 —
484 Frank and Mary Coady, Lytham
　　　St Annes
485 Dorothy and David Hindle, Grimsargh
486 Emma and Richard Edwards, Freckleton
487 Alan and Irene Whiteside, Freckleton
488 Anthony Francis, Freckleton
489 Mary Gregg, Freckleton
490 Donald Brunton, Sydney, Australia
491 Paul and Adrienne Freckelton, Cudgen,
　　　Australia
492 David Freckelton, Orange, Australia
493 Peter and Alison Dawson, Freckleton
494 P. Torrible, Freckleton

495 Miss Mary Elizabeth Thompson, Freckleton
496 —
497 —
498 Vin and Sue Smith, Freckleton
499 Anne Gregg, Freckleton
500 Jane Parkinson, Freckleton
501 Mrs E. P. Marshall, Freckleton
502 E. and M. Cartmell, Freckleton
503 Mrs Anne Eales, Freckleton
504 Miss S. M. Billington, Freckleton
505 Roy Mason, Blackpool
506 Mr J. Arrowsmith, Warrington
507 David and Glenys Crossley, Weeton
508 Paul and Maureen Outhwaite (née Sidebotham), Freckleton
509 Alan and Edna Kirkham (née Salisbury), Esprick
510 Keith Stewart (Sidebotham), Sydney, Australia
511 Barry Stewart (Sidebotham), Newport, Australia
512 Mr Andrew Bamber, Freckleton
513 Doreen and Andrew Norris, Freckleton
514 Eileen and Brian Wilson, Kelmscott, Western Australia
515 David and Valerie Borrill, Freckleton
516 Rod Leach, Freckleton
517 John Eccles, Freckleton
518 Les and Gale Camp, Freckleton
519 Mrs S. Wright, St Anne's-on-Sea
520 Mrs Jane Finch, Freckleton
521 Robert Godson, Freckleton
522 Stephen Bell, Freckleton
523 Mr J. and Mrs M. E. Ashton, Longridge
524 Philip Whitehead, Freckleton
525 Ted Lightbown, Blackpool
526 Blackpool and Fylde Historical Society
527 Rebecca and Rosemary Braithwaite, Freckleton
528 Joan Thompson, Newton
529 Donald R. Hopper, Lytham St Annes
530 John Ashton, Longridge
531 Angela Jane Cossins, Greenhalgh
532 Georgie Hutchinson, Freckleton
533 Grace Smith, Freckleton
534 Mr and Mrs J. D. Wilkinson, Freckleton
535 Peter W. Tyson, Freckleton
536 Mr and Mrs T. F. Gooding, Freckleton
537 Mrs D. McCann, Freckleton
538 Peggy Livesey (née Rawcliffe), Freckleton
539 Dr M. C. Higham, Clitheroe
540 Mrs F. R. Longbottom, Penwortham
541 Mrs Rosemary Jolly, Freckleton

542 Patrick Jolly, Earby
543 Matthew Jolly, London
544 Charlotte Jolly, Derby
545 Vicky Barlow, Wesham
546 Doug Paulson, San Antonio, USA
547 Stephanie Brightey, Freckleton
548 Geraldine Dagger, Freckleton
549 Kevin Stevens, Freckleton
550 Lee Williams, Freckleton
551 David H. Moehring, Salem, Oregon, USA
552 Thomas Kenneth Townsend, Freckleton
553 Harold Banks, Preston
554 D. Taylor, Lytham St Annes
555 Eric and Glenys Clifton, Kirkham
556 Mr and Mrs A. Hibbert, Freckleton
557 Martin Ramsbottom, Kirkham
558 Keith and Anne Langley, Freckleton
559 Jill Heap, Freckleton
560 Cyril Jim Leech, St Annes
561 Joe Whiteside, Freckleton
562 Pauline Pio, Freckleton
563 June Johnstone, Warrington
564 Brian McDowell, Freckleton
565 Mr and Mrs D. J. Threlfall, Freckleton
566 David Forshaw, Lytham
567 Jane Callon, Freckleton
568 George and Valerie Sant, Freckleton
569 Mary Robertson, Freckleton
570 N. Hankinson, Blackpool
571 Mr I. Comber, Lytham St Annes
572 Teresa Harrison, Fulwood
573 Michael J. Wildman, Freckleton
574 Mr T. M. Shorrock, Kirkham
575 Cud and Irene Fare, Freckleton
576 Peter and Patsy Batson, Freckleton
577 Mrs Deborah E. Mather, Freckleton
578 R. C. Thompson, Lytham St Annes
579 Nigel Hare, Freckleton
580 Jason Michael Fox, Freckleton
581 R. A. Eastwood, Freckleton
582 Peter Benson, Warton
583 June Wilkins, Warton
584 Mr B. Firth, Warton
585 Wilfred Naylor, Kirkham
586 Peter Swindells, Freckleton
587 Joan Fisher, Freckleton
588 Barbara Adams, Freckleton
589 Christina Salisbury, Leyland
590 Mrs L. Gettings, Freckleton
591 Gemma Gale, Freckleton
592 Frank and Joan Lonsdale, Lytham St Annes
593 Susan and Michael McDade, Lytham St Annes